The Rest of the Story

CRITICAL ESSAYS ON ALICE MUNRO

D1525057

The Rest of the Story

CRITICAL ESSAYS ON ALICE MUNRO

Edited by

ROBERT THACKER

ECW PRESS

The publication of *The Rest of the Story* has been generously supported by the Government of Canada through the Book Publishing Industry Development Program.

CANADIAN CATALOGUING IN PUBLICATION DATA
Main entry under title:
The rest of the story : critical essays on Alice Munro

ISBN 1-55022-392-5

1. Munro, Alice, 1931-   – Criticism and interpretation.
I. Thacker, Robert.

PS8576.U57Z874 1999   C813'.54   C99-930876-9
PR9199.3.M8Z874 1999

Cover: Debby West, *Enter: The Muse*. Reproduced by permission of Gallery Contemporanea, Jacksonville/SuperStock.

Cover design and artwork by Guylaine Régimbald.
Imaging by ECW Type & Art, Oakville, Ontario.
Printed by AGMV Marquis Imprimeur, Cap-Saint-Ignace, Quebec.

Distributed in Canada by General Distribution Services,
30 Lesmill Road, Don Mills, Ontario M3B 2T6.
Distributed in the United States by General Distribution Services,
85 River Rock Drive, Suite 202, Buffalo, New York 14207.

Published by ECW PRESS,
2120 Queen Street East, Suite 200,
Toronto, Ontario M4E 1E2.
www.ecw.ca/press

PRINTED AND BOUND IN CANADA

TABLE OF CONTENTS

ABSTRACTS

CAROL L. BERAN

The Luxury of Excellence: Alice Munro in the *New Yorker*

Alice Munro published thirty-four stories in the *New Yorker* between 1977 and 1998. The magazine has broadened her readership, affected her writing slightly through its editorial policies, and provided an additional context in which to read her stories. Those who read recent Munro stories in the *New Yorker* rather than in a book of collected stories are frequently distracted by ads, cartoons, sketches, poems, and brief articles. The marginalia of "The Love of a Good Woman" in the 23 and 30 December 1996 issue of the *New Yorker* present a lifestyle characterized by a search for health, adventure, collectible objects, and intimacy. The juxtaposition of her depiction of what she has termed "real life" with the vision that the marginalia imply causes magazine readers to experience the story differently from those who encounter it in a book with blank margins.

ILDIKÓ DE PAPP CARRINGTON

Recasting the Orpheus Myth: Alice Munro's "The Children Stay" and Jean Anouilh's *Eurydice*

In an ironic intertextualization of Jean Anouilh's *Eurydice*, "The Children Stay" subversively recasts the roles of the Anouilh characters, complicating, combining, and multiplying them to define the paradoxical meanings of the story's title and to reject Anouilh's conception of a pure, fated love. To preserve Eurydice's purity, Anouilh's Orphée joins her in death. To satisfy her sexuality, Munro's protagonist abandons her children for her lover. By choosing this "death," she becomes both Orphée and Eurydice. That her lover only seems to be Orphée and is also M. Henri, Anouilh's director and messenger of death, prefigure her choice's irony.

DENNIS DUFFY

"A Dark Sort of Mirror": "The Love of a Good Woman" as Pauline Poetic

This article discusses a number of factors — particularly the story's recapitulation of familiar motifs — that render "The Love of a Good Woman" a landmark in the Munro oeuvre. The treatment concludes with an examination of the tone of disgust with the physical that marks the story, and suggests a Pauline origin for this motif.

NATHALIE FOY

"Darkness Collecting": Reading "Vandals" as a Coda to *Open Secrets*

"Vandals" serves as a coda to *Open Secrets* because it not only resembles the other stories in the collection in its multiple layers of narrative but also picks up narrative threads of the stories that precede it. The darkness in "Vandals," at first seemingly inconsistent with the sense of Munro's veneration of fiction evident in the other stories, sheds light on aspects of her reverential relationship with her craft.

DEBORAH HELLER

Getting Loose: Women and Narration in Alice Munro's *Friend of My Youth*

This essay considers *Friend of My Youth* as a collection of stories about characters —
principally women — who, in one way or another, "get loose": from the roles expected
of them by other characters, from the roles that readers may expect them to play in
predictable plots, and from the narrator's own knowledge and control. They thereby
often discover unexpected affinities with apparently dissimilar women. Through a
reading of a number of stories, and in particular of "Friend of My Youth," "Meneseteung," and "Goodness and Mercy," this paper shows how *Friend of My Youth*
returns to the mother-daughter material familiar from Munro's earlier "autobiographical" stories while at the same time offering new departures and exploring it in
fresh ways.

ROBERT LECKER

Machines, Readers, Gardens: Alice Munro's "Carried Away"

"Carried Away" explores the ways in which reading and writing are historically
conditioned — in this case by the economic and social impacts of two world wars and
the Depression. This essay discusses the impact of this conditioning on personal
and communal self-creation. The postindustrial and postwar emphasis on reading did
not necessarily lead to self-improvement: because there is no self beyond story, the
more one reads, the more one creates multiple selves in search of an elusive centre.
There is no integrated self, either before or after "the machine" inhabits "the garden,"
a fact that the characters confront through a welter of texts.

W.R. MARTIN AND WARREN U. OBER

Alice Munro as Small-Town Historian: "Spaceships Have Landed"

Alice Munro has been praised as a social historian, but her stories are much more than
a mere record: she writes not "just *about*" life to the east of Lake Huron but also
"*through*" it." She explores the depth and the range of universal human feelings and
experiences not only by the quality of her writing but also through the intersections
of her texts with others in our literary heritage. In "Spaceships Have Landed,"
small-town Carstairs becomes an archetypal community and its hundred years a
history of human civilization in all its complexity, diversity, change, and permanence.

JOANN MCCAIG

Alice Munro's Agency: The Virginia Barber Correspondence, 1976–83

"She got me into the *New Yorker*," Alice Munro once said of her American literary
agent, Virginia Barber. However, correspondence from the Virginia Barber Literary
Agency, collected in the Alice Munro Papers at the University of Calgary, makes it
clear that both the author and her "cultural banker" share the credit for this
breakthrough. Barber's letters to Munro describe a partnership between two women
seeking empowerment within a patriarchal literary culture. The correspondence shows
how ideologies of nationality, gender, genre, and economics leave their marks on
cultural products and how a strong friendship between two determined women can
defeat or at least push aside some of the barriers to authority.

Introduction:
Alice Munro, Writing "Home":
"Seeing This Trickle in Time"

ROBERT THACKER

> A place that ever was lived in is like a fire that never goes out.
> It flares up, it smolders for a time, it is fanned or smothered
> by circumstance, but its being is intact, forever fluttering within
> it, the result of some original ignition. Sometimes it gives out
> glory, sometimes its little light must be sought out to be seen,
> small and tender as a candle flame, but as certain.
>
> — Eudora Welty, "Some Notes" (286)

> This ordinary place is sufficient, everything here touchable and
> mysterious.
>
> — Alice Munro, "Everything" (33)

"LOOK AT THE ROAD MAP OF HURON COUNTY, . . ." Magdelene
Redekop begins her essay in this volume — that advice seems ever
more pertinent to readers who approach, take up, savour, and — as
much as possible — understand the art of Alice Munro. With her
ninth volume, *The Love of a Good Woman* (1998), just awarded the
Giller Prize (having been passed over, ridiculously, in the Governor
General's Literary Award competition), with its title story the inspiration for the cover of the *New Yorker*'s 1996 holiday fiction issue
(itself reprised in the 1997 issue containing Munro's "The Children
Stay") and featured in the O. Henry Awards "Best of 1997," with
the massed bulk of the *Selected Stories* (1996) asserted and confirmed,
the accomplishment of Munro's work is now both unquestioned
and unquestionable. And, in ways not altogether clear to reader and
critic alike, "The Love of a Good Woman" became, almost at the
instant of its publication in the *New Yorker* in 1996, a central Munro
text — such are its style and its extent, so clear are its echoes of
previous Munro stories, so comprehensive and mysterious are its
interleavings that critics — and most emphatically Dennis Duffy
here — saw in it a key, virtuoso instance of its author circling

back, retaking up, probing once more the "open secrets" of being, of having grown up, and of having lived in, and of having left, and of having remembered, and of having returned to, and above all of having made texts out of Huron County, Ontario.

Indicative passages, chosen almost at random, resonate within and between Munro's works. In "Walker Brothers Cowboy," for instance, the narrator recalls her younger self and especially her amazement over her father's attitude toward time: "The tiny share we have of time appalls me, though my father seems to regard it with tranquillity" (*Dance* 3). Equally indicative and even more resonant is "Of course it's my mother I'm thinking of . . .," which Munro writes as she concludes "Friend of My Youth," just before she offers as the literal conclusion (relevant to some of the story's characters) a historical summary of the sect called the Cameronians — or Reformed Presbyterians — one of whose "ministers, in a mood of firm rejoicing at his own hanging, excommunicated all the other preachers in the world" (*Friend* 26). Beyond this panache, the explicit meaning of this paragraph in relation to the story just told stands contextual but mysterious.

In another story in *Friend of My Youth*, "Meneseteung," Munro creates the discovery of a nineteenth-century Huron County poet, Almeda Joynt Roth, whose book of poems *Offerings*, said to have been published in 1873, contains a poem entitled "Champlain at the Mouth of the Meneseteung" (52). Writing of the relationship between Roth, the character, and the first-person narrator (also, of course, a character), who discovers Roth through the local paper, the *Vidette*, Pam Houston asks a question and offers an answer that together are a fit departure for meditating on Munro's intricate time- and place-based art: " 'Does the landscape, then, exist separately from the way these women see it?' And neither woman can answer. The two women have momentarily become one voice, bound together by the metonymic qualities of language, and by the inability of a metaphor to speak its name" (89).

Also bound up with these two women's voices is Munro's own voice through her pen, moving across pages, making and remaking texts. Munro, the creator, the person who, between the first publication of "Meneseteung" in the *New Yorker* and its inclusion in *Friend of My Youth*, made a change — as she often has done (in *The Love of a Good Woman*, notably, she even points out the extent of the changes between the *New Yorker* publication of the stories and their appearance in the book). In "Meneseteung," the narrator describes her search for Roth's gravestone and her discovery of it; the *New Yorker* version ends thus:

> I made sure I had got to the edge of the stone. That was all the name there was — Meda. So it was true that she was called by that name in the family. Not just in the poem. Or perhaps she chose her name from the poem, to be written on her stone.
>
> I thought that there wasn't anybody alive in the world but me who would know this, who would make the connection. And I would be the last person to do so. But perhaps this isn't so. People are curious. A few people are. They will be driven to find things out, even trivial things. They will put things together, knowing all along that they may be mistaken. You see them going around with notebooks, scraping the dirt off gravestones, reading microfilm, just in the hope of seeing this trickle in time, making a connection, rescuing one thing from the rubbish. (38)

Munro left her *New Yorker* readers with a hopeful sign — making sense of what in "Carried Away" she has referred to as a "devouring muddle" (*Open Secrets* 50). Yet, when "Meneseteung" appeared in *Friend of My Youth*, Munro dropped the phrase "knowing . . . mistaken," and this additional paragraph had been added (or reattached once the editors at the *New Yorker* had been satisfied) to offer a different ending: "And they may get it wrong, after all. I may have got it wrong. I don't know if she ever took laudanum. Many ladies did. I don't know if she ever made grape jelly" (73). With this addition, the previous hopeful sign has been dashed, and, more troubling to some (though certainly not to Munro herself, given her various comments, especially surrounding *Open Secrets*), the narrator's authority, despite the foregoing twenty pages, is utterly compromised if not altogether dashed. Welcome, again, to Alice Munro — in whose fiction everything is both "touchable and mysterious," a world in which each character, especially those who narrate or serve as centres for Munro's wonderings, is raptly aware of myriad difficulties in the "hope of seeing this trickle in time" or in "making a connection." It is a world rooted in the times and the touchable surfaces and characters of Huron County, a place lived in since the early 1800s by Munro's ancestors (as she writes, apparently, in "A Wilderness Station" in *Open Secrets*), one that she has taken in all its depths.

Take, as an indicative introduction here, a key instance in Munro's art: the story "Home," published in 1974. It offers a basis for further meditation on the ways by which Munro makes her connections. It is one of the few of her published stories not to have been collected in a book (those first appearing in the *New Yorker*, Carol Beran points out here, are "Wood" [1980] and "Hired Girl" [1994]). In "Home," Munro writes of the circumstances of her father's declining health — a subject that she returned to in "The Moons of Jupiter" (1978). Like "The Ottawa Valley," also published in 1974, "Home" is patently autobiographical and metafictional; it reflects the circumstances of Munro's return to Ontario after living in British Columbia for over twenty years. That it hasn't been republished in a book, I would guess, has as much to do with its metafictional uncertainties — for tentative and uncertain the narrator shows herself to be there — as with anything else (though Munro has commented in interviews in a tone of resigned rejection over these attempts at metafictional techniques; see, for example, "Alice Munro"). Yet "Home" is an apt text for both this essay and this volume: set in the centre of Munro's oeuvre, "Home" reveals her techniques, her focus, and her concerns. As such, it introduces, connects with, and illustrates her own hopeful "seeing" of "this trickle in time."

In "Home," accompanying her ill father to the hospital, the narrator/Munro — I conflate the two knowingly, be assured — writes:

> So I sit beside him . . . and we follow that old usual route. Victoria Street. Minnie Street. John Street. Catherine Street. The town, unlike the house, stays very much the same, nobody is renovating or changing it. Nevertheless it has faded, for me. I have written about it and used it up. The same banks and barber shops and town hall tower, but all their secret, plentiful messages drained away. Not for my father, perhaps. He has lived here, nowhere else; he has not escaped things by this use. (143)

This passage proclaims a conclusion — "used it up" — that has since been proven false by Munro's further writings: Munro returned to southwestern Ontario after her first marriage ended, but she had not at all "used it up," whatever she may have thought then. Rather, she began to use it differently — another story title — the difference born of her time away, her changed perspective born of distance and experience, the deepened complexities of her art, and her myriad imaginative connections within and between her stories.

Thus, Munro wrote, also in 1974, of the Maitland River (which the Natives called the "Menesetung"), contradicting some of what she had written in "Home":

> We believed there were deep holes in the river. We went looking for them, scared and hopeful, and never found them, but did not stop believing for that. Even now I believe that there were deep holes, ominous beckoning places, but that they have probably silted up. But maybe not all. Because I am still partly convinced that this river — not even the whole river but this little stretch of it — will provide whatever myths you want, whatever adventures. I name the plants, I name the fish, and every name seems to me triumphant, every leaf and quick fish remarkably valuable. This ordinary place is sufficient, everything here touchable and mysterious. ("Everything")

This short essay, published when Munro was described as "a writer living in London, Ontario," shortly after the appearance of *Something I've Been Meaning to Tell You*, was prescient: her art since then has largely been one of visiting and revisiting the same places, the same people, shifting emphases, altering structures, moving in time, "rescuing one thing from the rubbish." The narrator in "Home" heads out from a London-like city on a succession of buses so as to visit her father and stepmother, Irlma, who live outside a Wingham-like town. The "Meneseteung" — the spelling altered from Munro's first use of it — becomes the title of the story featuring Almeda Joynt Roth, the Native name that the character uses for the Maitland River in her poem. That river, though renamed the Peregrine, manages with its holes to obscure Mr. Willens's fate in "The Love of a Good Woman." That river thus proves to Munro's imagination to be an "ominous beckoning place" indeed, its flow a metaphorical equivalent to the passage of time, to the ongoing processes of her art.

Meandering thus through the lowlands of Huron County, near the lake, following its flow from Wingham to Goderich — "this little stretch of it" — is what Munro's fiction has done from the first stories of the early 1950s up to *The Love of a Good Woman*. In its own flow, her art defines and details the rapt mystery with which Munro sees being, and these details define a complex web of connections, reconnections, summations, and seeming conclusions that hold for a time but ultimately are insufficient. Like Frost's notion that every poem clarifies something, Munro's stories offer readers moments of insight, perhaps epiphanies: "Breathing spaces, is that all?" one of her narrators wonders (*Progress* 273). These moments both clarify and mystify — and Munro has returned to them, *The Love of a Good Woman* further shows, in progressively more complex ways.

Critics have tried to keep up to Munro yet largely have not — although eleven single-author critical books on Munro have been published, the ability of critics to encompass her and her work within an overarching rationale has been paltry (see Thacker, "Conferring Munro," "Go Ask Alice," and "What's 'Material'?"). Indeed, owing to the shape and the scope of Munro's art — story following upon story, reconnecting, redefining — the critical monograph is not really up to Munro at all. Rather, individual articles on individual stories or connected groups of them now seem, to me at least, to offer the better critical course. Thus, the rationale for this volume, is that it better follows its subject's inclinations, its subject's art. Following up on Louis K. MacKendrick's *Probable Fictions: Alice Munro's Narrative Acts* (1984), this volume offers essays that explore little-examined aspects of Munro's art — JoAnn McCaig and Carol Beran, for instance, make significant use of the Alice Munro Papers at the University of Calgary to define and understand Munro's long relationships with, respectively, Virginia Barber, her agent, and the *New Yorker*, the showcase magazine in which many of Munro's stories have first been published through Barber's agency. As I have said elsewhere and am about to demonstrate again through my discussion of "The Progress of Love" based on the Calgary archive, the Alice Munro Papers represent an exceptional resource still largely ignored by her critics. Several authors here take up the stories contained in *Open Secrets*, a volume that has not yet received much attention, save from Ildikó de Papp Carrington, who here has pressed her work into the stories in *The Love of a Good Woman* with her source study of "The Children Stay." Broadening the textual relationships within *Open Secrets*, Nathalie Foy, W.R. Martin and Warren U. Ober, and Robert Lecker treat stories that resonate both within and beyond that volume — and the latter two essays extend historian John Weaver's important characterization of Munro as a historian of her time and place. Likewise, Marianne Micros and Magdalene Redekop have defined influences on Munro that have not yet been examined, and Deborah Heller has dealt broadly with *Friend of My Youth*.

Following "Home" to "The Progress of Love"

Returning to "Home," I want to continue this introduction by using an extended quotation that offers text for the balance of this essay — my consideration of the ways by which Munro's stories lend themselves to what Helen M. Buss has called "mapping." That is, "Home" offers a textual grounding that, when understood in relation to what is available in the Calgary archive, forecasts a subsequent relation to "The Progress of Love" and to "Friend of My Youth." At the same time, "Home" both looks backward and looks forward in its detailing of Munro's characteristic concern with, even obsession with, fictional renderings of her relationship with each of her parents. "My Mother's Dream" in *The Love of a Good Woman* offers yet another version — fantastic and delightful as it is — of the mother-daughter relationship. So, when seen at the centre of Munro's work, "Home" both resonates and illustrates the ongoing connections in her art, wherever one looks.

Toward the beginning of "Home," the narrator/Munro meditates on changes made to the house in which she grew up:

> The front rooms have been re-papered. The paper has red and silver vertical stripes. Wall-to-wall carpeting — moss green — has been put down. . . .
>
> Even the outside of the house, the red brick whose crumbling mortar let in the east wind, is disappearing under clean white metal siding. My father is putting this on himself. So it seems now that the whole house is being covered up, lost, changed into something ordinary and comfortable, and I do not lament this loss as I would have done at one time. I do say that the red brick was really lovely, and that people in the city pay a good price for old bricks, but I do this mostly because I think my father expects it. He can explain again about the east wind and the cost in fuel and the difficulties of repair. It cannot be claimed that the house now being lost was a fine or handsome house in any way. A poor man's house, always, with the stairs going up between the walls. A house where people have lived close to the bone for a hundred years; and if my father and Irlma, combining their modest prosperities, wish it to be comfortable, and — this word is used by them without quotation marks, quite simply and positively — *modern,* I am really not going to wail about the loss of a few charming bricks, a crumbling

wall. But I am shy of letting my father see that [the] house does not mean to me what it once did, and that it really does not matter much to me how he changes it. 'I know you love this place,' he says to me, apologetically yet with satisfaction. I don't tell him that I am not sure now if I love any place, any house, and that it seems to me it was myself I loved here, some self I have finished with, and none too soon. I used to go into the front rooms and rummage around looking for old photographs, and sheet music. I would sit at the piano where mice were nesting — banished now by Irlma — and try to play the opening bit of the Moonlight Sonata. I would go through the bookcase looking for my old Latin Poetry, and find the best sellers of some year in the nineteen-forties when my mother belonged to the Book-of-the-Month-Club (a fine year for novels about the wives of Henry the Eighth, and for three-name women writers, and for understanding books about Soviet Russia). Also limp-covered classics bought by mother before she was married, her maiden name written in lovely, level, school-teacher's writing on the watered end-paper. *Everyman I will go with thee, in thy most need be by thy side*, it says above my mother's name. Reminders of my mother in this house are not easy to find, though she dominated it for so long, filled it with her astonishing, embarrassing hopes, and her dark and helpless, justified complaint. She was dying for many years of Parkinson's disease, which was an illness so little known to us, and so bizarre in its effects, that it did seem just the sort of thing she might have made up, out of perversity, and her true need for attention, and stranger dimensions to her life. This attention was what I was bound not to give, not to be blackmailed into giving. I give it now, being safe. (135–36)

Readers of Munro will see at once the connection between this passage and "The Progress of Love," the title story of her sixth story collection — there the story's narrator, Phemie, revisits the house that she grew up in and notices, among many other things, that in one place the wallpaper — which she had put up with her mother — "hadn't been stripped off when this new paper went on." She can "see an edge of it, the cornflowers on a white ground" (*Progress* 27). Equally, readers will see in the narrator's mother in "Home" similar figures in "The Peace of Utrecht," "The Ottawa Valley," and "Friend of My Youth," to name only the best-known instances — in all of them, Munro's mother, Anne Chamney Laidlaw, who died in 1959 of Parkinson's disease, served as a model for much of the detail about the character and her circumstances.

What readers do not generally know, though, is the path by which Munro arrived at her finished stories — thus, the balance of this essay will, first, treat the composition of "The Progress of Love" and, second, extend the consideration beyond this single story to the larger issue of Munro's continuing writing and rewriting of her parents, especially her mother. Literally and emphatically, I am arguing that in writing "Home" Munro has been writing home — that her life has been her text, that Huron County, Ontario, has been her imaginative nexus, and ultimately that her career has demonstrated that this "ordinary place" has been "sufficient" for her needs. "The Love of a Good Woman," whether in the *New Yorker*, *Prize Stories 1997*, or *The Love of a Good Woman*, has shown as much, again, and most complexly.

One might argue for the pivotal status of the title story in each collection — thus, "The Progress of Love" is set apart by titling the collection, as are "The Moons of Jupiter" and "Friend of My Youth" in their respective collections. (One might wonder, though, about the inevitability of this status: "The Moons of Jupiter" was to be the penultimate story in *Who Do You Think You Are?* as originally configured [Alice Munro Papers (hereafter cited as AMP), MsC 38.4.6.f6], and the arrangement of the stories in *The Progress of Love* was established late in the process — "The Progress of Love" had been the seventh story [AMP, third accession, 11.3].) Each story, however, is arguably pivotal for better reasons: each continues Munro's apparently lifelong meditation on who is fit for parenthood, on her relationships with her parents (especially her mother — here "Chaddeleys and Flemings" needs to be added as a companion to "The Moons of Jupiter"), and on the cultural legacy of a Protestant rural southwestern Ontario upbringing during the 1930s and 1940s.

The first appearance in the Alice Munro Papers of one of the central incidents in "The Progress of Love," the threatened suicide by Phemie's grandmother, is in "Suicide Corners," one of the vignettes for an Ontario photo album by Peter D'Angelo, for which Munro was to have written the text; although she worked on it for some time during the 1970s, the book was never published (MsC 37.13.10.14). According to Catherine Sheldrick Ross, Munro got the idea of the hanging from her second husband, Gerald Fremlin, whose father had been a policeman in Clinton and had been called to stop such a suicide

(87). It appears again in a fragment, apparently part of *Who Do You Think You Are?* There Flop Morgan threatens to hang himself because his wife has called him a liar. Rose's father talks him out of it — the scene contains the same detail as that published in "The Progress of Love": the rope isn't tied, but subsequently this character succeeds: "Flop dangling from the beam in his barn was just doing what his name has always predicted" (MsC 37.16.12).

The hanging appears in a draft story in a notebook included in the second accession, a story that Munro entitled "Suicide Ladies." Told from the point of view (drafts exist of both first- and third-person versions) of a girl named Winona, the suicide attempt is made by a Mrs. Cole at the end of a pregnancy. Winona's mother, Winifred, and her family are being visited by three relatives (Iris, Marianne, and Flora), and the news of Mrs. Cole's attempt at suicide is delivered by her son, Franklin, who says, " 'She says she's going to hang herself in the barn' . . . and then he did laugh, in embarrassment and dread and apology. He began to hiccup." The text continues:

> Franklin's mother was in the barn, just as he had said. She was standing on a kitchen chair in the middle of the space her husband usually parked the car in, and she had a noose around her neck. Phylis and Margory and the dog were hanging around the barn door.
>
> "Oh, Mrs. Cole!" said Winona's mother in a tired voice[.] "Come down out of that."
>
> Mrs. Cole's figure made a stunning impression on Winona. At that time women did not go out when in an advanced state of pregnancy, and she had never seen anyone so disfigured. Mrs. Cole was a tall, thin woman normally and as sometimes happens with narrow hipped women she seemed to be carrying the baby not as something fitted into her body but as something precariously hinged on; it didn't seem possible her skin could have stretched so far. She wore the shapeless kind of housedress that poor women wore, several sizes too big; it kept sliding off one shoulder; her hair also was cut in the style of a poor woman[:] short, straight, held back with a bobby pin.
>
> "I said I was going to do it." She said in a high voice. This was the first time I had heard her say anything except when she called the children or dog Wig, from her back door. (MsC 38.11.2)

Such passages — coupled with the advantages of hindsight — define connections between stories. This one suggests that Munro had the hanging incident in the story that became "Chaddeleys and Flemings: 1. Connection" (1978) because Iris, Marianne, and Flora are likely the visiting cousins in that story; here they see the threatened hanging as the "entertainment" of a summer's morning. There are, as well, connections between this passage and "Miles City, Montana" (1985), another meditation on parenting and parenthood. Thus, this anecdote, consistent in its particulars, was to have been included (at least) in the photo text, *Who Do You Think You Are?*, and "Chaddeleys and Flemings: 1. Connection" (itself once just "Chaddeleys and Flemings" — it was first submitted for publication as one very long story but later divided into "Connection" and "Chaddeleys and Flemings: 2. The Stone in the Field") before it became an essential part of "The Progress of Love." There, of course, it is a visible explanation of Phemie's mother's hatred for her father, a hatred so deep that she burned the money he left her in his will — her legacy — in the family stove.

This, the second major incident in "The Progress of Love," may also be seen working toward its ultimate place through more than one version. There is, for example, an autograph draft story called "Money to Burn" for which there are two versions of the beginning. The first begins with the unnamed narrator going to town one evening with her aunt Tizzy, who is referred to simply as Tizzy. The time period is probably the early 1940s: "The radio ran on batteries. There was no electricity in the house — a fact I remembered only when the lamps were lit." The news we listened to at home made you feel the world was full of doom, but under control. The news here indicated that the world beyond the farm was a jumble of disasters and sprees and jokes of nature that even a man as cocky and worldly wise as the newscaster has trouble crediting. (AMP, third accession, 6.7)

Tizzy has been married twice, and there is a mystery to her first marriage: she went on her honeymoon but came back unmarried, though pregnant, and then lived with her parents before marrying Wyck, the narrator's uncle. In the second draft, the details are much the same, though Tizzy has become Aunty and Wyck has become Wick.

Munro uses the name Wick in "A Queer Streak" (1985–86), and the aunt suggests Beryl in "The Progress of Love" (whose visit there echoes the visits of Del Jordan's American uncle in *Lives of Girls and Women* [1971] and that of the cousins in "Chaddeleys and Flemings:

1. Connection"). In the same notebook is evidence that Munro tried to use the burning-money episode in the story that became "Fits" (AMP, third accession, 6.7). Here too she was working on the story about Franklin; it is much bigger than "The Progress of Love" and derives from the notebook work that uses characters from "Chaddeleys and Flemings: 1. Connection"; it contextualizes Marietta — the grandmother in "The Progress of Love" — offering much more family detail. Indeed, as the story developed, Franklin's role became Marietta's in the finished version.

I could continue to compare details; my comparisons here address some of the material found in autograph drafts. In another one, for example, Bob Marks initiates sex while he and Phemie are visiting her girlhood home — his desires are evident in the completed story. Such handwritten material is then changed further — and sometimes changed back again — in the authorial typescripts that follow and in the typist's typescripts that follow those. Or the story could be taken further yet, into the differences between its first publication in the *New Yorker*, where the point of view is third person, and its subsequent publication in book form, where the point of view is first person (both points of view are found in draft materials).

Elsewhere I have argued for the appropriateness of Eudora Welty's essay "How I Write" to Munro's compositional methods; two passages from that essay are worth quoting again here: first, "The story is a vision; while it's being written, all choices must be its choices, and as these choices multiply upon one another, their field is growing too"; second, "Relationship *is* a pervading and changing mystery; it is not words that make it so in life, but words have to make it so in a story. Brutal or lovely, the mystery waits for people wherever they go, whatever extreme they run to" (245, 250). Both comments — from one of Munro's admitted influences — speak directly to her composition of "The Progress of Love" as revealed in the little-examined Alice Munro Papers at the University of Calgary Library. "The story is a vision . . .": when applied to the evidence in the archive, which admittedly is random in that it is made up of what has been saved (doubtless much was lost, and probably some burned: see 37.14.28), one can see several stories in gestation at the same time, each overlapping the other, some destined to emerge transformed, many destined not to emerge at all.

Throughout, Munro may be seen shaping, adjusting, honing, and sharpening her articulation until she finds it satisfactory. This trying out of incidents such as a threatened suicide or the seemingly senseless burning of three thousand dollars is at the source of her method. Her literal source of material is almost always Huron County. Such personal anecdotes are necessary for Munro, as she wrote eloquently in a story called "Material"; speaking of a story written by her ex-husband, Hugo, derived from their time together, the narrator thinks, "how strange it was for me to realize that what was all scraps and oddments, useless baggage, for me, was ripe and useable, a paying investment, for him" (*Something* 43). And because, as Welty wrote, "Relationship *is* a pervading and changing mystery . . .," Munro uses words "to make it so in a story. Brutal or lovely, the mystery waits for people. . . ." For Munro, the mystery of being shapes her stories until the shapes cohere, until they seem fit and proper.

In "Suicide Corners," one of the vignettes from the photo text, Munro wonders, "More men seem to come to it [suicide] than women. Is that the truth? And if it is the truth, why?" (AMP, MsC 37.13.10.14.f2). What the Munro archive reveals is that, after its numerous tryings out in various stories drafted over a decade, the threatened hanging at the core of "The Progress of Love" still yields a mystery. It is the incident through which the story's most essential question is asked; it is the incident that fosters the burned money, which perplexes Phemie still. As she says, wondering about her parents in a phrase that echoes "Suicide Corners," "It seems so much the truth it is the truth; it's what I believe about them. I haven't stopped believing it. But I have stopped telling that story" (*Progress* 30). Munro may have stopped telling the story that is "The Progress of Love," but the Calgary archive reveals that the story is always one that confirms that "Relationship *is* a pervading and changing mystery . . .," and *her* words certainly make it so.

"The Bitter Lump of Love": Mothers, Fathers, and Autobiographical Sequence

The image of Phemie wondering about her parents might be seen as something of a tableau in Munro's writing; as is widely acknowledged, one of her key focal points is on the relationships between generations, especially between daughters and mothers. Although well known among critics, the means by which Munro managed this, like the previous discussion of the Calgary archive, indicate ways in which her stories might be better understood. I have put forward an autobiographical approach to Munro generally; nowhere, probably, does that approach better apply than in her various depictions of her father and, especially, her mother: her relationships with them, both literally and through memory, make figures based on them commonplace throughout her work (see Thacker, "So Shocking"). There are two groups of stories relevant to this configuration, one involving the mother, the other the father. Of the first group, most depict Munro's mother as a person who is dying or has died of Parkinson's disease. Intimations of this figure are seen in other stories in *Dance of the Happy Shades*, but the first really extended treatment of her is in "The Peace of Utrecht" (1960), included in that first collection. She appears — emotionally if not precisely — in *Lives of Girls and Women* as Ida, in *Something I've Been Meaning to Tell You* in "Winter Wind" and "The Ottawa Valley," and, during the same year of publication, in "Home." Usually characterized by the narrator as an overtly haunting, now long-dead, mental presence, she returns in "Friend of My Youth." These stories offer a type of "family resemblance" born of their autobiographical provenance, and, when looked at sequentially, they create a deeper understanding.

By returning again and again to subjects of autobiographical obsession, Munro is, as she has said, editing her life as she goes along (Carrington 196), but she is also creating a broader fictional world, one born of her sequences and one that, given time and continued publication, may eventually be seen as almost Faulknerian in its complexity — James Carscallen has tried to argue as much in *The Other Country: Patterns in the Writing of Alice Munro* (1993), and, given Duffy's analysis here, such is what is found in "The Love of a Good Woman." Indeed, Munro's sequencing may well help to account for the minimal — though not unheard — dissent over her return to materials that readers have seen before in her stories — most apparent in *Who Do You Think You Are?*, which many reviewers thought in many ways a redone *Lives of Girls and Women*.

Although some critics grant mothers a more important place in Munro's work than fathers and offer good reasons for thinking so — gender identity, female desire, as well as others (Irvine 91–110) — such judgements are of less moment than their presences throughout the stories. Moreover, the autobiographical facts suggest something of what may be apprehended as the author's very different relationship with each parent, given only the determinant of available time: Munro's mother died in 1959, when Munro was twenty-eight, and her father lived until 1976, when she was forty-five. Taking up the early fiction, if stories are to be attributed on the basis of mothers and fathers in *Dance of the Happy Shades*, then it is about a draw, with two stories ("The Peace of Utrecht" and "Red Dress — 1946") concerned primarily with mothers, two with fathers ("Walker Brothers Cowboy" and "Images"), and one pitting the roles against each other ("Boys and Girls"). In *Lives of Girls and Women*, however, Del's father is something of a nonpresence, living out at the farm bachelor-style, with the hired man, while Del, her mother, and their boarder live in Jubilee; yet throughout that book the theme of gender roles dominates, and, if not represented by fathers, then male characters — Mr. Chamberlain and Del's boyfriends, Gerry Story and Garnet French — are certainly important.

These themes continue diversely in *Something I've Been Meaning to Tell You*, with a story such as "Material," a meditation on men's power, and the title story, about human secrets. In "The Ottawa Valley," though, the vision of Munro's mother reappears, focusing on another moment in their relationship from its predecessor, "The Peace of Utrecht," but the relationship is unmistakable. In the earlier story, the narrator returns to Jubilee from the West Coast to visit her sister, Helen, and her two small children. Their mother, who suffered a long decline, died earlier, and the purported "peace" of the story's title is as much between the two sisters as it is between the narrator, the facts that she learns about her mother's death, and the responsibility that she shares with her sister (see Thacker, "Connection"). Carrington discusses the autobiographical details of this story thoroughly, noting that Munro, in her reminiscence "Working for a Living," describes her "adolescent attitude toward her mother's disease: 'Most of the time I was angry at her, for her abdication and self-absorption. We argued' " (186).

In "The Ottawa Valley," Munro focuses not on the details of death but on that critical remembered moment when the narrator, as a young girl visiting the valley, testing its reality against her mother's mythic descriptions of it as her home place, recognized for the first time that her mother's infirmity would get the best of her:

> "So, are you not going to get sick at all?" I said, pushing further. I was very much relieved that she had decided against strokes, and that I would not have to be the mother, and wash and wipe and feed her lying in bed, as Aunt Dodie had had to do with her mother. For I did feel that it was she who decided, she gave her consent. As long as she lived, and through all the changes that happened to her, and after I had received the medical

explanations of what was happening, I still felt secretly that she had given her consent. For her own purposes, I felt she did it: display, of a sort; revenge of a sort as well. More, that nobody could ever understand. (*Something* 195)

Such a passage is precisely Munro: the immediacy of here and now is connected immediately with then and gone, with what is remembered. The "reckless" and "stubborn" inquisitiveness of the young girl is not to be allayed, so she pushes on, asking "Is your arm going to stop shaking?" and demanding that her mother "promise" her what she needs. "But she did not do it. For the first time she held out altogether against me. She went on as if she had not heard, her familiar bulk ahead of me turning strange, indifferent" (195).

But the passage from the story that has received the most attention from critics — and that I have quoted myself elsewhere — is the final, metafictional paragraph, a separate summing up in which Munro questions the very process of creating fiction; indeed, she comments on what has gone before in her own voice or in the narrator's, beginning with "If I had been making a proper story out of this . . ." and going on to realize that the central impetus of this story has been to purge herself of her mother, to "*get rid* of her." Munro concludes that this attempt has not worked, because her mother is still there in memory; "she weighs everything down," for "she looms too close, just as she always did" (246). Memory is obsessive indeed.

Judging from "Friend of My Youth" and "My Mother's Dream," Munro's mother is still looming. The former, a story within a story, tells of the family relationships of Flora Grieves, with whom the narrator's mother boarded while teaching school before her marriage and whose story is fascinating to the narrator herself; it is framed by the narrator's description of her dreams of her dead mother, a woman who bears the attributes of the mothers in "The Peace of Utrecht," "The Ottawa Valley," and "Home." The frame begins thus:

I used to dream about my mother, and though the details in the dream varied, the surprise in it was always the same. The dream stopped, I suppose because it was too transparent in its hopefulness, too easy in its forgiveness.

In the dream I would be the age I really was, living the life I was really living, and I would discover that my mother was still alive. (The fact is, she died when I was in my early twenties and she in her early fifties.)

. . . She would be looking quite well — not exactly youthful, not entirely untouched by the paralyzing disease that held her in its grip for a decade or more before her death, but so much better that I remembered that I would be astonished. Oh, I just have this little tremor in my arm, she would say, and a little stiffness up this side of my face. It is a nuisance but I get around.

. . . I would say that I was sorry I hadn't been to see her in such a long time — meaning not that I felt guilty but that I was sorry I had kept a bugbear in my mind, instead of this reality — and the strangest, kindest thing of all to me was her matter-of-fact reply.

Oh, well, she said, better late than never. I was sure I'd see you someday. (*Friend* 36)

Munro then turns to the story of Flora and her sister, Ellie, who is impregnated by Robert, Flora's betrothed, who then marries her, continuing to live with both sisters, though they physically divide the house into separate apartments. Ellie dies of too many failed pregnancies followed by cancer, and, romance be damned, instead of marrying Flora (finally), Robert marries Audrey Atkinson, an officious nurse who looked after Ellie. Atkinson is reminiscent of Mary McQuade in "Images" and anticipates Enid in "The Love of a Good Woman" (this is another textual "progress" derived from the mother that ought to be traced further). Eventually, Flora leaves the farm to them and takes a clerk's job in town. The connection to the narrator's mother is left hanging in the air, as it were, until deftly taken up again: Flora is the "friend of my youth" of the title, a form of address that the narrator once saw on one of the numerous letters that her mother, in her infirmity, began but seldom completed — written in the same schoolteacher's handwriting mentioned in "Home." Munro's concern is with the mysteries of sex in her mother's generation ("'sex' was a dark undertaking for women. She knew that you could die of it" [22]), her attachments to long-unseen friends such as Flora, and ultimately the narrator's connection with her mother as a separate being.

In a frequent device that characterizes the later stories, Munro concludes her story, completes her frame, echoes her earlier stories, and offers an equivocal insight in her final paragraphs:

Of course it's my mother I'm thinking of, my mother as she was in those dreams, saying, It's nothing, just this little tremor; saying with such astonishing lighthearted forgiveness, Oh, I knew you'd come someday. My mother surprising me, and doing it almost indifferently. Her mask, her fate, and most of her affliction taken away. How relieved I was, and happy. But now I recall that I was disconcerted as well. I would have to say that I felt slightly cheated. Yes. Offended, tricked, cheated, by this welcome turnaround, this reprieve. My mother moving rather carelessly out of her old prison, showing options and powers I never dreamed she had, changes more than herself. She changes the bitter lump of love I have carried all this time into a phantom — something useless and uncalled for, like a phantom pregnancy. (48)

Adding to the equivocation here, or to the mystery, is the story's final paragraph. There Munro offers the seemingly factual, but also ambiguous, definition of the Cameronians — the sect to which the Grieveses belonged — ending, as I noted at the outset, with the panache of one of the Cameronian "ministers," who, "in a mood of firm rejoicing at his own hanging, excommunicated all the other preachers in the world" (26). Although it is tempting to brush that paragraph aside and deal merely with the concluding, resonant image of the story proper (the narrator's "bitter lump of love" transformed "into a phantom"), Munro does not allow it. The penultimate ending echoes numerous other stories — "The Peace of Utrecht" and "Home" generally and "The Ottawa Valley" explicitly, even down to some of the same language ("Of course" with reference to summarizing her mother) — and it extends to the substance of the "Janet Stories" ("Chaddeleys and Flemings" and "The Moons of Jupiter") in the multiple mysteries of the bonds in families. It also suggests a reasonably clear summing up — an epiphany — of the sort found in Munro's early stories in *Dance of the Happy Shades* and in some of the recent stories in *The Love of a Good Woman* (e.g., "Rich as Stink"). Yet "Friend of My Youth" ends not with the words "something useless and uncalled for, like a phantom pregnancy," but with the triumphant Cameronian minister excommunicating all the others. And there that paragraph sits, mysterious, suggesting its meaning, offering not closure but continuance "just in the hope of seeing this trickle in time, making a connection, rescuing one thing from the rubbish." Alice Munro, writing "Home," tracing "The Progress of Love," finding "The Friend of [Her] Youth," wondering over the touchability and mystery of being, of being from and within Huron County, Ontario. Alice Munro, writing on. . . .

The Alice Munro Papers. Special Collections Division, U of Calgary Library.

The Alice Munro Papers: First Accession. Ed. Apollonia Steele and Jean F. Tener. Calgary: U of Calgary P, 1986.

The Alice Munro Papers: Second Accession. Ed. Apollonia Steele and Jean F. Tener. Calgary: U of Calgary P, 1987.

Buss, Helen M. *Mapping Our Selves: Canadian Women's Autobiography in English.* Montreal: McGill-Queen's UP, 1993.

Carrington, Ildikó de Papp. *Controlling the Uncontrollable: The Fiction of Alice Munro.* DeKalb: Northern Illinois UP, 1989.

Carscallen, James. *The Other Country: Patterns in the Writing of Alice Munro.* Toronto: ECW, 1993.

Houston, Pam. "A Hopeful Sign: The Making of Metonymic Meaning in Munro's 'Meneseteung.'" *Kenyon Review* 14.4 (1992): 79–92.

Irvine, Lorna. *Sub/Version.* Toronto: ECW, 1986.

MacKendrick, Louis K., ed. *Probable Fictions: Alice Munro's Narrative Acts.* Downsview, ON: ECW, 1984.

Munro, Alice. "Alice Munro." Interview with Douglas Freake et al. *What* 6 (1986): 8–10.

___. *Dance of the Happy Shades.* Toronto: McGraw, 1968.

___. "Everything Here Is Touchable and Mysterious." *Weekend Magazine* [*Toronto Star*] 11 May 1974: 33.

___. *Friend of My Youth.* Toronto: McClelland, 1990.

___. "Home." *New Canadian Stories: 74.* Ed. David Helwig and Joan Harcourt. Ottawa: Oberon, 1974. 133–53.

___. "Meneseteung." the *New Yorker* 11 Jan. 1988: 28–38.

___. *The Progress of Love.* Toronto: McClelland, 1986.

___. *Something I've Been Meaning to Tell You.* Toronto: McGraw, 1974.

Ross, Catherine Sheldrick. *Alice Munro: A Double Life.* Toronto: ECW, 1992.

Thacker, Robert. "Alice Munro and the Anxiety of American Influence." *Context North America: Canadian-U.S. Literary Relations.* Ed. Camille La Bossière. Ottawa: U of Ottawa P, 1994. 133–44.

___. "Conferring Munro." *Essays on Canadian Writing* 34 (1987): 162–69.

___. "Connection: Alice Munro and Ontario." *American Review of Canadian Studies* 14 (1984): 213–26.

___. "Go Ask Alice: The Progress of Munro Criticism." *Journal of Canadian Studies* 26.2 (1991): 156–69.

___. "So Shocking a Verdict in Real Life: Autobiography in Alice Munro's Stories." *Reflections: Autobiography and Canadian Literature.* Ed. K.P. Stich. Ottawa: U of Ottawa P, 1988. 153–61.

___. "What's 'Material'? The Progress of Munro Criticism, Part 2." *Journal of Canadian Studies* 33.2 (1998): 196–210.

Weaver, John. "Society and Culture in Rural and Small-Town Ontario: Alice Munro's Testimony on the Last Forty Years." *Patterns of the Past: Interpreting Ontario's History*. Ed. Roger Hall, William Westfall, and Laura Sefton MacDowell. Toronto: Dundurn, 1988. 381–402.

Welty, Eudora. "How I Write." *Virginia Quarterly Review* 31 (1955): 240–51.

___. "Some Notes on River Country." *The Eye of the Story: Selected Essays and Reviews*. 1944. New York: Vintage, 1979. 286–99.

Alice Munro and the
Scottish Nostalgic Grotesque

MAGDALENE REDEKOP

LOOK AT THE ROAD MAP of Huron County, Ontario, and you will find that Wingham (the place where Alice Munro grew up) and Clinton (where she lives now) are in the middle of a region generously sprinkled with Scottish names: Culloden, Fingal, Kincardine, Melrose, Iona, Dungannon, Ailsa Cragg, New Dundee, and many more. Of course, Ontario also has a Dublin, a Stratford, a Paris, and even a Sparta (not to mention Brantford, named after the Mohawk chief Joseph Brant), but there is no question that the area is especially resonant with displaced Scottish history. Munro has described it as a "rural culture with strong Scots-Irish background . . . that has become fairly stagnant. With a big sense of righteousness. But with big bustings-out and grotesque crime. And ferocious sexual humour . . ." (qtd. in Ross 26).

Tour guides suggest a visit to Goderich, in the heart of this area:

> An excellent way of having an overall view not only of the harbour but of the Maitland River, which drains into Lake Huron, is by walking across the Menesetung Bridge. . . . Menesetung is the Chippewa name for the Maitland River and interpretations for the word include "laughing water" — thought to refer to the sound of the water running over rocks in the river. (Kilpatrick)

Other travel books translate the Ojibway word *menesetung* as "healing water." Laughter, they say, is the best medicine, and when a name or a "saying" comes out of an oral culture there is no way of finally confirming the correct meaning or spelling by "looking it up." Munro spells it Meneseteung, and in earlier stories it is the Wawanash. Her comments about the river — whatever its name — are often quoted: "This ordinary place is sufficient, everything here touchable and mysterious" (qtd. in Ross 24). The idea that a mysterious river is somehow the original source of all her stories, however, can be misleading, luring critics down a nostalgic garden path that leads to a dead end. Although she does not write satire of the sort that John Kenneth Galbraith does in his wry book *The Scotch*, there is not another contemporary writer as unsentimental and antinostalgic as Munro.

Catherine Sheldrick Ross writes that, "when Munro looks at Huron County, she sees a whole geology and archeology of meaning" and that she "has an archeological sense of layers of human history" (26). Critics have typically collapsed Del Jordan into Alice Munro when referring to Del's passionate desire to get it all in, "every layer of speech and thought, stroke of light on bark or walls, every smell, pothole, pain, crack, delusion, held still and held together — radiant, everlasting" (*Lives* 210). The deliberate hyperbole of the last two words in that layered sentence opens up an ironic distance between Munro and Jordan. For Munro, this aesthetic goal is complicated by a profound respect for layers beyond her experience. This respect is what makes her archaeology so meticulous and her dilemma so fierce. She does not attempt to write from either the Chippewa or the Ojibway point of view about the Meneseteung River, but neither does she turn a blind eye to those or any other layers. She does not idealize lost oral cultures, but neither does she stay grimly within the confines of a realistic representation of the world around her. The present tense, for her, is dynamic, not static. It is the present of the act of writing or telling and the act of reading or listening. The listener has a share in this dynamic process: there is no innocent or passive ear. It is this dynamic approach that for her makes of an "ordinary place" a crossing like those in fairy stories, a place where wonderful transformations can happen, where stories are exchanged like gifts.

From the seminal early story "Images" to the most recent one, "Save the Reaper," Munro's stories are full of the simple wonder of what might happen next. The focus in her latest story is on the possibility of alien invasion, but the magic is the same as it would be if the "invaders" were fairies. Indeed, despite the shift in point of view from child to grandmother, the conclusions of "Images" and "Save the Reaper" are almost interchangeable. Like the grandmother in "Save the Reaper," the father in "Images" returns to tell of the adventure. He teases Mary McQuade by telling her how Joe Phippen gave whisky to a cat. Both stories conclude with a secret pact between adult and child. In "Images," Mary becomes suspicious and protective of the child: "Was he feeding the whisky to her too?":

"Not a drop," said my father, and looked steadily down the table at me. Like the children in fairy stories who have seen their parents make pacts with terrifying strangers, who have discovered that our fears are based on nothing but the truth, but who come back fresh from marvellous escapes and take up their knives and forks, with humility and good manners, prepared to live happily ever after — like them, dazed and powerful with secrets, I never said a word. (*Dance* 43)

In "Save the Reaper," the child, Philip, looks up at his grandmother with "a flat look, a moment of conspiratorial blankness, a buried smile, that passed before there could be any demand for recognition of it. It seemed to mean that, however much or little he knew, he knew about the importance of keeping things to yourself" (135). Taken together, the two stories are like companion tales of innocence and experience that draw attention to Munro's ongoing profound connection with oral storytelling traditions.

The fairy tales that work as intertexts here and in other stories are not, of course, specifically Scottish. It is possible to see the sinister Mary McQuade and the genial storytelling father as two sides of Scottishness for the child in "Images." What I want to argue, however, goes beyond the thematic level. I want to demonstrate, through an exploration of the interworkings of orality and print, that a Scottish oral tradition informs Munro's craft at the deepest level, particularly as it has come to her through the writings of her ancestor James Hogg. Her 1979 story on "The Irish" (see "Better Place"), although moving, is written in a fairly straightforward representational style and demonstrates none of the complexity that results from the Scottish influence. Although Munro is of mixed Scots, Irish, and English descent, she seems to identify most with her father's Scottish ancestors. The most recent evidence of this affiliation is the marvellous piece entitled "Changing Places," in which the very obliqueness of her passing references to Hogg (as if his perspective is a given) argues for his importance to her.

An explicit nonfictional narrative by Munro about her ancestors is a rare thing, but the Scottish emphasis, however implicit, has always been there. The narrator of the semiautobiographical "Connection" — in a sentence significantly beginning with "It is a fact . . ." (*Moons* 7) — comments on how Canadians of Scottish and Irish descent boast of their poverty, while Canadians of English descent claim lost aristocracies. She scorns her mother's cousins for admiring their snobbish grandfather Chaddeley:

> I had too much Scottish blood in me, too much of my father. My father would never have admitted there were inferior people, or superior people either. He was scrupulously egalitarian, making it a point not to "snivel," as he said, to anybody, not to kowtow, and not to highhat anybody, either, to behave as if there were no differences. I took the same tack. (*Moons* 9–10)

"Scrupulously egalitarian" is an apt phrase to describe Munro's fiction, but the image of Scotland that emerges from it is complex and even contradictory. It is hard to reconcile the egalitarianism, for example, with the intolerance of the fanatical Presbyterians who people her fiction. Del's mother in *Lives of Girls and Women* worries that fanaticism may be hereditary. In "The Progress of Love," one wonders if the narrator's mother's fanaticism is as bizarrely Scottish as the narrator's name, Euphemia. In an often-quoted phrase, Munro has referred to the "extremely crazy Calvinism" that she works with in herself (qtd. in Truss). The repressed aunts in "The Stone in the Field" — like Milton Homer's Methodist aunts in "Who Do You Think You Are?" — are grotesque in their life-denying rigidity, yet one could argue that Munro's own scrupulosity about ethical issues is characteristic of both Methodism and Presbyterianism.

Munro's more recent stories contain increasingly explicit Scottish references. "Friend of My Youth" contains tantalizing allusions to Hogg's *The Private Memoirs and Confessions of a Justified Sinner, Written by Himself*, so much so that Lynne Truss observes that "the presence of James Hogg signalling wildly from the past is impossible to overlook." (Not so impossible for Canadian and American readers, it must be said.) The story is rich with historical details that Hogg also used as raw material. He sometimes viewed Cameronians sympathetically; they appear in Munro's story as some "freak religion from Scotland" (*Friend* 5). Most spectacular in its implications for the debate about orality and print is the book burning. Although it is only imagined, it is shocking nonetheless, particularly in a story by Munro: "Those smelly old books. . . . The elect, the damned, the slim hopes, the mighty torments — up in smoke. There was the ending" (21). It is a smoke signal saying to me that, whatever else, her views on closure, like Hogg's, are informed by her response to the Calvinist doctrine of predestination. Against these horrific scenes of a fixed Calvinist fate and the fixed words of print, Munro sets the frail speech act of the salutation: *Friend of My Youth*. Despite the associations of that phrase with grief, guilt, and nostalgia, it is like a trace, left by her mother's hand — not a transparent sign leading to transcendental significance but an opaque chirographic that acts as a catalyst for an ongoing dynamic storytelling exchange.

An equally complex interworking of orality and print is apparent in "Wilderness Station." The frequent repetition of the word *saying* signals the central importance of orality in this story. Munro plays on the split between the kind of saying that is incantatory and the kind of saying that constitutes a speech act. The "minister came and said the service" (*Open Secrets* 229). "We went out and said the Lord's Prayer" (249). Annie is able to sew up the corpse only by saying something — anything: "I sewed on, and every bit of him I lost sight of I would say even out loud, there goes, there goes" (244). The urgency of her orders to George — "I said, listen" and "All you have to do is say you are sorry" (246) — underscore that the various ways of saying and seeing are related to the issue of control and power. Her random appeal to the printed Bible — "It says so in the Bible" (247) — is undermined and rendered absurd by the traces on her body: the "black and blue marks" that she tries to hide, that are an open secret to the reader (248).

Even this cursory look at a few stories suggests to me that the Scottish connection needs to be seen as more than a blurry background for interpretations of Munro's fiction if one is to understand the complex interplay of orality and print. Because they have not been interrogated, assumptions about this background have contributed to misreadings of Munro that categorize her as a writer of realism that is somehow both grim and nostalgic. The Scottish connection is important on a deeper level, one that ultimately aligns her not with that kind of realism but with what Mikhail Bakhtin has called "grotesque realism" (18). Her response to the Scottish experience enables her to resist even as she acknowledges the power of nostalgia.

It is becoming increasingly obvious that the shapes of Munro's stories cannot be accounted for without some reference to orality. As her stories get longer and longer, they push at the limits of generic categories. Are they just very long short stories? If they get long enough, can we call them novels? The context of oral tradition helps to explain the layered nature of Munro's stories, how they meander like a river toward no conspicuous goal. Of course, the issue gets instantly more complicated when we acknowledge the coexistence of orality and print. That her stories meander through the columns of the *New Yorker* is, after all, a large factor in the particular pleasures that they offer. This complexity is apparent in her titles, which reflect an oral bias yet acknowledge the realities of the publishing business. Munro tends to reject static titles (e.g., *The Beggar Maid*) in favour of more unwieldy titles, which are sometimes actual speech acts: *Something I've Been Meaning to Tell You, Who Do You Think You Are?* It is not "The Grim Reaper" but an urgent imperative, "Save the Reaper." Walter Ong notes that "label-like titles as such are not very operational in oral cultures" (126). When Munro does use them, she seems to favour place names that suggest transience or are ironically displaced tourist destinations: "Marrakesh," "Miles City, Montana," "Jakarta," "Meneseteung." Although the names are like printed signposts, there is always suggested movement, the sense of stories that come out of life and feed back into life.

Munro is a storyteller. No matter how long her stories get, she will never be a novelist. Walter Benjamin differentiates the novel from "the fairy tale, the legend, even the novella" in that it "neither comes from oral tradition nor goes into it" (87). The storyteller, by contrast, "takes what he tells from experience — his own or that reported by others. And he in turn makes it the experience of those who are listening to his tale" (87). Munro's stories are notoriously resistant to interpretation because they are like gossip: the best response is an answering story. Her profound connection with orality similarly accounts for her popularity, for that feeling you have when reading a Munro story that you are reading about your own life and, conversely, for those uncanny moments, while you are busy living your life, when you become convinced that you are inside a Munro story. Like Homer, Munro is a genius at deploying the formulas and commonplaces that make up our lives. She is not a writer of that epiphanic kind of short story that Benjamin describes, that has "removed itself from oral tradition and no longer permits that slow piling one on top of the other of thin, transparent layers which constitutes the most appropriate picture of the way in which the perfect narrative is revealed through the layers of a variety of retellings" (93; see also Ong 144). Munro has described her method in words much like Benjamin's:

> what I want . . . is a lot of overlap. I want things to come in as
> many layers as possible, which means the stories have to come

from as many people as possible, with their different baggage of memories. And then I have to hold them still in one frame. (qtd. in MacFarlane 54)

Holding still in a frame — a still — is a cinematic metaphor, more so than "held still and held together" (*Lives* 210). Both images remind us, however, that this is a craft actually worked out in print and that Munro must out-Homer Homer.

How does the fact that Munro's own baggage is mainly Scottish influence her craft? James Carscallen comments briefly on her Scottish allusions (75–77). He draws attention to Blaikie Noble, in "Something I've Been Meaning to Tell You," with his "Scottish name and romantic wooing," who tells Char and Et that the "Scottish ballad singer" is drunk and wears corsets. Blaikie is "Scottish and lordly," but also a "born loser," and Scotland in Munro's stories "is connected with her imagery of misfortune and death" (75). Carscallen observes that Munro "admits to weeping at the thought of Mary's execution," and he notes that Del Jordan wallows in histories in which "Mary and other great losers go to their deaths in the most romantic ways imaginable" (76). One thinks of great losers such as Bonnie Prince Charlie and the lost Jacobite cause that inspired so much poetry, including poems by James Hogg. Nostalgia is clearly an inevitable part of the Scottish baggage that must be unpacked.

T.C. Smout blames the nostalgic approach to Scottish history on the fact that the achievement of Sir Walter Scott "mesmerized his contemporaries." Underlying all Scott's art, according to Smout, is a "nostalgia for the Scottish past that seems to say that that which is Scottish and that which is past must therefore be admirable" (467). With expectations conditioned by Scott, readers of the time did not "much like anything that came nearer the bone." As Smout notes, Hogg's *The Private Memoirs and Confessions of a Justified Sinner*, which did so and which violated those expectations, is now seen by many as "the most interesting Scottish novel ever written," but it met with "a uniformly hostile and indifferent reception" at the time (468).

It would be difficult to exaggerate the influence of Hogg on the writing of Munro. With the notable exception of Ildikó de Papp Carrington's excellent article, however, that influence has gone virtually unnoticed. This is a pity, because a dose of Hogg's exuberant parody would be a useful corrective to misreadings of Munro that involve her in the very nostalgia that she resists. It is not so much Hogg himself as his self-constructions that we need to consider. In

The Performing Self, Richard Poirier sees self-parody (with the exception of Laurence Sterne) as a recent phenomenon. His description of Jorge Luis Borges, however, could apply as well to Hogg, who "won't allow *any* element" "to become stabilized or authoritative," and who himself "cannot be located in most of his writing" (43). These features endear Hogg to increasing numbers of contemporary critics, but his precocious genius was not without problems in his own time, not the least of which was his abject poverty. His tendency to self-parody was exploited by the Edinburgh literati for their own purposes. "The Ettrick Shepherd" was a regular participant in the *Blackwood's* series called the *Noctes Ambrosianae*. Indeed, Hogg was the life of the party. His ambivalent participation in this exercise has provided enough material to keep scholars occupied for a long time. Caroline McCracken-Flesher has recently argued persuasively that Hogg was "fully aware of the tourist refiguration of Scotland" and of his part in that business. Although he often objected vehemently to misrepresentations of him, at other times, when it suited him, "he wrapped himself in his plaid and posed as 'The Ettrick Shepherd' " (35).

The postcolonial Scots "functioned as tourists in their own land, even as they were reconstructed as the sight to see," writes McCracken-Flesher (33). The discomforts of such exotic ethnicity are familiar to me as a Mennonite.

> After leaving Goderich, head into the countryside [near St. Jacobs] where buggy makers still ply their trade, and farmers plow fields behind huge workhorses — pulling five abreast. Better still, drive out early on a Sunday morning when backroads are crammed with scores of buggies heading to their separate meeting places: bearded old men and their wives, stiff young bachelors riding alone, grinning kids in straw hats. Little has changed since their ancestors came. It's a scene right out of history. (Fulton and King J4)

Don't forget to take your camera, but remember that some of the Amish still have an aversion to being photographed. In *Camera Lucida: Reflections on Photography*, Roland Barthes tries to account for the pain of being photographed: "each time I am (or let myself be) photographed, I invariably suffer from a sensation of inauthenticity, sometimes of imposture (comparable to certain nightmares)" (14). A non-Amish Mennonite travelling into Amish territory is similar to the wandering postcolonial Scot who "stood displaced not just from his land, but from his image; a new, tartan-clad self loomed romantically in his place" (McCracken-Flesher 31). My awareness of this shared dilemma now colours my memory of how I became a lover of Scottish songs as a child growing up on a Mennonite farm in Manitoba. It must have been just after the Russians launched Sputnik that my mother gave me a "rocket radio" for Christmas. (I remember the Low German joke: *Shput Nik. Daut mut nik.* "Mock not. You must not.") It was small enough to hold in one hand. The plastic bulb at the end of a cord went into one ear. By pulling up the metal knob at the top of the rocket, I could tune in to the local station, CFAM. The reception was excellent.

Television was forbidden, and the single radio was permitted only for religious broadcasts, but with this gadget I had instant secret access to the world outside our Mennonite community. My private ritual was to tune in every night at eleven, after all the lights were out, to a program called *Songs of the Nations.* I had never met anyone from Scotland, and there were no books about that country in the one-room school that I attended, but this lack of knowledge was no barrier to the potent charm of the Scottish songs. Like Plato, my father (had he known) would have viewed this charm as dangerous. I lay in my bed in the prairie dark, listening with impunity to the voice of Kenneth McKellar. Places such as Loch Lomond had a strange resonance for me, as if I already knew them well. *Loch* was the Low German word for "hole"; the *vota loch*, or "water hole," was the largest body of water I had seen.

The Scots dialect and Low German (my mother tongue) are in fact both closer to Old English and to each other on the English-language tree than they are to standard contemporary English and German. Mine was a borrowed nostalgia nonetheless. I could not yet conceive of a construction of my self that would be able to survive outside the Mennonite walls, so I shamelessly appropriated the secondhand trappings of the Scottish other offered to me via the illusion of remote control. Like a souvenir, my rocket radio could only "evoke and resonate to," could "never entirely recoup," authentic experience (Stewart, *On Longing* 135). Even as I acknowledge its inauthenticity, however, I feel a renewed and stubborn loyalty to my old flame. The image of the "tartan-clad" Scot may well have been constructed by an imperial power for economic reasons, but mine was not a visual experience. I still feel a sort of "blind gratitude" (Hyde 16) toward the invisible source of my midnight aural consolations. It still seems to require from me some answering gesture, however oblique.

My love of Scottish songs continued after I left the farm, so much so that my husband called me Maggie McFalk when we were courting. Having done its work, however, the Scottish spirit (like a household Brownie) made herself scarce as I went on to reinvent myself in terms more true to my Mennonite origins. My interest in things Scottish went underground, so I considered myself lucky when I happened upon James Hogg in a library just when I was expected to write a doctoral dissertation. While scholarly work on Hogg legitimized my love affair with Scotland, I continued to keep a wary distance from my unfamiliar/familiar other. Moving to Ontario was not free of culture shock for me. Sometimes I think that I will never feel at home in a place where it is improper to weep at funerals. The more I experienced of this Anglo-Saxon reticence, the more I was fascinated by Hogg's vacillation between clever self-concealing dramatization and reckless self-exposure.

These issues came briefly to the fore when I had the pleasure of meeting Cliff Hanley, the man who wrote the lyrics for "Scotland the Brave," the very words sung into my ear by Kenneth McKellar those many years ago. I was astonished to find that the words had an author who was alive and well and living in Glasgow. I must have assumed that they were so ancient as to have been born, not made. Hanley was the Scottish writer-in-residence at Glendon College in Toronto from 1979 to 1980. I *had* to meet him, in order to be convinced of his existence, so my husband and I invited him to dinner. Like Hogg, Hanley was self-taught and given to mendacious self-dramatization. He wrote thrillers as Henry Calvin and satirical Scots verse as Ebenezer McIlwham. I was fascinated and entertained and still treasure his gift, a chapbook of selected poems signed "Yer aul' frien' an' scribe, Ebenezer." I could not help noticing, however, that my friends with Scottish names responded ambivalently to the author of "Scotland the Brave." Gradually, I have become aware of a strange figure shadowing the singers of the Scottish songs that comforted me as a youth. The tourist version of this Scottish nostalgic grotesque consists of a mishmash of plaids and bagpipes pointing every which way so drunkenly as to result in an embarrassing spectacle. This is not — let's be clear on this — either Hanley or Hogg. It is my aul' frien' Ebenezer McIlwham, and it is The Ettrick Shepherd in some of his guises.

When I began work on Munro, I had no idea that she was related to Hogg. I was aware that her father was Scottish, and I had even written a review of his novel *The McGregors* in 1980. Beyond that,

I did not give much thought to what might be "Scottish" about her. As I think about it now, it strikes me that her connection to Hogg, The Ettrick Shepherd, must be like having a trickster for an ancestor — a trickster who could not always control his shape-shifting. Perhaps her aesthetic of conscious, clowning failure has its roots in her understanding of Hogg's dilemma. In *Roland Barthes*, Barthes observes that "You are the only one who can never see yourself except as an image" (qtd. in Jefferson 170). Ann Jefferson isolates the resulting problem: "Since the body is what others see and what the subject does not, the subject becomes dependent upon the Other in a way that ultimately makes the body the focus of a power struggle with far-reaching ramifications" (153). This was Hogg's problem, as many of his readers now see it. They lament the fact that Hogg was condemned to a repertoire of images that lay "in the hands of the Other" (170).

My own view is not so bleak, because I see Hogg's response to his dilemma as resulting in a vigorous comic aesthetic. Because critics who choose to write about Hogg have to endure endless bad puns about pigs, we develop considerable empathy for him in this regard. We have all rehearsed the obvious defences, that *hogg* is really a small sheep in Scots, and so on. Hogg himself rejects such defensiveness and plays a carnivalesque game with his name. In their "social semiotics of the pig in its relation to 'low' discourses, the body and the fair," Peter Stallybrass and Allon White note that "pigs seem to have borne the brunt of our rage, fear, affection and desire for the 'low' " (44). Hogg was the victim of an ambivalence that they describe as typical: "But disgust always bears the imprint of desire. These low domains, apparently expelled as 'Other', return as the object of nostalgia, longing and fascination . . ." Just as "idealization and phobic avoidance" are two sides of the same coin (191), so too anonymous disgust for Hogg's supposed vulgarities was expressed in *Blackwood's* alongside drooling descriptions (not usually anonymous) of his natural unschooled genius.

Although Munro is luckily not burdened with Hogg's name, she and Hogg are not only relatives but also kindred spirits in their approaches to art. It seems logical to begin an investigation of these shared issues with the figure of Milton Homer in "Who Do You Think You Are?" He is a low entertainer with a high name who pigs out on "date squares, hermits, Nanaimo bars and fruit drops, butter tarts and brownies" (*Who* 244). When he performs his mock christenings, he opens his mouth wide and takes up "each phrase with a deep grunt" (236), but his name is not Hogg. Like the blind leading the blind, Milton, the name of a puritan epic writer, stands in front of an older oral epic tradition represented by the name Homer. His aunts, Hattie and Mattie Milton, on the other hand, represent a puritanical rigidity specifically associated with a print culture. Hattie assigns verbatim memorization, a "text-based concept" (Ong 61), and insists that each student first pass through a laborious chirographic stage: "One day she wrote a long poem on the board and said that everyone was to copy it out, then learn it off by heart, and the next day recite it" (Who 242). In skipping the first step, Rose stays with the oral stage, thus provoking from Hattie the challenge taken up as the book's title: "Who do you think you are?" (243).

Visitors who see Milton Homer ask "Who is that?" But he is "not all there" (239). In his apparent lack of individual identity, he is a parody of Bakhtin's carnival body. Inflated as a mocking version of King Billy, he is the body of grotesque realism paraded as a walking "egotistic form" pretending to be universal (Bakhtin 19). However, Munro makes his performance a means to a celebration that is more like what Bakhtin seemed to have in mind. Rose mimicking Ralph mimicking Milton Homer is a different parade, one in which the "material bodily principle is contained not in the biological individual, not in the bourgeois ego, but in the people, a people who are constantly growing and renewed" (Bakhtin 19). This parade is not represented. It is available only by means of our participation in Munro's comedy. Participation acts out a dissolution of ego that moves to carnival through parody of the "flaming bigotry" that is so often coloured orange (Who 237). By itself, the "Orange Walk was the most splendid of all the parades" (237), and a spectator might be distracted by the gorgeous silk banners. Fanaticism and bigotry are made visible through the "ferocious gifts" of Milton Homer (238).

Thinking of Hogg, the man advertised as a natural talent but also a "mimic of ferocious gifts" (238), it is tempting to see Milton Homer as a parody of an oral bard. Instead of words coming out of his mouth, there is food going into it. He is also, however, a parody of a writer. Instead of writing with the pen, he "put the pen in his mouth, too, so that ink had blotched his lips" (Who 245–46). This is the writer as clown. Although it seems to be an apt image for Hogg, I am not suggesting that Milton Homer is Munro's representation of James Hogg. He is one of various embodiments of what I am calling the Scottish nostalgic grotesque. To imagine The Ettrick Shepherd as joining the parade of mimics helps to demonstrate how far Munro is from a transparent, classic realism that capitulates to nostalgia. The "grotesque realism" of the bodies in the parade — Rose mimicking Ralph mimicking Milton Homer — insists on the present reality of performance and on a dynamic process that dissolves the boundary between spectator and participant. Munro's wicked parody, her play on low and high views of art, her construction of a grotesque body that resists nostalgia by posturing it — these techniques are informed by her understanding of Hogg.

Such an emphasis on the body is a direct consequence of a focus on orality. As Ong points out, the spoken word "never exists in a simple verbal context, as a written word does. Spoken words are always modifications of a total, existential situation, which always engages the body" (67). Does it matter whether the body in question is male or female? This is an interesting question to ask in relation to the issue of ballad transmission. In 1988, when I first wrote to Munro, it was the grotesque body of the constructed mother that intrigued me. I was well into my book on Munro, my dissertation on Hogg receding into the hazy past, when somebody at a conference in Scotland casually mentioned that Munro was a descendant of Hogg. Curiosity eventually drove me to write to Munro to ask if this was true. "Yes," she wrote in her letter of 30 May 1988. "One of Margaret Laidlaw's brothers (she was James Hogg's mother) was my direct ancestor. We came from Ettrick."

Alice Munro related to James Hogg's mother? Alice Munro a descendant of the woman who was a source for many of the ballads printed by Sir Walter Scott in *Minstrelsy of the Scottish Border*? I found it hard to believe, but there it was in a handwritten letter signed by Munro herself. Looking at her generous, flowing handwriting, I was intensely conscious of the fact that Hogg did not learn to read and write (or so he claimed) until he was an adult. I had read his story of how his mother scolded Scott: "there was never ane o' my songs prentit till ye prentit them yoursell, an' ye hae spoilt them a'thegither. They war made for singing, an' no for reading; and they're nouther right spelled nor right setten down" (*Memoirs* 62). I had heard this anecdote often repeated as an expression of nostalgia for a vanished oral tradition, and I couldn't connect it with Munro at all.

Where does Margaret Laidlaw fit in that mockingly linear literary history going from Homer to Milton to Chapman to Keats to Milton Homer through Ralph through Rose to Alice Munro? Marshall McLuhan's definition of primary orality was not much help. Recent theories have questioned the chasm that McLuhan constructed between primary orality and print, and this development brings Laidlaw's role into sharper focus. Ruth Finnegan, for example, stresses that oral communication is not "natural" but based, like print, on "social and cultural conventions" (14) and that these conventions vary depending on "particular historical conditions" and "specific individuals, groups and cultures" (176).

In a recent book, Penny Fielding considers the specific case of Scott and Hogg within this new "broader historical perspective which resists the idea of the sudden death of orality" (14). She retells the famous anecdote about Laidlaw's complaint to Scott, noting that it presents a "seemingly unbridgeable gulf between an oral recitation and a written record," whereas the actual "mixture of sources" involved an "inevitable blurring of the oral and the literary" (47). Percy, Ritson, and Scott, she claims, "made ballad literature popular among a fashionable readership, yet, at the same time, actual orality was systematically demoted as the production of socially inferior classes" (44). The "best kind of memory," for Scott, was "not the historical palimpsest of oral memory, but the imagined documentary accuracy of writing" (56). He eventually posited a "highly gifted individual" as the ballad maker and moved "towards a view of authorship which in fact eliminates the ballad's transmitters" (57).

McCracken-Flesher faults Hogg for his part in this elimination. She argues that he "participated in the nineteenth century's tourist reconstruction of Scotland" and that, by acting as "a conduit for his mother's songs to Scott and thence to the English proto-tourist audience, he himself deserves the criticism Mrs. Hogg levelled at the Sheriff" (34). This judgement evades a central dilemma — namely, that Hogg himself recorded his mother's speech and that the anecdote itself may have been written with tourist consumption in mind. It is true, however, that Laidlaw's contribution, in this new theoretical context, looms much larger than it did before, and her role should be of particular interest to readers of Munro.

Mary Ellen Brown notes that "Students of balladry and song have come late to the consideration of 'gender,'" but recent studies have shown that gender may influence "the subject matter chosen, the style and venue of performance, and the meaning/significance of the material" (51). She takes part of her title, "Old Singing Women," from a heading written by William Motherwell in his collection notebook (44). In her discussion of fieldwork, she describes the excitement resulting from "the discovery of an individual with an extensive repertoire, an individual who might be called a specialist in oral balladry and song" (46). She uses as her main example "Mrs. Brown of Falkland," an educated woman who would have wanted, instead, to be known for her literary verse (49). Catherine Kerrigan notes that all the "major male collectors of the ballad . . . refer to women as a primary source of their material" and that "women played such a significant role as tradition bearers and transmitters that it can be claimed that the ballad tradition is one of the most readily identifiable areas of literary performance by women" (2).

No story speaks more explicitly and more profoundly about the importance of the singing old women than "Hold Me Fast, Don't Let Me Pass" in *Friend of My Youth*. The story stages the Scottish nostalgic grotesque as a tourist destination. In an astonishingly bold gesture, Munro reinstates the figure of the ballad transmitter eliminated by the ballad collectors. The effect, for me at least, is a kind of extratextual scene of recognition. In the story, Hazel goes to Scotland to track down her dead husband's old flame, but the lines of her inquiry get hopelessly crossed, and that scene of recognition never happens. As the story moves around the central figure of Margaret Dobie, the old woman who recites "Tam Lin," there is a gradual recognition of the historical importance of this figure. I am saying not that she is or represents Margaret Laidlaw but that I couldn't read the story without awareness of this extratextual knowledge. There is a sense in the story of boundaries collapsing. Anything might happen in a story that takes place near a fairy crossing.

Munro's history-making inclusion of the old female ballad transmitter *as* a maker of history is consistent with the new approach to orality developed by John Miles Foley in *The Singer of Tales in Performance*. In the terms of this new theory, Margaret Dobie's recitation not only transmits but also *constitutes* tradition. The details of social history excluded by the male collectors of ballads are all parts of this performance and visible in the situation that elicits the recitation. The story in "Hold Me Fast, Don't Let Me Pass" is a formulaic love triangle (two overlapping triangles, in fact), but the emotion in those relationships is discharged by the performance of the old woman.

There is a frightful amount of pain in the story. It seems to me, in fact, that the pain would be unbearable without the recitation, during which Judy stuffs herself with the cake that was intended as a gift for Dudley. "The gift turned inward," in May Sarton's words, "unable to be given, becomes a heavy burden, even sometimes a kind of poison. It is as if the flow of life were backed up" (qtd. in Hyde 146).

Absurdly, one hears another Antoinette say "Let them eat cake," and, when Antoinette vomits by the roadside on the return trip, it seems that the wrong woman is vomiting. Gifts are given and not received; messages are sent and lost. Even the focus on Judy's hair, "glorious — a ripply fan of red hair, shining over her shoulders" (*Friend* 91), is ominous. The visual sense, unlike the aural sense, has a cutting effect, and the "flamboyance" of the "spread-out hair," brushed to a gloss and arranged "on show," has the effect of separating her head from her body. Her expression is like that of a child "holding back a howl" (94), and this silencing seems to fuel the fear of decapitation, as if only a release of her voice could reconnect her head to her body (see Eilberg-Schwartz and Doniger 6). When Dudley asks if she still has her "wonderful red hair" and Hazel responds with "Did you think she would have shaved it off?" (*Friend* 100), I had a fleeting image of the decapitated Mary, Queen of Scots, and thought of Munro weeping.

Perhaps the cake was poisoned, Dudley suggests later. *Gift* is, in fact, the German word for "poison." One thinks of Snow White, the wicked queen, the dwarfs — but all the roles are grotesquely distorted, like the hideous, swirling shapes of the changing elf in the ballad. "In the midst of this an old woman" sits on a high-backed chair. Her arms and legs are thick, and she wears men's shoes (a gender blurring reminiscent of the Scottish ballad singer who is pictured wearing a corset in "Something I've Been Meaning to Tell You"). She volunteers to "say" a recitation and does so — some "rigmarole about fairies" (*Friend* 95). Somewhere, in the midst of the swirling deception and confusion, a gift is given, and somewhere else a gift is received. Although the exchanges taking place at this crossing are not all visible, there is no question about the generosity of Margaret Dobie. The story reads like a tribute to her.

There is an interplay here between language used as incantation and language used to send messages or signals. The central incantatory text is the ballad "Tam Lin." Except for a change of name from Janet to Jennet, Munro seems to be working with the version of the ballad in Scott's *Minstrelsy of the Scottish Border*. This version, Scott writes, was "prepared from a collation of the printed copies with a very accurate one in Glenriddel's MSS, and with several recitals from tradition" (472). He does not say whether one of these recitals was by Margaret Laidlaw, nor does he specify on what basis he judged the Glenriddel version to be "very accurate" (see also Child 335–58).

It is unusual for Munro to interpolate quotations of poetry within her stories. When she does — in "The Ottawa Valley" and in "Meneseteung" — it is in aid of an exploration of history charged with an emotion so intense that it seems to require the stabilizing addition of metrical regularity. As if to accentuate the boldness of the poetic interpolation, Munro does not transcribe Margaret Dobie's speech as a simulation of the Scots dialect. Although we are told that the Scottish accent thickens during the recitation, the distinction between Hazel's Canadian speech and Dobie's Scottish speech (or Dudley's, for that matter) is not apparent in print. This rejection of printed dialect prevents readers from letting the old woman slip back into that quaint and primitivist oral realm that celebrates the speaker even as it eliminates her, but it also heightens the archaic effect of the ballad itself.

When Dudley and Hazel make a joint effort to remember, leading to a second full (understood) recitation of the ballad, the reader hears the meter as a kind of subtext or underground river. Hazel "tentatively" offers a line of iambic tetrameter and one of iambic trimeter: "First dip me in a stand of milk? . . . Then in a stand of water?" Dudley follows up with another two lines of the same: "But hold me fast, don't let me pass. . . . I'll be your bairn's father!" (100). Together they complete a quatrain. The regularity of the metrical pattern is signalled by the title and undergirds the entire story. The language of the title works both as incantation and as speech act, and this collapse of functions that are usually divided is a part of the story's special power. This power lies in an acceptance of failure, in the awareness of all that can never be said or known but that may be contained in the sheer sound of poetry. In "Lyric Possession," Susan Stewart accounts for some of this power:

> Meter has its own internal history, its own evolution, and along that temporal path it accrues a weight of allusion. . . . Ballad, hymn and other song forms using this structure are meters with a particularly rich legacy of accrued meanings. To use these forms means that one carries over into writing an enormous weight of social and cultural resonance. (40–41)

If, as Fielding argues, Scott reduced the singing old women to "mindless mimics" who were "separated from their own stories" (55), then Munro's singing woman is certainly a forceful contrast. She is a maker of the history that she sings, the focal point within the overlapping layers of stories that contain her. She exhibits what

Benjamin refers to as the social function of story (see 108), and her recitation of "Tam Lin" — partly because of the omission of the text of the ballad in the story — puts the focus on the lines connecting the ballad to the overlapping stories. To adapt a sentence that Fielding uses in another context, Dobie "performs a version of it that is relevant at the moment of narration" (105), yet any effort to spell out the precise nature of that relevance will result in failure and return readers to the reality of sheer sound. Significantly, it is during the recitation, in the moment of acceptance of this inevitable failure, that Hazel abandons her futile quest.

Munro tends to construct the nostalgic as grotesque, the better to repudiate it, but Dobie is not the wicked wolf disguised as grandmother. Despite her oddly assembled costume, she is very much herself, precisely because she is fully absorbed into the present of performance. As a tourist destination, she is redeemed from triviality and erasure by that performance and by its importance to the people around her. Poirier notes that "Performance creates life in literature in the sense that it is itself the act and evidence of life. It is a way of being present, in every sense of that word" (44).

I see that I have constructed a happy ending for myself that could be dismissed by a cynic as routine catharsis. "Hazel thought how little was required, really — a recitation — to turn her mind from needling to comforting" (*Friend* 102). A feminist cynic might go on to note that it is not Dudley, after all, who is most in need of comfort. Soon after the ballad has "stirred and eased his heart," his thoughts turn to casual sex, and Hazel is reminded of Jack's promise *"I could make you very happy"* (103). So much for a happy ending. Munro's story does not end, in any case, where I was trying to hold it fast. It passes on to a closing double take that is typically Munro. Hazel reflects on happy endings for women, then observes that what makes a man happy "must be something quite different" (105).

Contingency is what causes this inevitable collapse into failure. Poirier comments that the

> literature of self-parody is bound by its allegiance, minute by minute, to the passage of time. Its practitioners are doing what Griffith thought of doing with his camera: of holding it on a scene so long that the scene would have to break up. Hold the camera, that is, on the noble rider until he climbs down. . . . The passage of time distorts any shapes proposed by art. . . . (36–37)

Poirier's image brings to mind the Polaroid picture that disintegrates after being left in the sun in "Lichen." Time, of course, may as easily expose cynicism. In "The Children Stay," there is an atmosphere of impending doom, of a threat to the safety of the children; hold the camera on the children until they are grown up, however, and the fairy-tale horror story vanishes as the maternal anxiety of the past is put into perspective by the obvious well-being of the grown children.

A printed story, however, has to end somewhere, the "endless tale" being an oral phenomenon that publishers fail to understand. Munro somehow has to hold all the layers "still in one frame" (MacFarlane 54). Frequently, she uses the framing device of a visit, the visit to Scotland in "Hold Me Fast, Don't Let Me Pass" being one example. Departure and return comprise a formula familiar to oral narrative, *The Odyssey* being a prime example. Travel is a frequent image in Munro's stories, and travel blurs our ideas about beginnings and endings, always leaving open the possibility that we may arrive at the crossing where anything can happen. I am often travelling, in fact, while reading a Munro story for the first time. Riding home on the subway with the *New Yorker* burning a hole in my briefcase, I can never wait until I get home. This was my situation when I read "Carried Away" for the first time. I nearly missed my stop, in fact, because I was so engrossed in the section called "Tolpuddle Martyrs." You might say that I was no longer on the subway. I was with Louisa in that makeshift bus depot in the "dilapidated house," hanging on every word of the bizarrely disorienting scene of nonrecognition, when "a group of oddly dressed folk" comes across the gravelled yard. "The children were dressed just like their elders, even to the bonnets and hats" (*Open Secrets* 55). That's what gave it away for me. Louisa's companion jokingly and mistakenly calls them "The Tolpuddle Martyrs" (55), but I recognized them before Louisa does, and I felt a thrilling mixture of hope and fear. The fear was what I feel for the Amish whenever they are on exhibit for tourists. The hope was that Munro would resist the rush toward borrowed nostalgia. As, of course, she does. In the midst of the anarchy, the threatening muddle, these people are identifiable, and Louisa's recognition of them is crucial to the restoration of sanity. What Louisa experiences when she sits down with them is what Mennonites would call *mitsein*, or "being together." This is not closeness or identification; it is, rather, a comfortable acceptance of recognizable difference: "But these Mennonite settlings are a blessing. The plop of behinds on chairs, the crackling of the candy bag, the meditative sucking and soft conversations" (56). After sucking on a butterscotch candy given to her by a little girl, Louisa notices a string of "little colored bulbs" that makes her "think of festivities. Carnivals" (57).

It would be hard for any Mennonite reader not to get "carried away" with Louisa, not to be tempted by the carnival lights into staying put. As if to remind me not to miss my subway stop, Louisa asks the woman beside her, "What place is this?" (57). The question takes us back to the earlier misnomer: The Tolpuddle Martyrs. In this muddle, these muddy puddles, with this narrator called Mud, what should one make of these odd and displaced people? That they are not so odd after all? The Mennonite story of martyrdom, going back to the Reformation, is not remotely like that of The Tolpuddle Martyrs, "men who had been tried and found guilty for administering illegal oaths" in England and for this "peculiar offense" had been transported to Canada (46). Mennonites, in fact, are peculiar in that they refuse to swear oaths (obeying the "Swear not . . ." of Matthew 5.34) and opt for plain speech: let your yea be yea, and your nay be nay (see Matthew 5.37).

It was by invoking the context of Munro's stories about aliens and fairies at crossings that I began to account for the presence of Mennonites in this story. When tourists in Ontario opt for borrowed nostalgia, Mennonite-style, they travel to the rural areas where they can gawk at horses and buggies and women in bonnets. Like the tourists who buy into the Romantic image of natural Scottish bards, these people think that they are mourning the loss of a more simple, natural life. That simplicity, in fact, is a construct and can be used to sell a lot of things besides shoofly pie and quilts. A Mennonite writer representing these lives might do well to construct a Mennonite nostalgic grotesque. Munro signals her awareness of all this by a deliberate distortion of representation that communicates respect for difference. "Doing consciously what time does more slowly, parody can work to distort the shapes of art," writes Linda Hutcheon (97). Without pointing an intrusive camera at Louisa's Mennonite neighbours, Munro keeps them in her frame long enough to celebrate a gift exchange. These Mennonites, significantly, are not at home. They too are at a crossing, on their way from somewhere to somewhere else.

What place is this? Not a place of nostalgia but a place of *mitsein* and of gift exchange. There is in all Munro's stories, no matter how painful or sad, the experience of a celebratory high that comes when

40

a gift changes hands. Lewis Hyde notes how frequently gift exchange accompanies a transformation; "it is when art acts as an agent of transformation that we may correctly speak of it as a gift" (47). Like the candy given to Louisa by the Mennonite girl, the gift "must always be used up, consumed, eaten" (8). It moves in circles so that you don't get a gift from the same person to whom you gave one. You "give blindly" and end up feeling "a sort of blind gratitude" (16).

ACKNOWLEDGEMENTS

For their invaluable help, I would like to thank the students in my 1998 summer course on Canadian women writers. I am particularly indebted to Michelle Levy, Katrina Onstad, Vikki Visvis, and Samantha Zacher.

WORKS CITED

Bakhtin, Mikhail. *Rabelais and His World*. Trans. H. Iswolsky. Cambridge, MA: MIT, 1968.

Barthes, Roland. *Camera Lucida: Reflections on Photography*. Trans. Richard Howard. New York: Hill, 1981.

Benjamin, Walter. "The Storyteller: Reflections on the Work of Nikolai Leskov." *Illuminations*. Ed. Hannah Arendt. Trans. Harry Zohn. 1955. New York: Schocken, 1969. 83–109.

Brown, Mary Ellen. "Old Singing Women and the Canons of Scottish Balladry and Song." *A History of Scottish Women's Writing*. Ed. Douglas Gifford and Dorothy McMillan. Edinburgh: Edinburgh UP, 1997. 44–57.

Carrington, Ildikó de Papp. "Double-Talking Devils: Alice Munro's 'A Wilderness Station.'" *Essays on Canadian Writing* 58 (1996): 71–92.

Carscallen, James. *The Other Country: Patterns in the Writing of Alice Munro*. Toronto: ECW, 1993.

Child, Francis James, ed. *The English and Scottish Popular Ballads*. Part 2. Cambridge, UK: Riverside, 1884.

Eilberg-Schwartz, Howard, and Wendy Doniger, eds. *Off with Her Head: The Denial of Women's Identity in Myth, Religion, and Culture*. Berkeley: U of Califorina P, 1995.

Fielding, Penny. *Writing and Orality: Nationality, Culture, and Nineteenth-Century Scottish Fiction*. Oxford: Clarendon, 1996.

Finnegan, Ruth. *Literacy and Orality: Studies in the Technology of Communication*. Oxford: Blackwell, 1988.

Foley, John Miles. *The Singer of Tales in Performance*. Bloomington: Indiana UP, 1992.

Fulton, Barbara, and Paul King. "Mohawks to Mennonites." *Toronto Star* 13 June 1998: J1, J4.

Hogg, James. *Memoirs of the Author's Life and Familiar Anecdotes of Sir Walter Scott.* Ed. Douglas S. Mack. Edinburgh: Scottish Academic, 1972.

___. *The Private Memoirs and Confessions of a Justified Sinner, Written by Himself.* Ed. John Carey. London: Oxford UP, 1969.

Hutcheon, Linda. *A Theory of Parody: The Teachings of Twentieth-Century Art Forms.* New York: Methuen, 1985.

Hyde, Lewis. *The Gift: Imagination and the Erotic Life of Property.* New York: Vintage, 1979.

Jefferson, Ann. "Bodymatters: Self and Other in Bakhtin, Sartre, and Barthes." *Bakhtin and Cultural Theory.* Ed. Ken Hirschkop and David Shepherd. Manchester: Manchester UP, 1989. 152–77.

Kerrigan, Catherine. Introduction. *An Anthology of Scottish Women Poets.* Edinburgh: Edinburgh UP, 1991. 1–11.

Kilpatrick, Ken. "Goderich Delightful Place to Lose Yourself." *Toronto Star* 13 June 1998: J18.

MacFarlane, David. "Writer in Residence." *Saturday Night* Dec. 1986: 51–55.

McCracken-Flesher, Caroline. "You Can't Go Home Again: James Hogg and the Problem of Scottish 'Post-Colonial' Return." *Studies in Hogg and His World* 8 (1997): 24–41.

Munro, Alice. "A Better Place than Home." ["1847: The Irish" — originally a screenplay broadcast on CBC Television in 1978 as part of the series *The Newcomers/Les Arrivants*.] *The Newcomers: Inhabiting a New Land.* Ed. Charles E. Israel. Toronto: McClelland, 1979. 113–24.

___. "Changing Places." *Writing Home: A Pen Canada Anthology.* Ed. Constance Rooke. Toronto: McClelland, 1997. 190–206.

___. "The Children Stay." the *New Yorker* 22 and 29 Dec. 1997: 90–103.

___. *Dance of the Happy Shades.* 1968. Toronto: McGraw, 1988.

___. *Friend of My Youth.* 1990. Toronto: Penguin, 1995.

___. Letter to the author. 30 May 1988.

___. *Lives of Girls and Women.* 1971. Toronto: Signet, 1974.

___. *The Moons of Jupiter.* 1982. Toronto: Penguin, 1986.

___. *Open Secrets.* 1994. Toronto: Penguin, 1995.

___. "Save the Reaper." the *New Yorker* 22 and 29 June 1998: 120–35.

___. *Who Do You Think You Are?* 1978. Toronto: Penguin, 1996.

Ong, Walter. *Orality and Literacy: The Technologizing of the Word.* London: Routledge, 1982.

Poirier, Richard. *The Performing Self: Compositions and Decompositions in the Languages of Contemporary Life.* New Brunswick, NJ: Rutgers UP, 1992.

Ross, Catherine Sheldrick. *Alice Munro: A Double Life.* Toronto: ECW, 1992.

Scott, Sir Walter. *Minstrelsy of the Scottish Border: Consisting of Historical and Romantic Ballads.* London: Murray, 1869.

Smout, T.C. *A History of the Scottish People: 1560–1830*. 1969. London: Fontana, 1972.

Stallybrass, Peter, and Allon White. *The Politics and Poetics of Transgression*. Ithaca: Cornell UP, 1986.

Stewart, Susan. "Lyric Possession." *Critical Inquiry* 22.1 (1995): 34–63.

___. *On Longing: Narratives of the Miniature, the Gigantic, the Souvenir, the Collection*. Baltimore: Johns Hopkins UP, 1984.

Truss, Lynne. "Alice in Memory's Looking-Glass." *Independent* [London, UK] 14 Oct. 1990: 33.

Et in Ontario Ego:
The Pastoral Ideal and the
Blazon Tradition in
Alice Munro's "Lichen"

MARIANNE MICROS

"O, MISTRESS MINE, where are you roaming?" sings David in Alice Munro's story "Lichen" in *The Progress of Love* (51), but his ex-wife, Stella, remembers another line of this song from Shakespeare's *Twelfth Night, or What You Will*: "What's to come is still unsure" (2.3.46). Neither character mentions the last line of that song, "Youth's a stuff will not endure" (2.3.49),[1] yet the "absent presence" (Sidney, Sonnet 116) of that truth underlies the emotions of both David and Stella. "Lichen" is a story of absent presences and present absences, of attempts to communicate that do not succeed: the photographed body of an absent woman, a woman made silent and invisible, becomes merely a sign to both her male and her female interpreters, each of whom reads the sign differently.

In addition to the quotations from *Twelfth Night*, "Lichen" contains a subtext of allusions to sixteenth-century literary conventions, especially conventions of pastoral poems and love sonnets. Munro, in a story with a multitude (even for her) of descriptions of physical bodies, uses several conventions popular in sixteenth-century literature in England, France, and Italy. The pastoral, the blazon, and the love sonnet were not new to the Renaissance period, but they were sometimes blended in original ways to idealize the love object, the landscape, or love itself, though not without an awareness that this idealization conflicted with reality. Munro also blends elements of these conventions while parodying and deconstructing all three.

"Lichen" is set in a pastoral locale — cottage country along Lake Huron, where Stella lives in a summer house overlooking the lake and in a community that consists mostly of people who have left the city for various reasons; this group includes a woman who raises sheep, "spins the wool," and "weaves it into cloth" (Munro 47, 48). As Peter V. Marinelli explains in *Pastoral*,

The case of the modern author is complicated by the fact that there is no common myth to which he can appeal for a pastoral art; in effect, he is forced back upon his own imagination for the creation of such a myth. Most likely, he will attempt to create it from a real landscape with which he is familiar, from a set of local circumstances that have coloured his vision. (55)

This is indeed the case with Munro, who has chosen a landscape familiar to her since childhood.

The use of the pastoral locale as a place away from the city where shepherds could discuss subjects such as love, poetry, and religion was established by the idylls of Theocritus and the eclogues of Virgil. Edmund Spenser's shepherds in the *Shepheardes Calender*, for example, discuss poetry, religion, current events, love, and moral behaviour.[2] Likewise, Munro's Stella belongs to the local historical society, a play-reading group, a church choir, a wine-makers' club, and a group that meets for dinner parties and entertainment. The pastoral locale was a place for self-exploration and discussion, a place created by "the desire of the weary soul to escape" (Marinelli 12).

Nevertheless, an important aspect of the pastoral genre, from classical times through the Renaissance, was an awareness that this situation could not be permanent and was already threatened by outside forces. The love of the shepherd was frequently unrequited, his poetic talent had dried up, and he had little desire to live. Marinelli writes, "To arrive in Arcadia by whatever means (and there are many) or for whatever purpose . . . is merely to have one's problems sharpened by seeing them magnified in a new context of simplicity, by seeing Art against Nature and of being forced to conclusions about them" (11). The interloper from the city, in this case David, visits Stella, bringing memories of her past that threaten to disrupt her artistic lifestyle, just as the outside world always disrupts and threatens the existence of the pastoral ideal. Nor can David escape his problems by returning to this landscape.

Despite this lack of permanence, the pastoral locale was considered "a positive ideal. It was an ideal of the good life, of the state of content and mental self-sufficiency which had been known in classical antiquity as *otium*" (Smith 2). Poets of the sixteenth century in England sought this ideal, though their awareness of the difficulty, or even impossibility, of reaching it permeates their poetry. Sir Philip Sidney, in *A Defence of Poetry*, defines the poet as someone who can make something that is "better than nature" (23): "Nature never set forth the earth in so rich tapestry as divers poets have done; neither with so pleasant rivers, fruitful trees, sweet-smelling flowers, nor whatsoever else may make the too much loved earth more lovely. Her world is brazen, the poets only deliver a golden" (24). Yet when Sidney, in his *Astrophil and Stella* and in his *Arcadia*, describes attempts by human beings to implement these neoplatonic ideals, we can see that these theories do not easily translate into practice in the human world.

In "Lichen," as well, Stella cannot sustain the peace and integrity of her ideal landscape or of her artistic vision. Nor can David create for himself the world that he fantasizes about, a world that, like the one described in Christopher Marlowe's "The Passionate Shepherd to His Love," is static, always beautiful, and without any possibility of ageing or dying. David would not understand the famous line "Et in Arcadia ego," which can be construed as "Death is even in Arcadia," with Death as the speaker of the line (Panofsky 26). David cannot believe that he will ever look like Stella's father, with his "[b]luish-gray skin, with dark-blue spots, whitened eyes, a ribbed neck with delicate deep hollows, like a smoked-glass vase" (Munro 68); he imagines that he will always be young and attractive to women.

The names of the two main characters in the story also evoke the pastoral ideal. David, "perhaps the most romantic figure in the Old Testament, was a shepherd, as well as being the principal poet and singer of songs among the ancient Hebrews" (Smith 3). Stella is the name of the idealized loved one in Sidney's sonnet sequence *Astrophil and Stella*. David himself is much like Astrophil as he whines about his new love. He sings, as does Astrophil, and his voice is described by Stella as "peculiarly artificial": "This special voice of his is rather high-pitched, monotonous, insistent, with a deliberate, cruel sweetness" (Munro 56). The dialectic between David and each of his women is reminiscent of Astrophil's love of a woman whom he cannot have, whom he has idealized beyond human possibility and who causes conflict within him. Munro's Stella, however, unlike Sidney's Stella, is a middle-aged woman with an ageing body, a woman who refuses to hide behind conventions.

One of these conventions is a man's idealization of a woman's body, another example of the tendency to create an ideal through poetry and one sometimes integrated into the pastoral genre during the Renaissance period, though it developed separately. This form of poetry, called a blazon, describes a woman's body in terms of a series of metaphors; in "Lichen," however, the women's bodies described thus are not ideal, or cannot remain so, as the woman ages and the photograph fades. Munro subverts and demolishes the blazon form by describing women's bodies literally or by using metaphors ironically. By presenting several descriptions of women's bodies, each one seen through the eyes of either the male or the female protagonist, or both of them, Munro does much more than satirize the male view of women's bodies: she suggests the difficulties inherent in human image making — through metaphor, simile, photography, and language — and the isolation of the individual attempting to communicate something that is not certain or fixed.

In the blazon tradition, women's bodies and body parts could be compared to a number of things, including flowers, plants, buildings, jewels, planets, gods, and animals. Spenser's Sonnet 64 of the *Amoretti*, for example, compares the odours of parts of a woman's body to the odours of particular flowers:

> Her lips did smell lyke unto Gillyflowers,
>   her ruddy cheekes lyke unto Roses red:
>   her snowy browes lyke budded Bellamoures,
>   her lovely eyes lyke Pincks but newly spred,
> Her goodly bosome lyke a Strawberry bed,
>   her neck lyke to a bounch of Cullambynes:
>   her brest lyke lillyes, ere theyr leaves be shed,
>   her nipples lyke yong blossomd Jessemynes.
> Such fragrant flowres doe give most odorous smell,
>   but her sweet odour did them all excell. (ll. 5–14)

In Sonnet 15, Spenser describes his lady using metaphors of precious jewels:

> if Saphyres, loe her eies be Saphyres plaine,
>   if Rubies, loe hir lips be Rubies sound:
> If Pearles, hir teeth be pearles both pure and round;
>   if Yvorie, her forhead yvory weene;
>   if Gold, her locks are finest gold on ground;
>   if silver, her faire hands are silver sheene,
> But that which fairest is, but few behold
>   her mind adornd with vertues manifold. (ll. 7–14)

Spenser's extended blazon describing Belphoebe, in *Faerie Queene* 2.3.22–31, compares parts of her to flowers, planets and stars, gods, jewels, ivory, marble pillars, et cetera.

Sidney's Sonnet 9 of *Astrophil and Stella* interestingly describes Stella's face as a building:

> Queene *Vertue's* court, which some call *Stella's* face,
>   Prepar'd by Nature's chiefest furniture,
>   Hath his front built of Alablaster pure;
> Gold is the covering of that stately place.
> The doore by which sometimes comes forth her Grace,
>   Red Porphir is, which locke of pearle makes sure:
>   Whose porches rich (which name of cheekes endure)
> Marble mixt red and white do enterlace.
> The windowes now through which this heav'nly guest
> Looks over the world, and can find nothing such,
> Which dare claime from those lights the name of best,
> Of touch they are that without touch doth touch,
>   Which *Cupid's* selfe from Beautie's myne did draw:
>   Of touch they are, and poore I am their straw.

These women may seem ideal, but they are not: the imagery is extremely artificial, the metaphors of jewels and temples cold and hard — not really complimentary to a living woman. The women's bodies do not have the physicality of real bodies: they seem to exist only as metaphors, as examples of perfection, part of the nature, or even the architecture, surrounding them. We can understand Shakespeare's need to parody such poetry, as in Sonnet 130: "My mistress' eyes are nothing like the sun" (l.1).[3]

Munro's descriptions of women, through David's and Stella's eyes, use many of the same metaphors, but not in order to idealize the women. Rather, when Munro compares women to animals or to plants, we see them as even more dehumanized than are the women in blazons. Munro focuses on the actual body, with its flaws and fat and warts, showing a different kind of depersonalization — woman as mere flesh, especially as she ages, but also woman as "lichen," mere pubis, dependent on a man's desire for her body.

Munro's descriptions, like those of Renaissance poets, present parts of a woman's body in no clear order. Nancy J. Vickers, in "'The blazon of sweet beauty's best': Shakespeare's *Lucrece*," finds the term "blazon" to have originated with the French *blassoner*, which means to proclaim, as well as to publish (95). The speaker of a blazon "displays" a body, first dividing it into parts in a manner that allows him to possess and control the parts. Vickers proposes, in "Diana

Described: Scattered Woman and Scattered Rhyme," that the purpose for the "scattering" of body parts in a blazon can be explained by the Diana-Actaeon myth, alluded to by Petrarch and by the English poets whom he influenced (as well as by Shakespeare in *Twelfth Night*). Because Actaeon has seen her naked body, Diana turns him into a stag, to be hunted and torn apart by his own hounds. Consequently, the male poet describes a woman's body as consisting of scattered parts, dismembering her in retaliation for Diana's destruction of Actaeon (103).

The Renaissance male poet, therefore, creates an idealized image of a woman described not only by her particular parts in isolation from each other and in jumbled order (e.g., Spenser, in Sonnet 64, gives these body parts in this order: lips, cheeks, brows, eyes, bosom, neck, breast, nipples; in Sonnet 15, he describes eyes, lips, teeth, forehead, locks, and hands and then leaps to mind) but also by metaphors that do not give a clear picture of her as a human being. Usually, the woman is not permitted a voice of her own, and the male author speaks of her and for her: "A modern Actaeon affirming himself as poet cannot permit Ovid's angry goddess to speak her displeasure and deny his voice; his speech requires her silence" (Vickers, "Diana Described" 109). She becomes not a real woman but an image.

Patricia Parker describes the blazon as an "inventory" that displays the body through rhetorical language that points to an economic purpose — to publicize and sell the merchandise (129–32). She quotes as an example a scene from *Twelfth Night* in which Olivia describes herself: "It shall be inventoried, and every particle and utensil labell'd to my will: as, *item*, two lips, indifferent red; *item*, two grey eyes, with lids to them; *item*, one neck, one chin, and so forth" (1.5.231–34). As in Shakespeare's Sonnet 130, the convention of the blazon is parodied, just as Munro parodies it in our time.

The descriptions of women in Munro's "Lichen," whether related by David or by Stella, not only tear the woman's body into scattered parts but also deconstruct the sonnet or any other poetic form that imposes control and unity on the depiction of the body. Munro's "sonnet" is the photograph, which, like the love sonnet, presents an image. Some of the blazons, however, occur within David's or Stella's thoughts and are entirely subjective and changeable.

David creates in his mind a "blazon" of Stella, who, as an older woman, is not idealized — just the opposite. He thinks that she has "turned into a troll" (43). He resents her refusal to hide the ageing of her body and describes her, and other women of her age, in this way: "There's the sort of woman who has to come bursting out of the female envelope at this age, flaunting fat or an indecent scrawniness, sprouting warts and facial hair, refusing to cover pasty veined legs, almost gleeful about it, as if this was what she'd wanted to do all along" (43). Unlike Renaissance poets (but like Olivia's description of herself in *Twelfth Night*), David does not use metaphor here, except for the image of her body "bursting out of the female envelope." This woman does not look like a garden or a temple or a jewel or a planet; she is not described, as was the ideal Renaissance goddess/woman, according to cosmic metaphors that relate one woman to the whole, one body to heavenly bodies. Like Renaissance poets, David scatters her body: warts, facial hair, and "pasty veined legs" are not connected to each other and do not form a whole human being. Unlike those poets,[4] he describes an ageing woman, one who no longer meets the criteria required to be his lover and, worse, one who does not care. To David, women should remain within "the female envelope," confined by their relationships with men and by society's gender restrictions.

David does find that, "Close up, Stella looks a bit better — with her smooth, tanned skin, childishly cropped hair, wide brown eyes" (44). Again he focuses only on the physical, not idealizing or turning into symbol or image these dissociated parts. As is often the case in pastoral writing, David is nostalgic about the past, one created by his memory and based on a photograph of Stella that he has: "He saw her coming across the lawn at a suburban party, carrying a casserole. She was wearing a sundress. . . . Stella coming across the lawn, with her sunlit hair — the gray in it then merely made it ash blond — and her bare toasted shoulders . . ." (70). He contrasts that Stella with Stella now, a "white-haired woman walking beside him" who "dragged so much weight with her" (71) and who was "bloated with all she knew" (72). David prefers his women young and subservient, carrying casseroles, leaning on rocks, even, and perhaps especially, controlled by the confines of the photograph (which acts as a "female envelope"), just as the form of the sonnet or other lyric poem held a woman in whatever stable pose the poet preferred.

Just as David wishes to control, or to avoid seeing, Stella's ageing body, male writers have traditionally tried to control, with their pens, the "literary fat lady," a metaphor for the spreading text. As Parker points out, the image of the fat lady, the dilating and unmanageable enchantress who is the text, was described in literature in order to contain the matter within a form, to erase the woman who threatens the "execution of closure or accomplishment" as a way of "mastering or controlling the implicitly female, and perhaps hence wayward, body of the text itself" (11). In "Lichen," David contains his latest lover in a photograph and uses that image of a woman's body as a means of creating his own identity. He maintains her youth, her image just at the moment when their relationship is blossoming, a relationship that he will eventually control by ending it before the woman becomes old and fat.

David chops up women even in his thoughts, isolating a physical feature of a woman and highlighting its imperfections. He plans to give Catherine, his current partner, "the big chop" (57), perhaps because she, like Stella before her, no longer fits the image that he has created for her (as Stella learns when she tests the information that he has given her about Catherine [60]). David sees Catherine as "a tall, frail, bony woman with fair hair and sensitive skin. Her skin is so sensitive it won't stand any makeup at all, and is easily inflamed by colds, foods, emotions" (44). He criticizes her use of mascara, because "Blackening those sparse wisps of lashes emphasizes the watery blue of her eyes, which look as if they couldn't stand daylight, and the dryness of the skin underneath" (44). Like Shakespeare, David describes a woman whose "eyes are nothing like the sun," and, like Astrophil, he denigrates black eyelashes: "When Nature made her chiefe worke, *Stellas* eyes, / In colour blacke, why wrapt she beames so bright?" (Sidney, Sonnet 7 ll. 1–2). In "Lichen," David's women, unlike Sidney's and Spenser's, are growing old, and David is now more likely to describe them physically and literally. When Stella tries to imagine Catherine as David has described her, she sees her as the victim of his chopping, as an "amputee. Not much cut off, just the tips of her fingers and maybe her toes" (58).

David's description of his new love, Dina, also chops her into unrelated parts:

> Her clothes and hair always have a smell of curry powder, nutmeg, incense, added to what David thinks of as her natural smell, of cigarettes and dope and sex. Her cheeks bear a slash of crude color and her eyelids are sometimes brick red. She tried out once for a part in a movie some people she knew about were making. She failed to get the part because of some squeamishness about holding a tame rat between her legs. This failure humiliated her. (64)

Like Spenser in Sonnet 64, David describes a woman in terms of odours, and he describes her in terms of colours, as do Renaissance poets; these colours, however, do not heighten the beauty of the woman but make her seem almost clownlike. He also describes her in terms of something that she was unable to do — hold "a tame rat between her legs" — a metaphor that Stella will later remember. Perhaps this detail, which David singles out, attracts him to her — her lack of a phallus, with its association with masculine potency. Dina paints her face, drugs herself, is unable to hold a rat between her legs, even "a tame rat," and smells of spices and incense: she is a passive hippie and not a feminist. Perhaps David sees himself as the rat, the potent but "tame" man who cannot be contained by the woman's legs. Interestingly, he knows that he fictionalizes Dina, that she is not really "so wild, or so avid, or doomed, as he pretends she is, or as she sometimes pretends she is" (65), and he knows that, in ten years, she will no longer be the "trollop" that he describes her as.

Magdalene Redekop has discussed Dina's absence from the story and her silence (184). Dina is similar in this regard to Astrophil's Stella, who is silent unless Astrophil speaks in her voice. In "Lichen," David imitates a woman's voice: "Perhaps he could do a woman's voice, squeaky" (63). Elizabeth D. Harvey has recently referred to this appropriation of women's voices by male writers as "ventriloquism" (see 1–53).[5] These "ventriloquizations" in the Renaissance "fostered a vision that tended to reinforce women's silence or to marginalize their voices when they did speak or write" (5). Sidney, a male writer, writes Stella's lines as well as Astrophil's: Munro, a female writer, writes from both Stella's and David's points of view,[6] though Dina is not given a voice at all, having been reduced by David to an image. In the cases of both Sidney and Munro, the author either weights the argument in favour of the character of his or her own gender or gives that character the predominant voice.[7]

Stella herself creates blazons of women — something uncommon in the conventional Renaissance blazon — hers coloured by her failed relationship with David. She, like David, controls her reactions to his women by containing them through image and metaphor. She remembers Rosemary, David's first lover while married to Stella, as "a shrill trite woman," a "dark haired, childless, chain-smoking woman, given . . . to tantalizing silences," and she remembers David stroking Rosemary's "cold, brown, shaved, and prickly calf" (71). This childless woman was not fully feminine to Stella and, like the male-created female objects of love, was given to "silences," though she was "shrill" (a common criticism of women by misogynistic men). We might wonder, though, if her silences were "tantalizing" because they were engineered by Rosemary in order to entice David; they may have been silences filled not with passivity but with power.

Stella coldly describes the photograph of Dina, this time with metaphors from the Renaissance blazon that she uses ironically:

> There is a flattened-out breast far away on the horizon. And the legs spreading into the foreground. The legs are spread wide — smooth, golden, monumental: fallen columns. Between them is the dark blot she called moss, or lichen. But it's really more like the dark pelt of an animal, with the head and tail and feet chopped off. Dark silky pelt of some unlucky rodent. (55)

This "blazon" obviously deconstructs the blazon form. The body parts are not only scattered but also exist in distorted relations to each other, and the dismemberment seems actual, because the body resembles an animal with its "head and tail and feet chopped off." The way that Stella sees the photograph suits Vickers's explanation of the Renaissance blazon — this is David's dismemberment of his Diana figure, as he reverses the result of Actaeon's viewing of Diana's nakedness. It is also Stella's bitter interpretation of David's habit of labelling and discarding women — a type of ventriloquism because she sees Dina in a way that is coloured by David's treatment of her. Dina (perhaps an allusion to Diana: David says that her name is "Dina without an 'h'" [55]; her name can also be read as Diana without the "a") is a creation of the male photographer; her body looks like lichen against the rock — the woman reduced by the male artist to a blur, to an image dependent on his description of her. All that David says about the photograph is "See her legs?" (55): to Stella, Dina is all legs, which are spread out to receive yet release the rat that she cannot hold.

Munro uses several traditional metaphors: the legs are compared to columns — here, however, fallen ones, in a destruction of the temple image used by Sidney and others. Instead of decorously comparing parts of the woman's body to flowers, Stella compares the pubic hair to moss or lichen — a parasitical plant.[8] She also compares the pubic hair to "the dark pelt of an animal, with the head and tail and feet chopped off" — not unlike Actaeon as a dismembered stag. Here the pelt is compared to that of an "unlucky rodent." Perhaps Stella has unconsciously remembered the story about Dina and the rat; here the pubic hair looks like the rat that Dina refused to hold between her legs, the "tame rat" becoming, to Stella, an "unlucky rodent." The rat now signifies Dina herself, unlucky because David has effaced her, powerless because she has been flattened against the male rock, her "silky pelt" now only a "dark blot," having become a parasite clinging to a man who has chopped off her head, tail, and feet — now she is only pubis, which has no meaning. Dina has become, at least in Stella's mind, the rat that she once feared.

The fact that David has left the photograph of Dina with Stella reveals something about his attitude to Stella, now a mother figure, sister (as she herself says), or confidante to him. He is "selling" Dina's image to Stella to signify the power and the youth that he thinks he possesses, though his potency is contradicted by the very existence of Stella, a former lover who has not been erased or silenced. It is also obvious that he has been unable to break his ties to her completely, that her presence in his life affects his relationships with other women, for he entrusts her with this secret photograph of his new lover.

The figure in the photograph, however, undergoes another transformation, one that is compatible with Stella's view of David's relationships with women. In Stella's description of the figure, the pubic hair is *like* "the dark pelt of an animal," but *she calls it* "moss" or "lichen." Stella corrects herself when she later finds the photograph again and discovers that simile has become metaphor: "She said it was lichen. No, she said it looked like lichen" (73). For Munro, as for a variety of modern theorists, language can create reality.[9] As a result, meaning is dependent not on a word itself but on the way the word is used, the way in which it relates to other words and to the world around it. Now Stella sees that "her words have come true" — the picture has faded, and the figure has become lichen: "The outline of the breast has disappeared. You would never know the legs were legs. The black has turned to gray, to the soft, dry color of a plant mysteriously nourished on the rocks" (73). The legs, so important to David, are now unrecognizable as legs. This fading, to Stella, is a transformation that always occurs in his relationships with women and mirrors the future of his relationship with Dina. Stella, however, thinks that her words have made this happen — it is her way of seeing David and his women that has caused the fading. The image changes according to one's interpretation of it. In addition, Stella is speaking of the image in the photograph, not of reality. This is an image of a woman's body, an image subject to the frailty of the photograph and a sign open to different interpretations.[10]

The body, especially for David, determines identity — the identity that he gives to a woman, based on how he visualizes her, and his own identity. Peter Brooks observes that "The body is both ourselves and other, and as such the object of emotions from love to disgust" (1). If a body is a sign or image of a self, rather than an actual self, then it is unstable, subject to change and mortality. Whereas David creates an image of a young woman's body by means of photography, in order to complete the image of himself that he needs to have, Stella uses language to re-create the bodies whose representations by photography or by another person's words she rejects. The tension between word and meaning,[11] between image and interpretation, is evident in their different responses to an image, Stella's affected by her knowledge of David and by her bitterness.[12]

Perhaps David, like the sonneteers (e.g., Sidney, Spenser, Shakespeare), thought that he could make immortal the youth and beauty of his love objects. The photograph, like the sonnet, can be thought to fix a moment in time. Nevertheless, the photograph in "Lichen" does not do so: it is a poorly taken Polaroid, dark and blurred, and the picture itself fades. This photograph, then, does not convey a clear picture of a woman's body, nor does it convey an absolute truth: "Contrary to what is suggested by the humanist claims made for photography, the camera's ability to transform reality into something beautiful derives from its relative weakness as a means of conveying truth" (Sontag 112). Roland Barthes writes that the presence of something in a photograph is an indication of its absence and that photography is therefore "hallucination" (*Camera Lucida* 115). Dina has become merely an image, a symbol, but one with no definite meaning. Unlike monuments, designed to immortalize a person, the photograph is perishable: "Attacked by light, by humidity, it fades, weakens, vanishes; there is nothing left to do but throw it away" (Barthes, *Camera Lucida* 93). Dina will be attacked by age and, like the photograph, will be discarded by David. The photograph is not a monument but an image of death. This photograph does convey a meaning, however, for it accurately reflects not the woman but the personality of the photographer, who expects the woman to fade, to eventually allow her "disguise to crack," making it necessary for him to "move on" (66).

Munro has shown that words and photographs are arbitrary signs subject to various interpretations — especially when they attempt to define human beings. The characters in "Lichen" never know each other except subjectively and inadequately. Stella can predict David's behaviour, but even her knowledge is touched by uncertainty, part of her predilection for storytelling, making metaphors, playing with words and their shifting meanings. Even in a pastoral locale and the pastoral mode, there is death — along with isolation, loneliness, and displacement.

Munro has combined the pastoral locale and various pastoral signifiers with the conventions of love poetry and the blazon to create an atmosphere of lost ideals and faded romance. She has, however, changed the conventions by giving the woman her own voice, by making her a shepherd-poet, by allowing her to ponder and shatter ideals. Nevertheless, Stella is left alone with her words, though there is hope in "the flow of the days and nights" — the continuity in human life and human thinking. However, there are also the pauses and "harsh little breaks" (74) — the separation of women from men, the isolation of the individual, the distance between creator and created, image and reality, art and nature — the frustrating gaps that we bridge and cannot bridge over and over again. Still, it is Stella, or any human being, who keeps "the days and nights" going — who has the potential for survival, for self-respect, for continuity, for discovering some significance in the shifting signs.

NOTES

[1] Dr. Neil Carson of the Department of English, University of Guelph, mentioned this omission to me.

[2] Other Renaissance poets, of course, wrote pastoral poetry and pastoral romance. I have confined my examples to a few writers of the sixteenth century because Munro seems to focus on the time of Shakespeare in her allusions. However, the cynicism and irony that entered the genre in the seventeenth century, as in the poetry of Andrew Marvell, is somewhat present in "Lichen." I believe, though, that the naïve shepherd, expecting some fulfilment in his quest for ideal love with the ideal woman, while egotistically creating his own version of woman and love, is much more prevalent in late-sixteenth-century poetry and much more like Munro's David.

[3] Hannah Betts, in her recent article " 'The Image of this Queene so quaynt': The Pornographic Blazon 1588-1603," discusses the nature of sexually explicit blazons during this period, blazons that included "accounts of the female genitalia, typically using geographical metaphors. These catalogs convey the sexual organs in graphic, predominantly tactile detail, as soft, smooth, moist, slippery, and downy" (162). These descriptions served as a "denigration of the Petrarchan mistress," who is "displaced by

heroines who resemble her, but whose sexual proclivities imply a critique of her behavior" (162). These pornographic blazons are very interesting in comparison to the photograph of Dina in "Lichen" and the attitudes of David and Stella to Dina's depiction.

[4] Renaissance poets *did* describe the bodies of old, evil hags, as does Spenser in *Faerie Queene* 1.8.46-48. When Duessa is stripped, her body parts are not scattered but described in the correct order — perhaps because there is no more fear of her seducing and dismembering the male poet — from her bald head, rotten teeth, sour breath, dried dugs, and scabby skin to her shameful "neather parts" (1.8.48.1), with a rump from which hung a "foxes taile, with dong all fowly dight" (1.8.48.4). Duessa is shamed by this uncovering of her real body and her true age; Stella is not.

[5] Harvey writes of classical and Renaissance texts that, "although written by male authors, they are voiced by female characters in a way that seems either to erase the gender of the authorial voice or to thematize the transvestism of this process. This phenomenon, which I call transvestite ventriloquism, accentuates the issues of gender, voice, and authorial property in ways that illuminate both Renaissance conceptions of language and their relation to the gendered subject, and also twentieth-century notions of the author and their link (or lack of connection) to the gendered body" (1).

[6] Ildikó de Papp Carrington, in *Controlling the Uncontrollable: The Fiction of Alice Munro*, discusses the alternating points of view in "Lichen" (159), the use of a male, as well as a female, protagonist.

[7] The presence of two alternating narrators here echoes, to some extent, the convention of the song contest in pastoral eclogues, in which two or more speakers sing or debate, usually with a winner declared, though sometimes, as in Spenser's *Shepheardes Calender*, ending in a draw or leaving us with no winner and no authorial stance.

[8] Smaro Kamboureli, in "The Body as Audience and Performance in the Writing of Alice Munro," writes of the roles demanded of the feminine body in a male culture: "When the feminine body enacts these roles it simply enunciates its own malaise of the feminine as parasite in a culture where the role of host is invariably assigned to the Name-of-the-Father" (35). However, as she discusses, some of Munro's female characters deconstruct this signification through discourse and through the use of their bodies as performances: "These women reverse the signifiers they are supposed to be" (34). Stella, for example, now flaunts her body, despite its flaws, and does not play the homemaker who carries casseroles.

[9] See Hawkes 57–91 for an overview of twentieth-century language theory.

[10] David and Stella misinterpret each other's words or perhaps unconsciously communicate unintended but relevant meanings. For example, when Stella says, "That's your affair" in relation to David's plans for

Catherine, she has not intended the pun. When David replies, "Very funny," Stella says, "I didn't even mean it to be. Whenever something slips out like that, I always pretend I meant it, though" (57). This unintentional pun indicates how communication and the interpretation of signs can be problematic.

¹¹ Ajay Heble, in *The Tumble of Reason: Alice Munro's Discourse of Absence*, writes of Munro's "paradigmatic discourse," which indicates "the unresolvable gap between all writing and the reality which writing attempts to re-present" (5). This discourse questions the relationship between language and meaning in a new way, by which "meaning itself depends on and is determined by traces of absent and potential levels of signification" (7). This theory can also be applied to the photograph of a woman's body, the absent woman having become the man's text, the signification of the woman's body based upon absence and interpretation.

¹² Roland Barthes writes in *Image, Music, Text* that the reading of a photograph is "always historical" (28), depending on the reader's knowledge and cultural situation.

WORKS CITED

Barthes, Roland. *Camera Lucida: Reflections on Photography*. Trans. Richard Howard. New York: Hill, 1981.

___. *Image, Music, Text*. Trans. Stephen Heath. 1977. New York: Noonday, 1988.

Betts, Hannah. "'The Image of this Queene so quaynt': The Pornographic Blazon 1588–1603." *Dissing Elizabeth: Negative Representations of Gloriana*. Ed. Julia M. Walker. Durham: Duke UP, 1998. 153–84.

Brooks, Peter. *Body Work: Objects of Desire in Modern Narrative*. Cambridge: Harvard UP, 1993.

Carrington, Ildikó de Papp. *Controlling the Uncontrollable: The Fiction of Alice Munro*. DeKalb, IL: Northern Illinois UP, 1989.

Harvey, Elizabeth D. *Ventriloquized Voices: Feminist Theory and English Renaissance Texts*. London: Routledge, 1992.

Hawkes, Terence. *Metaphor*. London: Methuen, 1972.

Heble, Ajay. *The Tumble of Reason: Alice Munro's Discourse of Absence*. Toronto: U of Toronto P, 1994.

Kamboureli, Smaro. "The Body as Audience and Performance in the Writing of Alice Munro." *A Mazing Space: Writing Canadian Women Writing*. Ed. Shirley Neuman and Kamboureli. Edmonton: Longspoon-NeWest, 1986. 31–38.

Marinelli, Peter V. *Pastoral*. London: Methuen, 1971.

Munro, Alice. "Lichen." 1986. *The Progress of Love*. Toronto: Penguin, 1987. 42–74.

Panofsky, Erwin. *"Et in Arcadia Ego." Pastoral and Romance: Modern Essays in Criticism.* Ed. Eleanor Terry Lincoln. Englewood Cliffs, NJ: Prentice-Hall, 1969. 25–46.

Parker, Patricia. *Literary Fat Ladies: Rhetoric, Gender, Property.* London: Methuen, 1987.

Redekop, Magdalene. *Mothers and Other Clowns: The Stories of Alice Munro.* London: Routledge, 1992.

Shakespeare, William. Sonnet 130. *Shakespeare's Sonnets. William Shakespeare: The Complete Works.* Ed. Alfred Harbage. 1969. Baltimore: Penguin, 1974. 1475.

———. *Twelfth Night, or What You Will. William Shakespeare: The Complete Works.* Ed. Alfred Harbage. 1969. Baltimore: Penguin, 1974. 305–34.

Sidney, Sir Philip. *Astrophil and Stella. The Poems of Sir Philip Sidney.* Ed. William A. Ringler, Jr. Oxford: Clarendon, 1962. 163–237.

———. *A Defence of Poetry.* Ed. J.A. Van Dorsten. 1966. Oxford: Oxford UP, 1989.

Smith, Hallett. *Elizabethan Poetry: A Study in Conventions, Meaning, and Expression.* Ann Arbor: U of Michigan P, 1968.

Sontag, Susan. *On Photography.* New York: Dell, 1978.

Spenser, Edmund. *Amoretti. The Yale Edition of the Shorter Poems of Edmund Spenser.* Ed. William A. Oram et al. New Haven: Yale UP, 1989. 598–658.

———. *The Faerie Queene.* Ed. Thomas P. Roche, Jr. London: Penguin, 1987.

Vickers, Nancy J. "'The blazon of sweet beauty's best': Shakespeare's *Lucrece.*" *Shakespeare and the Question of Theory.* Ed. Patricia Parker and Geoffrey Hartman. New York: Methuen, 1985. 95–115.

———. "Diana Described: Scattered Woman and Scattered Rhyme." *Writing and Sexual Difference.* Ed. Elizabeth Abel. Chicago: U of Chicago P, 1982. 95–109.

Getting Loose:
Women and Narration in Alice Munro's
Friend of My Youth

DEBORAH HELLER

ABOUT MIDWAY through Alice Munro's *Friend of My Youth*, the protagonist of "Oranges and Apples," recalling his mother's disparagement of his wife, reflects on the phrase "loose woman":

> When he heard people say that, he'd always thought of an unbuttoned blouse, clothes slipping off the body, to indicate its appetite and availability. Now he thought that it could also mean just that — loose. A woman who could get loose, who wasn't fastened down, who was not reliable, who could roll away. (132)

Most of the stories in *Friend of My Youth* are about characters — principally, but not exclusively, women — who in one way or another "get loose," are not "fastened down." They get loose from the roles expected of them by other characters in their fictional lives and from the roles that readers may expect them to play in predictable plots. In crucial instances, characters also seem to get loose from the narrator's knowledge and control. The image of the "woman who could get loose" is thus suggestive for the collection as a whole, hovering as it does at the intersection of substance and technique, subject matter and the manner of its narration.

The openness of Munro's characters to metamorphosis, as well as her refusal of closure in favour of open-ended narrative structures, have received considerable critical attention.[1] This essay is concerned more specifically with Munro's new departures in her seventh collection of stories and with how, even as Munro revisits familiar situations, structures, and concerns there, she develops them in fresh ways. The opening story, "Friend of My Youth," immediately points in several directions at once, introducing strategies and motifs — including that of getting loose — that are picked up throughout the eponymous collection while also returning to material familiar from earlier "autobiographical" stories, notably "The Peace of Utrecht" in *Dance of the Happy Shades* and "Winter Wind," "Memorial," and "The Ottawa Valley" in *Something I've Been Meaning to Tell You*: the mother's debilitating illness and the young daughter's inability to respond adequately to the challenge of her mother's needs, her youthful shame, and her adult guilt, experienced as especially powerful and tenacious in retrospect.

Although critics have commented on the broad similarity between the mother-daughter situation in "Friend of My Youth" and earlier versions of Munro's treatment of what appears to be the same material, none has noted how the crucial framing dream in "Friend of My Youth" echoes and reworks an earlier account of a dream in "The Peace of Utrecht," the story in which Munro "first tackled personal material" (Munro, "Real Material" 21).[2] In both stories, these are presented as recurrent wish-fulfilment dreams, revealing a narrator-daughter's fantasy that if only the mother had not been so ill, had not made so many demands, how simple it would have been to be a better daughter and not to have had to be guilty. In the early story, the account of the dream is brief, momentarily emerging out of the adult narrator's reflections about her mother on her first visit home after her mother's death. Moving from painful memories of her long suffering mother and her own failures to meet her mother's demands, the narrator recalls how

> the disease is erratic and leisurely in its progress; some mornings . . . she wakes up better . . . [and] tries to make up for lost time, tidying the house, forcing her stiff trembling hands to work a little while at the sewing machine. She makes us one of her specialities, a banana cake or a lemon meringue pie. Occasionally since she died I have dreams of her . . . in which she is doing something like this, and I think, why did I exaggerate so to myself, see, she is all right, only that her hands are trembling — (*Dance* 200)

The dream breaks off, and, even though the story is concerned with the two sisters' different ways of coping with the aftermath of their mother's illness and death, we do not hear of it again.

Until, that is, it resurfaces in the framing dream of "Friend of My Youth":

> I used to dream about my mother, and though the details in the dream varied, the surprise was always the same. The dream

stopped, I suppose because it was too transparent in its hope-fulness, too easy in its forgiveness.

. . . Sometimes I would find myself in our old kitchen, where my mother would be rolling out piecrust . . . or washing the dishes. . . . But other times I would run into her on the street, in places where I would never have expected to see her. . . . She would be looking quite well — not exactly youthful, not entirely untouched by the paralyzing disease that held her in its grip for a decade or more before her death, but so much better than I remembered that I would be astonished. (*Friend* 3)

But when Munro returns after more than twenty years to the recurrent dream of the daughter's wish to find her mother alive again and almost well, in the very early stages of her illness, she uses it in a much more purposeful and deliberate fashion. Prominently placed at the opening of the story, the dream is virtually deconstructed before it is recounted, by the narrator's unsparing explanation of why it stopped. But the narrator is then free to develop the dream fantasy more amply and leisurely, revealing its comfort value directly after she has denied its legitimacy. "I recovered then what in waking life I had lost — my mother's liveliness of face and voice before her throat muscles stiffened and a woeful, impersonal mask fastened itself over her features . . .," her "casual humor," and her "lightness and impatience and confidence" (3–4). The "recovered" dream-mother does more than forgive her daughter; she renders superfluous any apology or guilt:

I was sorry I had kept a bugbear in my mind, instead of this reality — and the strangest, kindest thing of all to me was her matter-of-fact reply.

Oh, well, she said, better later than never. I was sure I'd see you someday. (4)

Although offering an already discredited comfort, the recounted dream, by helping her to recapture the youthful mother, then serves as a springboard from which the narrator launches into a story told to her by her mother, stemming from her mother's single days teaching in a one-room country schoolhouse and boarding with the Grieves family, whose tangled lives form the substance of her tale. In the narrator's recounting of her mother's story, we successively witness the apparent self-effacement of two storytellers, for the narrator seems to disappear in giving voice to her mother's tale, and then the mother is lost to view within *her* story, which constitutes the bulk of "Friend of My Youth." Just when we have all but lost sight of any storytelling presence, however, the apparent self-sufficiency of the tale is abruptly undercut by a series of codas that jolt us into an awareness of the mediating role of the narrative voice. The codas provide glimpses of successively shifting stages in the narrator's own development and in her relation to her mother, each constituting a different attempt to understand the recalcitrant mother material. The last coda returns to the dream, which now upstages the story that it frames. The closing dream provides a new take on the mother-daughter drama at the same time that it offers suggestive avenues of approach to the stories that follow; for these stories ring their own variations both on Munro's familiar albatross story and on the wider issues raised in the codas to "Friend of My Youth" — issues of women's relations to one another and of "relation" itself, in the sense of narration.

The central story in "Friend of My Youth," which concerns the strict Cameronian Flora, twice betrayed by her one-time fiancé Robert, has been pieced together by the narrator's mother from firsthand experience and from gossip and letters telling of events before and after her stay in the community. The account ends with an exchange of letters between the mother and Flora in which the mother writes from afar to express sympathy and profess outrage and in which Flora replies to reject the sympathy and outrage and, essentially, to tell her former friend to mind her own business. At this point, the apparent neutrality of the account comes to a sudden end. The original narrator, temporarily lost to view, reemerges, offering successive codas, or exegeses, to the interpolated story that we have just read. First, reminding us of the source of the story, the narrator resentfully recounts her mother's attempt to package it as a moral tale:

> In later years, when she sometimes talked about the things she might have been, or done, she would say, "If I could have been a writer — I do think I could have been; I could have been a writer — then I would have written the story of Flora's life. And do you know what I would have called it? 'The Maiden Lady.'" (19)

If I could have been a writer. . . . The mother's wistful evocation of her unfulfilled potential highlights the fact that the lively, often comic, rendition of the sad tale that we have been reading is the achievement of the narrator-daughter, the real writer after all. The story of Flora's life emerges as a site of contestation between the narrator and her mother, implicitly posing the questions of who will give it definitive voice and to what end. Next, the narrator recalls her teenage rejection of her mother's reverential account of Flora as "a noble figure, one who accepts defection, treachery, who forgives and stands aside, not once but twice" (19). More than Flora is at stake in the narrator's dismissive youthful response to her mother's moralizing:

> In her own plight her [the mother's] ideas had turned mystical, and there was sometimes a hush, a solemn thrill in her voice that grated on me, alerted me to what seemed a personal danger. I felt a great fog of platitudes and pieties lurking, an incontestable crippled-mother power which could capture and choke me. . . . I had to keep myself sharp-tongued and cynical, arguing and deflating. Eventually I gave up even that recognition and opposed her in silence. (20)

Although recognizing the vulnerability and the impulse to self-preservation behind her teenage rejection of her mother's "reading" of Flora's tale, the adult narrator nonetheless judges her former self harshly, immediately undercutting the sympathetic presentation of her adolescent self that she has just written: "This is a fancy way of saying that I was no comfort and poor company to her when she had almost nowhere else to turn" (20).

Still, this unsparing, mature judgement on her younger self does not keep the narrator from relating that self's competing construction; in scornful contrast to her mother's wistful evocation of unfulfilled potential, the adolescent daughter "didn't think that I could have written a novel but that I would write one. I would take a different tack." As if anticipating the narrator's literary practice in "Meneseteung," she tells us, "I saw through my mother's story and put in what she left out" (20). The narrator then provides an account of her own youthful imaginings, which lead to an altered ending in which Flora emerges as a Presbyterian witch who gets her comeuppance in a lurid gothic finale.

The mature narrator of "Friend of My Youth," however, now rejects the competition of codas that she has just sketched, seeking instead a more dispassionate and deeper comprehension of their conflict: "What made Flora evil in my story was just what made her admirable in my mother's — her turning away from sex" (22). Moving beyond guilt and self-recrimination, the narrator meditates on the different worldviews inherent in their different exegeses, seeing in them atti- tudes beyond conscious, individual choice: "My mother had grown up in a time and in a place where sex was a dark undertaking for women. She knew that you could die of it" (22). Indeed, within the mother's story, Ellie *does* seem to have died of it (though by a logic that is clearer morally than physiologically).

So she honored the decency, the prudery, the frigidity, that might protect you. And I grew up in horror of that very protection, the dainty tyranny that seemed to extend to all areas of life. . . . The odd thing is that my mother's ideas were in line with some progressive notions of her times, and mine echoed the notions that were favored in my time. This in spite of the fact that we both believed ourselves independent, and lived in backwaters that did not register such changes. (22–23)

Her meditation concludes with a stunning image for the *Zeitgeist*: "It's as if tendencies that seem most deeply rooted in our minds, most private and singular, have come in as spores on the prevailing wind, looking for any likely place to land, any welcome" (23). Words of remarkable generosity and humility, which enable the narrator to transcend the mother-daughter competition for narrative authority through an understanding of the wider context of their conflict.

The narrator does not, however, bring her story to a close on this note of understanding and wisdom. Like the narrator of "The Ottawa Valley" in *Something I've Been Meaning to Tell You*, she pushes beyond the easier ending, adding yet another coda to the Grieves story. The mood of harmony as well as the competing codas that precede it are now displaced by the narrator's revelation that years later her mother received a letter from "the real Flora" (23), telling of her move to town and her clerking job in a store and, in an inversion of roles, offering sympathy to the mother for her debilitat- ing illness. Flora's letter leads the narrator to memories of her stricken mother's inability to get beyond writing the beginnings of letters (one of which started with "Friend of my youth") and of her "impa- tience with [her mother's] flowery language, the direct appeal for love and pity" (24).

Inevitably, the adolescent's impatience becomes guilt when recalled by the adult narrator. But the guilt is addressed by a circuitous route, which imperceptibly leads back to the opening dream. Although at the time of Flora's letter and her mother's illness the narrator "had lost interest in Flora," she has "thought of her since," imagining a happier ending to her story. In the narrator's more recent speculations, Flora is no longer the hateful, sex-rejecting witch of her youthful fantasies; her new, alternative ending springs Flora loose from her predictable stoic fate and the rigidities that defined and confined her in her mother's tale. The older narrator re-creates the formerly alien Flora as someone with whom she might even discover affinities. She spins an open-ended fantasy of Flora's progressive liberation, in which Flora, now working in a store, "might have had to learn about food blenders or chain saws, negligees, cosmetics, even condoms" (24). Each image suggests another, leading to a Flora who might "get a permanent, paint her nails, put on lipstick," or even "go on holidays . . . [and] eat meals in a restaurant . . . where drinks were served. She might make friends with women who were divorced. She might meet a man" (25).

From this fantasy of open-ended possibility, the narrator slips into a more personal one: "I might go into a store and find her." Immediately recognizing the impossibility of doing so ("She would be dead a long time now"), she nonetheless persists: "But suppose I had gone into a store — perhaps a department store" (25) — where she imagines meeting Flora, wanting to tell her that she knows her story, even "trying to tell her. (This is a dream now, I understand it as a dream)" (25–26). Whether or not we hear an echo here of the opening sentence of "The Ottawa Valley" — "I think of my mother sometimes in department stores" (*Something* 227), the dream of meeting a transformed Flora clearly echoes the opening dream of "Friend of My Youth" and quickly merges with it as the narrator now conflates the two long-dead women. When the dream-Flora responds to the narrator's claims with a mocking smile, "weary . . . of me and my idea of her, my information, my notion that I can know anything about her," the narrator recognizes that "Of course it's my mother I'm thinking of, my mother as she was in those dreams, saying, It's nothing, just this little tremor; saying with such astonishing lighthearted forgiveness, Oh, I knew you'd come someday. My mother surprising me" (26).

But the surprise surprises further by not being altogether pleasurable. Seeing her mother's "mask, her fate, and most of her affliction taken away," the daughter, though "relieved" and "happy," is also "disconcerted":

I felt slightly cheated. Yes. Offended, tricked, cheated, by this welcome turnaround, this reprieve. My mother moving rather carelessly out of her old prison, showing options and powers I never dreamed she had, changes more than herself. She changes the bitter lump of love I have carried all this time into a phantom — something useless and uncalled for, like a phantom pregnancy. (26)

In springing Flora loose from her fixed role in the mother's story, the narrator has also opened the way for her mother to get loose from "her old prison" — her illness and the narrator's fixed memories of her[3] — which in turn places the daughter in a new position. For with her new freedom and independence, the dream-mother also seems to have got loose from the narrator's knowledge and control. That this "turnaround," which destabilizes all that has preceded it, should prove disconcerting as well as "welcome" forces us to ponder why a part of the narrator suddenly seems to prefer the rigid and demanding mother. Why does she feel "cheated" at having to relinquish "the bitter lump of love" — presumably, the guilt with which she has lived for so long? (The lump is also an image that, within the story, looks back to Ellie's "growth" and unsuccessful — phantom? — pregnancies[4] and, elsewhere in the collection, forward to Barbara's lump in "Oranges and Apples.") Is it that by transforming her mother's story into narrative the narrator has automatically opened it up to the possibility of other directions that threaten the rigidity of her own mechanisms for dealing with the past? Or is it due to the threatened loss of narrative control once she begins to give free reign to her fantasies?[5] Or does her sense of being tricked and cheated point, as Carol Shields suggests, to a painful recognition of the fundamental unknowability of the mother, "her steadfast resistance to the notions of others" (22)?[6] In any case, as the mother is imaginatively freed from her prison, the narrator reveals needs and potentialities that we (and she) see for the first time. Perhaps most intriguingly, the destabilizing fantasy calls into question the truth value and the stability of any narrative, either imagined or remembered, reminding us that, as both memory and storytelling are constructions, creative acts, their content is always, in some sense, problematic and open ended. There is always another way of coming at the same material.[7]

The mother in the closing dream of "Friend of My Youth" may seem reminiscent of the mother at the end of "The Ottawa Valley," who is "indistinct," whose "edges melt and flow" (*Something* 246).

But while in the earlier story the mother "weighs everything down, . . . has stuck to me as close as ever and refused to fall away" (246), the self-sufficient dream-mother of "Friend of My Youth" eludes the narrator's grasp, seeming simply to slip away. Ultimately, her getting loose is experienced as more unsettling than liberating. Hence, while the narrator of "The Ottawa Valley" understands the final "purpose" of her (narrative) "journey" as an effort to *"get rid"* of the mother (246), the narrative of "Friend of My Youth" appears, instead, as an effort to recapture the mother, to bring her back.

The daughter's desire to recapture the mother in "Friend of My Youth" suggests another function of the daughter's tale. I have looked at the Grieves story as a site of competition between mother and daughter for narrative (and hence moral) authority. Additionally, though, we can see the story as a collaborative effort, even a kind of *hommage* to the mother, whose early illness and death perhaps prevented her from fulfilling her potential. In "Winter Wind," the daughter relates that her mother's "vocal cords were partly paralyzed" and that "Sometimes I would have to act as her interpreter, a job that made me wild with shame" (*Something* 195).[8] In the later "Friend of My Youth," the daughter finds a different, more affirmative, way to give a more permanent voice to the mother whose own voice was prematurely silenced.

Munro, of course, has always been interested in the process of storytelling, and her stories abound with fragments of stories and contradictory versions of characters and events. *Friend of My Youth*, however, viewed in its entirety, shows a newly focused interest in the construction of collaborative, shared narratives.[9] In addition to the complex title story, this interest is notable in the two other stories that directly treat a mother-daughter relationship — "Meneseteung" and "Goodness and Mercy." Before turning to them, however, we should dwell a moment longer on the destabilizing dream as well as on the fantasy that introduces it and the unexpected affinities that this fantasy suggests, for they illustrate motifs that reverberate throughout the collection. Just as the mother "moving . . . out of her old prison" points to characters in other stories who get loose from the bonds of predictable narratives, so too the narrator's fantasy of meeting an altered Flora and her desire to construct a happier ending for a woman whose fate has been presented to her as sealed in inescapable resignation or gloom are echoed in the impulses of other female protagonists in the collection.

In "Five Points," Brenda refuses to accept as final the dismal end for the adolescent Maria on which Neil's story from his past concludes. (After stealing money from her parents' cash register to pay boys to have sex with her, Maria was "sent to a place for young offenders" [*Friend* 40].) Brenda doggedly wants to know "what happened to Maria. . . . The story won't leave Brenda alone," and she goes on to imagine a more generous conclusion: "Well, maybe she got married. . . . Lots of people get married who are no beauties. . . . She might've lost weight and be looking good even" (42). Brenda's insistence on pushing beyond the known ending of Maria's incarceration to more open-ended possibilities provides the occasion for her first fight with her lover, Neil. Although it is not clear that his account of Maria's humiliating sexual need is intended to humiliate the attractive, sexy Brenda, her insistent desire to see Maria get loose from Neil's confining narrative shows an instinctive identification with the pathetic young woman whom she knows only from her lover's story.

A female protagonist's recognition of affinity in unexpected quarters and her impulse to write a more open ending through which an apparently dead-ended woman can get loose from a presumed foreclosed destiny reappear in "Hold Me Fast, Don't Let Me Pass." Having met the beautiful young Judy, whose illegitimate daughter, Tania, seems to confine her to a long dreary future looking after an isolated semi-invalid, Hazel speculates aloud (to Antoinette, Judy's older and successful rival for Tania's father), "It must be a lonely life for her," adding, "She might like to get married" (97). Just as Neil in "Five Points" rejects Brenda's hopeful scenario for Maria, so too Antoinette dismisses Hazel's generous thoughts about a happier future for Judy. And, like Brenda, Hazel refuses to back down: "It doesn't matter so much nowadays. . . . Girls have children first and get married later. Movie stars, ordinary girls, too. All the time" (97).

As suggested earlier, it is not only characters and narrators within the stories who offer liberating endings to foreclosed plots presented to them in interpolated tales; the characters themselves also get loose from expected, constricting story lines.[10] For example, Hazel is not simply the sympathetic imaginer of a more open future for Judy than her limiting circumstances might suggest but also someone who, years earlier, "broke open the shell of her increasingly doubtful and expensive prettiness; she got out"; even though she remained in a dreary marriage, she found a way to take "hold of her life" (82). In *Friend of My Youth*, unlike most of the earlier collections, some female characters are able to get loose from confinement — Hazel and Brenda, also Barbara of "Oranges and Apples" — even though they remain within their flawed marriages. (It is perhaps puzzling, but an example of the force of optimism, that both Brenda and Hazel, who have not exactly found marriage liberating themselves, should nonetheless construct it as such for others in their imagined narratives). At the same time, we also see the situation more familiar to Munro readers of a woman breaking free from her marriage,[11] described in ways that tie in with motifs present elsewhere in the collection. Joan in "Oh, What Avails," heeding the call of "a person not heard from in her marriage, and perhaps not previously heard from in her life" (199), "feels herself loosed" and "knows that she cannot go back to the life she was living or to the person she was before" (200). Georgia in "Differently," who similarly discovers that she "contained another woman" (233), is seen as confuting more conventional expectations familiar in literature (and in life): "you would have thought that after such scourging she'd have scuttled back into her marriage. . . . That was not what happened" (241). In "Wigtime," the divergent youthful paths of Anita and Margot seem early to cast them as contraries in a traditional good woman/bad woman dichotomy, but their later choices invert and then effectively dissolve this opposition (a staple of more predictable plots). The story ends with their renewed friendship, allowing Margot to tell of her frequent friendly visits to the now institutionalized ex-wife whom she has displaced. A similar rejection of clear divisions between recognizable types of women is present in "Hold Me Fast, Don't Let Me Pass" in the feelings of female loyalty and solidarity with which Hazel responds to both her dead husband's former lover, Antoinette, now respectable hotel owner and *soi-disant* widow, and the publicly stigmatized Judy.

"Meneseteung" is another story in which a protagonist gets loose from narrative expectations engendered by familiar, predictable plots, while it, too, presents unexpected affinities among three dissimilar women. Moreover, if, in Virginia Woolf's much-quoted words, "a woman writing thinks back through her mothers" (127), then this story of a female narrator seeking to recover a forgotten woman writer of the past may also be read as a version of the mother-daughter drama. Such recoveries have become a frequent subject of both fiction and historical research for contemporary women writers. Moreover, here, as in "Friend of My Youth," the narrator's treatment of material from a (literary fore)mother may be viewed as both competition and *hommage*.[12]

"Meneseteung" opens with a discussion of Almeda Joynt Roth's book of poetry *Offerings*, and excerpts from that volume provide epigraphs for each of the story's six sections. At the same time, the researching writer of "Meneseteung" — more successfully than the adolescent narrator of "Friend of My Youth" who "saw through . . . [her] mother's story and put in what she left out" (20) — portrays a denser and imaginatively richer world than that suggested by the pretty, sanitized poetry of her nineteenth-century foremother. Moving from Almeda's book of verse to her world in the second section of the story, the narrator, aided by old issues of the local *Vidette*, evokes a raw frontier town in which "Cows are tethered in vacant lots or pastured in back yards, but sometimes they get loose. Pigs get loose, too, and dogs roam free. . . . [A]nimals . . . leave horse buns, cow pats, dog turds that ladies have to hitch up their skirts for," young rowdies trundle a drunken Queen Aggie all over town in a wheelbarrow, "then dump her into a ditch" (54), and Almeda's bedroom window overlooks the disreputable Pearl Street at the edge of the swamp, to which "No decent woman ever would . . . [walk]" (56). Implicitly underscoring the greater authenticity of her re-creation of Almeda's world, the writer reminds us that "The countryside that she [Almeda] has written about in her poems actually takes diligence and determination to see. Some things must be disregarded. Manure piles . . . and boggy fields . . ." (61).

The various texts uncovered by the narrator — Almeda's poems, with her author's introduction and photograph, supplemented by *Vidette* entries — suggest a character recognizable from familiar plots: first, the decorous nineteenth-century maiden poetess, modest, if not downright apologetic, about her literary ventures, a baker of "fancy iced cakes and decorated tarts" (58); next, the not entirely over-the-hill spinster, embarking on a romance with her neighbour, Jarvis Poulter, presumably hoping for the closure of the marriage plot. The final *Vidette* entry fits Almeda into yet another female plot, that of the increasingly eccentric old maid who meets an ignoble end. Navigating among the "facts" and "documented" innuendo (supplied by the author of "Meneseteung"), however, the narrator enables Almeda to get loose from these familiar plotlines,[13] inventing for her a story of far greater drama and an inner life of far wider imaginative scope than any that one could hope to find in the pages of the *Vidette* or in the work of a nineteeth-century poetess.

The crucial imagined scene of the audible "ball of fire rolling up Pearl Street, shooting off sparks," followed by sounds of "a woman

. . . being beaten" (63) and the imperfectly glimpsed grappling figures at Almeda's back fence, with their "confused . . . gagging, vomiting, grunting, pounding" and the "choking sound of pain and self-abasement, self-abandonment," suggest to Almeda that she has witnessed "the sound of murder" and pose the question of her personal responsibility — "What is to be done, what is she to do"?[14] Although her immediate response is that "she must go out into the yard" (64), she succumbs to the medically (patriarchally) prescribed "nerve medicine" (62) and falls asleep. Waking, she imagines "a big crow sitting on her windowsill" and telling her, "Wake up and move the wheelbarrow. . . . [S]he understands that it means something else by 'wheelbarrow' — something foul and sorrowful" (64). While Almeda's gloss on wheelbarrow is certainly apt, if the narrator has found the account of Queen Aggie's treatment in the *Vidette*, then might not Almeda have read it there too? Additionally, a wheelbarrow is used to cart away rubbish, but the woman's body "heaped up" at the back fence is neither rubbish nor ready to be carted away, though it appears to Almeda's horrified gaze in dehumanized, brute animal — and vegetable — terms: "a bare breast let loose, brown nipple pulled long like a cow's teat, and a bare haunch and leg, the haunch showing a bruise as big as a sunflower. The unbruised skin is grayish, like a plucked, raw drumstick" (65). Fearing that her hesitation has been responsible for the woman's death, Almeda hastily summons Jarvis, who "looks down at" the body and "nudges the leg with the toe of his boot, just as you'd nudge a dog or a sow." In response, sustaining its closeness to brute animal life,

> The body heaves itself onto all fours, the head is lifted — the hair all matted with blood and vomit — and the woman begins to bang this head, hard and rhythmically. . . . As she bangs her head, she finds her voice and lets out an openmouthed yowl, full of strength and what sounds like an anguished pleasure. (66)

Whether or not we accept Dermot McCarthy's description of this woman as "Life itself in all its obscene splendor" (7),[15] she certainly serves as a graphic reminder of the animal nature of human — if not specifically female — life. After his encounter with the beaten, bruised woman and the dishevelled, agitated Almeda, Jarvis may still wish to preserve the fiction of two types of women, though he now "speaks to her [Almeda] in a tone of harsh joviality that she has never before heard from him" (67). Almeda, however, consciously or unconsciously, recognizes her bond with this other woman,[16] hitherto so remote from her fenced-in world and representing all that has been excised from her poetry, and Jarvis's contemptuous treatment of *her* signals the end of Almeda's romantic interest in *him*.

In a series of interlocking images, the blood that has congealed in the woman by the fence begins to flow in Almeda, as her menstrual flow merges with the grape juice overflowing its container, and both merge with the flow of words in her mind, staining the kitchen floor boards with a "stain [that] will never come out" (70). Almeda's newly recognized kinship with the other woman has irrevocably changed and stained her. The "[l]ittle jars of grape jelly" that Almeda has planned as "fine Christmas presents, or offerings to the sick" (62), are like her earlier literary *"Offerings"* — discrete units, attractively packaged and carefully contained. But Almeda and her new vision can no longer be contained so neatly. Like the genteelly crocheted roses in her tablecloth, which she soon imagines escaping into "floating independence" (70), Almeda has got loose from her previous moorings. Resembling another nineteenth-century fictional woman poised to rebel against patriarchal confinement, who obsessively watches the patterns of the wallpaper, seeing figured in these domestic surroundings her own imprisonment and then a promise of her escape,[17] Almeda "[surrenders] to her surroundings," watching the "garlanded wallpaper," curtains, floral carpet, and "sideboard spread with embroidered runners and holding patterned plates and jugs":

> For every one of these patterns, decorations seems charged with life, ready to move and flow and alter. Or possibly to explode. Almeda Roth's occupation through the day is to keep an eye on them. Not to prevent their alteration so much as to catch them at it — to understand it, to be part of it. (69)

As the "glowing and swelling" in Almeda begin "to suggest words . . . a flow of words" (69), she has a Whitmanesque vision of "one very great poem that will contain everything," including "the obscene racket on Pearl Street and the polished toe of Jarvis Poulter's boot and the plucked-chicken haunch with its blue-black flower" (70). Judging that the violence of climate and life can be "borne only if it is channelled into a poem," she decides that

> the name of the poem will be — it *is* — "The Meneseteung.". . .
> No, in fact it is the river, the Meneseteung, that is the poem —
> with its deep holes and rapids and blissful pools under the

summer trees and its grinding blocks of ice thrown up at the end of the winter and its desolating spring floods. (70)[18]

As the story has progressed, the narrator has gradually seemed to lose herself in Almeda, moving into her mind and shedding the cool detachment of the first section, with its almost pedantic observations about masculine and feminine rhymes. But here a glaring cliché suddenly reminds us of the distance between Almeda and the narrator, through whose mediation we have been reading her story, as we are shown Almeda's vision in what must surely be her own words: "Almeda looks deep, deep into the river of her mind and into the tablecloth, and she sees the crocheted roses floating" (70). Almeda is presented as a foremother who is granted a vision that, due to the limitations of her time, place, and culture, she lacks not simply the courage and the encouragement but also the adequate linguistic resources — the language — to express. Unlike the woman by the fence, Almeda does not, finally, find her voice. Yet while her all-embracing cosmic vision remains unwritten, the narrator's imagined rendering of decisive moments in Almeda's life and thought constitute her own "offerings" to a literary foremother. The narrator's story can be viewed as a collaborative creation in which a more privileged literary daughter gives voice to a disadvantaged predecessor who did not, ultimately, succeed in finding her own.

The final scene, as in "Friend of My Youth," brings us back to the frame. The narrator now distances us from Almeda through the *Vidette*'s report of her ignominious end, allowing us to draw ironic parallels between this account and the earlier accounts of Queen Aggie and the woman by the fence. But though we are brought back to the narrator as researcher, the detachment of the first section is gone. Looking for Almeda's gravestone, the narrator passionately begins "pulling grass and scrabbling in the dirt with my bare hands" (73), seeking to affirm her conjecture that the "Meda" mentioned in one of the poems is indeed Almeda Roth, author of the poems. The narrator on her hands and knees in the dirt (how else can we envision the scene?) suggests by her posture her own closeness to the animal life that she has imagined Almeda recognizing in herself on seeing the woman by the fence. Thus, the narrator's identification with Almeda is completed by her own final bodily identification with this other, unnamed woman.[19]

At the same time, there is a certain play in this frantic search, for the narrator's bold leap of imagination does not lie in her intuition that Meda was Almeda's nickname. The Almeda Roth who has come to interest the narrator (and us) is no longer primarily the Almeda Roth of the early book of poems and of the *Vidette* accounts but the author of the wholly imagined poem that remains unwritten — though the story that we have just finished reading may be seen as a prose approach to it. No sooner has the narrator prided herself on "scraping the dirt off gravestones, reading microfilm, . . . seeing this trickle in time, making a connection, rescuing one thing from the rubbish" than she concedes radical doubt: "I may have got it wrong. I don't know if she ever took laudanum. Many ladies did. I don't know if she ever made grape jelly" (73). These final sentences, added after the published *New Yorker* version, may be seen as part of Munro's increasingly characteristic refusal of definitive closure, and in light of issues raised earlier in this essay the disclaimer provides another example of a character escaping authorial control. But, of course, it is not the "facts" of laudanum or grape jelly that are in question, any more than whether Almeda was called Meda in her family. The narrator's apparent concern for historical accuracy is belied — even ignoring for a moment the fundamental fictionality of Almeda Roth — by the "fact" that even the (constructed) "record" gives no justification for the crucial events of the fracas on Pearl Street, the woman by the fence, the voice of the crow, and, indeed, all of Almeda's vibrant inner life in response to these experiences, including her unwritten poem. However, because the "record" — *Offerings*, the *Vidette* — *has been* invented, we cannot help but return at the end to the implied author behind the narrator who can never be wholly erased from our consciousness. So we are left with a series of refracted and related women, a sisterhood encompassing the invisible author, the narrator, Almeda/Meda, and the other woman.

Whereas "Meneseteung" presents a daughter generously reaching out across the gulf of historical time to resuscitate a forgotten foremother, "Goodness and Mercy" reworks the mother-daughter drama as a wish-fulfilment idyll. In contrast to Maddy's ten-year vigil caring for a mother whose "bizarre" disease inflicted "such unnecessary humiliation" on her daughters in "The Peace of Utrecht" (*Dance* 195), or the "decade or more" during which "the paralyzing disease" held the mother in "Friend of My Youth" "in its grip . . . before her death" (*Friend* 3), the companionable ocean voyage of Bugs and Averill (for which Averill has generously paid with "money left to her by the father she had never seen" [156]) lasts a mere ten days. Behind the figure of the "charming" (160), witty Bugs, minimizing her illness, continuing to jest, uncomplainingly absenting herself gradually from one meal or social occasion after another, yet still able to sing "with unimpaired — or almost unimpaired — sweetness" (167), we may see the shadows of other ailing mothers, far less attractive and easy to love: the mother in "The Peace of Utrecht," barely able to articulate, who demanded the love of her daughters "without shame or sense" (*Dance* 199), or the mother in "Friend of My Youth," who, with her "direct appeal for love and pity," refused to "withdraw with dignity, instead of reaching out . . . to cast her stricken shadow" (*Friend* 24). And, unlike the daughter-narrator in the earlier story left to lament that "the resources of love we had were not enough, the demand on us was too great" (*Dance* 199), or the daughter-narrator in the later story, who "was no comfort and poor company to her [mother] when she had nowhere else to turn" (*Friend* 20), Averill is unwavering in her devotion to her dying mother, the loving and dutiful daughter — except in her own eyes, as we learn when the captain tells "her perfectly secret story" aloud (177). Here Averill's story itself seems to get loose: "She had made it, and he had taken it and told it, safely" (178). For in telling it "safely," the captain, "alert to everything on the ship" and the embodiment of "peaceable authority" (166, 167), acknowledges her hidden fantasies and absolves her from guilt.

"Goodness and Mercy" hovers at the border of magic realism. The captain's wisdom and his knowledge of human nature may, of course, suffice to let him know that even a love as true and freely given as Averill's must have its ambivalent, dark side. Still, the story shared by Averill and the godlike captain seems to emerge as a mysterious collaboration, one that stands out from the collaborations between women that we have been looking at. Told by the captain, then amended (with his acceptance) by Averill, who recognizes it as her own, it slips loose from any fixed form, changing through successive versions in her fluid imagination and ultimately proving capable, through the captain's authority and participation, not only of absolving her from guilt but also of legitimizing the plenitude of her desires even in the face of loss and death.

The daughter's ambivalent feelings for the mother, implicit in the combination of competition and *hommage* in "Friend of My Youth" and "Meneseteung," are revealed here by the presence of the secret, liberating death wish that Averill harbours for Bugs alongside her profound love and solicitude. Except perhaps in Averill's free-floating fantasies or in the grace with which Bugs is dying, neither woman can be said to get loose from expected roles, escape authorial control, or discover surprising bonds with other women. Rather, "Goodness and Mercy" may be viewed as an idyllic replay of Munro's albatross story, creating a charmed space that corresponds to the "thing she [Averill] always felt, when her mother sang. The doors flew open, effortlessly, there was a lighted space beyond, a revelation of kindness and seriousness. Desirable, blessed joy, and seriousness, a play of kindness that asked nothing of you" (168). Unlike the mother's generous words in the opening dream of "Friend of My Youth," whose "transparent . . . hopefulness [and] too easy . . . forgiveness" the daughter is forced to deconstruct (3), Bugs's "gift" (168), though first presented as lasting only as long as her singing, seems endorsed at the end by "the captain's offering" (179). Within the idyllic space created by the story, Averill "is absolved and fortunate" (179), and the hope expressed in her hymn — "Goodness and Mercy all my life / Shall surely follow me" (169) — almost seems attainable. But Munro never wholly abandons her ironic edge. Underscoring the tenacity of the bond between daughter and mother, Averill first marries one man "chiefly because Bugs would have thought the choice preposterous" and then a second, who, with his "flippant and ironical manner," "either charmed people or aroused their considerable dislike" (179) — just like the flippant and ironic Bugs, whom people either consider "charming" or "can't stand" (160) — a sure indication of the daughter's abiding loyalty to the first friend of her youth.

NOTES

[1] On metamorphosis, change, and fluid boundaries, see Irving, who treats them as properties of *female* nature. On Munro's refusal of definitive closure, see Crouse; and Hoy 18–19. A number of critics observe that the self in Munro is shifting and multiple. See, for example, Blodgett 12, 68, and passim; Hoy 17; Stead 151–53; and Thacker 156.

[2] Speaking of her mother in another interview, Munro says of "The Peace of Utrecht" that "The first real story I ever wrote was about her" ("Alice Munro" 215).

[3] See also Carrington 187–88; and Stead 156. Earlier in "Friend of My Youth," the narrator writes of her mother's becoming "busy with her own life and finally a prisoner in it" (19).

[4] See also Redekop 215; and Stead 156.

[5] This fear would fit nicely into Carrington's thesis that "the most central and creative paradox of Munro's fiction is its repeated . . . attempt to control what is uncontrollable" (5).

6 Dermot McCarthy writes of the mother's affirming "her own impenetrable otherness" (12).

7 This suggests more radical doubt than is implied by the question in "Winter Wind" — "how am I to know what I claim to know?" (*Something* 201) — or than "the difficulty of getting to the truth," which W.R. Martin has described as a focus of *Lives of Girls and Women* and "The Progress of Love" (179). It leads into "the vexatious question of the nature of reality" (Hoy 12) and of Munro's relation to postmodernism and metafiction, which have been treated with increasing frequency by critics. Linda Hutcheon, for example, identifies Munro as a "postmodern metafiction writer" (45 and passim), while Stephen Regan comments on her willingness "to harbour intense doubts about the representational value of fiction and yet to persevere in the creation of something that is true to life" (124–25).

8 Also see "The Peace of Utrecht" (*Dance* 195, 199).

9 Katherine Mayberry discusses the development of the "communal cooperative narrative" in *The Moons of Jupiter* (though she locates it first at the end of *The Lives of Girls and Women*) (59). The kind of collaborative narrative that I am describing in *Friend of My Youth* is similar to, but not identical to, the narrative cooperation that she describes in the earlier books; our views of the impulse behind such narratives also differ somewhat. In a parenthetical remark, Mayberry does mention "Friend of My Youth" as an example of this "new configuration of narrative," but she does not elaborate (64).

10 Munro's rejection of anything like "a traditional plot" has become a basic premise of Munro criticism. See, for example, Mathews.

11 For example, Rose in *Who Do You Think You Are?* and Isabel in "White Dump" in *The Progress of Love*. The situation recurs in the recent stories "The Children Stay" and "Jakarta."

12 McCarthy 1 and Redekop 227 also speak of Almeda as foremother and offer various Canadian examples of this kind of recovery.

13 See McCarthy: "the 'plot' of the story is the project of freeing this imaginative ancestor from the patriarchal stereotype" (4).

14 McCarthy 20; Redekop 255; and Stead 159 all see "wrath" in Almeda's last name, Roth. Perhaps we can also see the Early Middle English "ruth," whose first definition in *The Shorter* OED, is "the quality of being compassionate; pitifulness; compassion, pity."

15 For Redekop, "this body is a parody of Mother Earth" (224).

16 See also Stead 161.

17 In Charlotte Perkins Gilman's *The Yellow Wallpaper*, the heroine obsessively watches movements behind the wallpaper, seeing there a woman behind bars struggling to get out. After "helping" the kindred woman by ripping off wide swaths of the wallpaper, she imaginatively merges with this phantom as she seeks her own escape.

[18] More than twenty years ago, Munro wrote of the "short river the Indians called the Menesetung [sic] and the first settlers . . . called the Maitland," which flowed past her father's land. Rising in spring to cover the flats, thus earning the nickname "the Flood," "shallow and tropical" in summer, and filled with myriad varieties of plants and fish, it offered a comprehensive image of the variegated abundance of ordinary experience: "We believed there were deep holes in the river. . . . I am still partly convinced that this river — not even the whole river, but this little stretch of it — will provide whatever myths you want, whatever adventures. I name the plants, I name the fish, and every name seems to me triumphant, every leaf and quick fish remarkably valuable. This ordinary place is sufficient, everything here is touchable and mysterious" (Munro, "Everything").

[19] While this scene has rightly been viewed as echoing the end of "The Stone in the Field" in *The Moons of Jupiter*, it may be more instructive to contrast the narrator's passionate "scrabbling" in "Meneseteung" with the narrator's rational decision in "The Stone in the Field" not to bother walking over to the rock pile.

WORKS CITED

Blodgett, E.D. *Alice Munro*. Twayne's World Authors Series, Canadian Literature. Boston: Twayne, 1988.

Carrington, Ildikó de Papp. *Controlling the Uncontrollable: The Fiction of Alice Munro*. DeKalb: Northern Illinois UP, 1989.

Crouse, David. "Resisting Reduction: Closure in Richard Ford's *Rock Springs* and Alice Munro's *Friend of My Youth*." *Canadian Literature* 146 (1995): 51–64.

Gilman, Charlotte Perkins. *The Yellow Wallpaper*. 1892. New York: Feminist, 1973.

Hoy, Helen. "Alice Munro: 'Unforgettable, Indigestible Messages.'" *Journal of Canadian Studies/Revue d'études canadienne* 26.1 (1991): 5–22.

Hutcheon, Linda. *The Canadian Postmodern: A Study of Contemporary English-Canadian Fiction*. Studies in Canadian Literature. Toronto: Oxford UP, 1988.

Irving, Lorna. "Changing Is the Word I Want." MacKendrick 99–112.

MacKendrick, Louis K., ed. *Probable Fictions: Alice Munro's Narrative Acts*. Downsview, ON: ECW, 1983.

Martin, W.R. *Alice Munro: Paradox and Parallel*. Edmonton: U of Alberta P, 1987.

Mathews, Lawrence. "*Who Do You Think You Are?* Alice Munro's Art of Disarrangement." MacKendrick 181–93.

Mayberry, Katherine J. "Narrative Strategies of Liberation in Alice Munro."

Studies in Canadian Literature/Études en littérature canadienne 19.2
(1994): 57–66.

McCarthy, Dermot. "The Woman Out Back: Alice Munro's 'Meneseteung.'" *Studies in Canadian Literature/Études en littérature canadienne*
19.1 (1994): 1–20.

Munro, Alice. "Alice Munro." *Canadian Writers at Work: Interviews with
Geoff Hancock*. Toronto: Oxford UP, 1987. 187–225.

———. "The Children Stay." *New Yorker* 22 and 29 Dec. 1997: 90+. (Rpt. and
rev. in Munro, *Love* 181–215.)

———. *Dance of the Happy Shades*. 1968. Toronto: McGraw-Hill, 1988.

———. "Everything Here Is Touchable and Mysterious." *Weekend Magazine*
[supp. to *Globe and Mail*] 11 May 1974: 33.

———. *Friend of My Youth*. 1990. Toronto: Penguin, 1991.

———. "Jakarta." *Saturday Night* Feb. 1998: 44–60. (Rpt. in Munro, *Love*
79–117.)

———. *The Love of a Good Woman*. Toronto: McClelland, 1998.

———. *The Moons of Jupiter*. 1982. Toronto: Penguin, 1986.

———. *The Progress of Love*. 1986. Toronto: Penguin, 1987.

———. "The Real Material: An Interview with Alice Munro." With J.R. (Tim)
Struthers. MacKendrick 5–37.

———. *Something I've Been Meaning to Tell You*. 1974. Toronto: Penguin,
1990.

———. *Who Do You Think You Are?* 1978. Toronto: Penguin, 1991.

Redekop, Magdalene. *Mothers and Other Clowns: The Stories of Alice
Munro*. London: Routledge, 1992.

Regan, Stephen. "'The Presence of the Past': Modernism and Postmod-
ernism in Canadian Short Fiction." *Narrative Strategies in Canadian
Literature*. Ed. Coral A. Howells and Lynette Hunter. Philadelphia: Open
UP, 1991. 108–34.

"Ruth." *The Shorter OED*. 3rd ed. 1973.

Shields, Carol. "In Ontario." *London Review of Books* 7 Feb. 1991: 22–23.

Stead, Kit. "The Twinkling of an 'I': Alice Munro's *Friend of My Youth*."
*The Guises of Canadian Diversity/Les Masques de la diversité canadi-
enne*. Ed. Serge Jaumain and Marc Maufort. Amsterdam: Rodopi, 1995.
151–65.

Thacker, Robert. "'So Shocking a Verdict in Real Life': Autobiography in
Alice Munro's Stories." *Reflections: Autobiography and Canadian Literature*. Ed. K.P. Stich. Ottawa: U of Ottawa P, 1988. 153–63.

Woolf, Virginia. *A Room of One's Own*. 1929. Ed. Morag Shiach. Oxford:
Oxford UP, 1992.

Alice Munro's Agency:
The Virginia Barber
Correspondence, 1976–83

JOANN MCCAIG

Dear Alice Munro:
I wonder if you've considered a literary agent? I believe your
work should be represented by someone, and I would very
much like to be that someone.
                    — Virginia Barber (Alice Munro Papers
                    [hereafter cited as AMP], MsC 37.2.47.2)

SO BEGINS VIRGINIA BARBER'S FIRST LETTER to Alice Munro,
dated 11 March 1976, a letter that initiated a long working relationship and friendship between the two women. Barber's New York
literary agency opened for business in 1974, and her approach to
Munro indicated her awareness of Munro's growing reputation in
Canada. However, Munro's publication record in the United States
was rather lacklustre. American editions of her first three books had
appeared by 1974, but her only successes in the magazine market
were three stories published in the mass-market women's monthly
McCall's. Munro had yet to crack the major literary venues of the
New Yorker and *The Atlantic Monthly*. It was through her association with Barber that this ambition was realized.

While a student at the University of Western Ontario in the early
1950s, Munro published several of her stories in the *Folio*, an
undergraduate literary journal. These early successes prompted her
to seek a wider audience. However, Canada was not her first choice
for marketing her work. In a 1994 *Paris Review* interview with Jeanne
McCulloch and Mona Simpson, Munro admits, "I sent all my early
stories to the *New Yorker* in the 1950's, and then I stopped sending
for a long time and sent only to magazines in Canada" ("Alice
Munro" 233). That Munro sent her stories to Canadian markets by
default is clear in the remark that follows: "the *New Yorker* sent me
nice notes though — pencilled, informal messages. They never signed
them. They weren't terribly encouraging. I still remember one of

them: 'The writing is very nice, but the theme is a bit overly familiar' "
(233).

Munro's relationship with the editor Robert Weaver began in the mid-1950s, and it was, in part, through her association with Weaver that Munro established her authority in Canada. In a discussion titled "Who Creates the Creator?" Pierre Bourdieu asks, "Who is the true producer of the value of the work — the painter or the dealer, the writer or the publisher?" (76). He comments on how "the ideology of creation . . . makes the author the first and last source of the value of his work," thus concealing the importance of the "cultural businessman" in the production of symbolic value (76). Weaver's importance in the first twenty years of Munro's writing career cannot be overstated. From the mid-1950s to the mid-1970s, Weaver functioned as mentor, editor, publisher, agent, advisor, and friend. He even served as head juror on the committee that selected Munro's first book, *Dance of the Happy Shades*, as winner of the 1968 Governor General's Literary Award for English-language fiction. In addition to his production work at the Canadian Broadcasting Corporation, Weaver was a founding editor of the *Tamarack Review* and functioned as editor-in-chief of many collections of Canadian short fiction. Sandy Stewart, in his history of Canadian radio, describes Weaver as "the godfather of Canadian writing" and adds that "Almost every successful contemporary writer in Canada has benefited from Weaver's guidance and encouragement" (155). Bronwyn Drainie concurs, saying that from the mid-1950s to the mid-1960s

> it's only the mildest form of Canadian exaggeration to say that Robert Weaver, through his twin outlets, CBC radio and *Tamarack Review*, kept fiction writing alive in this country. His great discoveries were Mordecai Richler and Alice Munro, but virtually every substantial fiction writer in Canada benefited from Weaver's understated and tireless devotion to the development of Canadian literature. (289–90)

The expansion and cultural aims of the CBC put Weaver in a unique position to help Canadian writers such as Munro. He joined the Talks and Public Affairs Department of the CBC in 1948 and worked for the CBC until his retirement in 1985. He was hired to produce CBC *Wednesday Night*, a program that provided "three hours a week of cultural entertainment [and was] an important outlet for the work of Canadian poets, authors, and playwrights" (Weir 275). Weaver later created the radio program *Anthology*, broadcast on the AM network of the CBC at his insistence, because he wanted to reach the largest audience possible. The program included "poetry and short story readings, talks, interviews and discussion, features and documentaries," and the bulk of the material selected for broadcast was by Canadian writers (275).

Outside the confines of the CBC, Weaver was also an important figure in marketing and promoting Canadian literature, short fiction in particular. In addition to founding and editing the *Tamarack Review*, he was well known for his work in anthologizing Canadian short stories. His first anthology appeared in 1952, just four years after he joined the CBC. Then he took on the editorship of an occasional series for Oxford University Press, called *Canadian Short Stories*. These collections appeared in 1960, 1968, 1978, 1985, and 1991. As Weaver notes in his preface to the 1991 edition, "only two writers have appeared in all five of these anthologies: Mavis Gallant and Alice Munro" (xi). In her foreword to *The* Anthology *Anthology*, Munro credits Weaver with "giving us [writers] what we needed most — his serious attention, his reasonable hopes, a real market" (x).

Bourdieu argues that "The art business, a trade in things that have no price, belongs to the class of practices in which the logic of the pre-capitalist economy lives on" (75). The field of cultural production is "the economic world reversed" (164), a world that functions "only by virtue of a constant, collective repression of narrowly 'economic' interest and of the real nature of the practices revealed by 'economic' analysis" (74). One example of such "repression" is that, in the Alice Munro Papers, all files pertaining to finances are restricted and can be viewed only by permission of the author. Another is the truism that no accusation could be more damning to a serious artist, a "literary" writer, than that of commercialism. The irony is that ultimately what Bourdieu describes as the "disinterestedness" of the serious artist facilitates economic gain, because "Symbolic capital is to be understood as economic or political capital that is disavowed, misrecognized and thereby recognized, hence legitimate, a 'credit' which, under certain conditions, and always in the long run, guarantees economic profits" (75). In short, by disavowing the economic, by denying an interest in anything but art for its own sake, the artist may make economic success possible. (This is not to say that disavowal of the economic *ensures* economic success — Ethel Wilson, Ralph Connor, and Ernest Buckler come to mind; rather, this disinterestedness is one of several "conditions" that must be in place for artistic consecration to occur.)

In the 1950s and 1960s, self-deprecating stories of the small size of the Canadian cultural audience abounded. For example, Stewart quotes Weaver as saying of *Anthology* that he was "the only producer who knew all of the show's listeners by their first names." Stewart then adds, however, that, "In fact, the show had an audience that exceeded 52,000" (155). Interestingly, Munro mentions a similar myth about the *Tamarack Review* in her interview with McCulloch and Simpson: "It was a nice little magazine, a very brave magazine. The editor said he was the only editor in Canada who knew all his readers by their first names" (235). It is probable that such self-effacing mythology is partly what allows "the logic of the pre-capitalist economy" to live on in Canadian culture. In "Writers and Publishers in English-Canadian Literature," Frank Davey asserts that literary publications in Canada in the previous century and in the early twentieth century were what Norman Feltes describes as " 'petty commodity productions' rather than capitalist productions" (94). In fact, according to Davey, despite the burgeoning of cultural nationalism and Canadian literature in the postwar years of this century,

> the petty-commodity mode remains the dominant form of literary publication in English Canada. Texts are written, even by experienced authors, with little conscious thought for the marketplace and with little input by publishers, whose staff generally lacks the man-power or talent to give such input. The audience inscribed in such texts, however, is a small, middle-class educated one, and very often with a regional or specifically ideological character. (95)

In the petty-commodity mode of production, therefore, the writer has the "autonomy" of a legitimate cultural producer. The "logic of the pre-capitalist economy" is tenable in such a market; obviously, the economic is easily disavowed when the stakes are small. The small scale of the Canadian literary scene, which Munro entered in the 1950s, is thus an important aspect of her self-formation as an author.

In Canada, however, the economic limitations on the cultural market make the role of restricted producer financially precarious. Davey notes that, "unlike in other countries where national publishers operate on a similar scale to that of the country's bookstores, and supply roughly 90% of the titles stocked by those stores, in English

Canada, national publishers have usually only had access to only 20% or less of bookstore sales" (90). This is a statistic of which Munro as a co-owner of a bookstore must have been aware. Her award-winning first book, *Dance of the Happy Shades*, for example, received an initial print run of 2,500 copies. Four years later, that print run had still not sold out. Her American gambit is risky in terms of her symbolic capital as a restricted producer; however, her formative years as a restricted producer in the limited Canadian market play a large role in her self-construction as an author in the market capitalist mode of American publishing. In forming a business relationship with Barber, Munro engages in a struggle between her own image of her position in the literary field and that of her new cultural banker, who operates in a market capitalist literary economy unlike the petty-commodity marketplace of Canadian literature.

Furthermore, in such a pursuit of a wider authority, gender inevitably comes to the foreground. Because women are defined in language — a public language constructed by and for masculine purposes in which male experience is the norm and women's experience is "unintelligible, unreal, unfathomable" (Spender 2) — to claim the status of "woman author" is to be in a problematic, contradictory, conflicted position. And it is in their female friendship that Barber and Munro find the resources to negotiate the ideological tensions of the cultural field.

If, as many critics suggest, Munro's published work wrestles with the question of female power, then her archive is a site where the conflict between gender and authority is explicit. It is in the archive that I witness the "conflicted psyche of an achieving woman" (Buss 126) as I observe the struggle of Munro the woman to become Munro the author, striving to take on the proprietary linguistic powers of the author function when her material, her life experience, and her very self are subject to the subordinating power of what Dale Spender calls "man made language."

In the Barber correspondence, Munro as writing subject in culture is visible in a gradual but necessarily incomplete process of empowerment. Or, in Chris Weedon's terms, she is visible as "an active but not sovereign protagonist" in a power struggle (41). Munro was attempting to expand her authority to the American market, and Barber herself, as Munro comments in her 1996 *Morningside* interview, was "just starting out too." Both women were acting out their efforts of self-empowerment inside a patriarchally defined cultural field. The correspondence contains evidence of the power struggle that occurs when women cultivate both female friendship and business dealings.

In a *Publisher's Weekly* article, Beverley Slopen describes the mid-1970s as a time when Munro's life took "two unexpected turns" (77). Her marriage ended in 1973, and Munro returned to Ontario with her youngest daughter. The first surprising turn was that Munro reencountered a former UWO classmate, geographer Gerald Fremlin; she subsequently married him and moved to Clinton, fewer than thirty miles from Wingham, the town where she had been born and raised. The second surprising turn, according to Slopen, was that, after the Canadian publication of *Something I've Been Meaning to Tell You* in 1974, Munro received

> a letter from US literary agent Virginia Barber asking to represent her. Feeling that she did not have enough material to offer, Munro replied diffidently, but subsequently she sent Barber some stories. The agent immediately sold two of them to the *New Yorker*, and made arrangements with Knopf to publish Munro's future works. (77)

Slopen's version of Munro's authorial story is undercut, or at least complicated, by the evidence of the archive, which shows that the process of empowerment and authority of the period was aided by the sisterhood of Barber but compromised and challenged by ideological biases related to nationality, genre, and gender and by the ideological structures of the cultural field. In effect, this "unexpected" turn was far less accidental and more ideologically grounded than Slopen suggests.

Slopen claims that Barber's initial contact with Munro occurred after the publication of *Something I've Been Meaning to Tell You* in 1974; the letter cited above bears the date of 11 March 1976, and it has the sense of a first direct contact between the two women. After stating her business, Barber enumerates her qualifications: she is interested in "good fiction," holds a Ph.D. in American literature from Duke University and has taught graduate courses in literature at Columbia University Teacher's College, is married to an editor with seventeen years' experience in the book trade, and is the mother of two. In the third paragraph, Barber gets to the heart of the matter: her personal response to and interest in Munro's work. And her words address the issue of authorial power head-on. Mentioning that "Material" is her favourite story, Barber writes,

My professors at Duke were fond of poems about the making of poems, or fiction about the artist or the making of fiction. I enjoyed these works too, although years later as I was changing diapers or scraping egg off plates, I wondered if Henry James would have changed places with me, allowing me to tell him it's "art which makes life" while I dined out the 355 evenings a year in his place. So I had an occasional sense of "It's not enough" in my own terms. "Material" put the subject in a perspective I hadn't seen but which has meant a great deal to me — the word authority calls to mind the whole story for me. (AMP, MsC 37.2.47.2)

That word is crucial here. What Barber saw in "Material" is a questioning of literary ideology that rewards metafictional reference and deconstructive cleverness and, through a feminist questioning of the omission of dirty diapers and egg-encrusted crockery, challenges the authority of the male author to make people and events "pass . . . into art" in the creative act, an act of "special, unsparing, unsentimental love" ("Material" 35). In short, Barber read a feminist subtext in the story, and the contract in which Barber hoped to engage Munro was not only about making a living but also about establishing a kind of female literary authority.

Barber's first letter politely closes with a gentle admonition to Munro to respond despite her reputed shyness. The archive suggests that Munro overcame her shyness quickly, because Barber's next letter is dated just eleven days later. It begins "Dear Alice" and quickly gets down to business, Barber explaining that she charges ten percent of the author's income on domestic sales and twenty percent on foreign sales. Barber is brisk and businesslike on the publishing game, describing her role as "matching" a book with a publisher, "matching" an author with an editor, negotiating the offer, overseeing the contract and book production and promotion, handling foreign sales and negotiating subsidiary rights (meaning the gruelling and not very lucrative task of trying to sell "excerpts of the book" to magazines). The agent also offers an optional "first reader" service but advises Munro to take her time deciding whether she wants to sign on, because "no good agent would want a reluctant client" (AMP, MsC 38.2.63.1).

That Barber mentions foreign sales as a foregone conclusion stands in sharp contrast to the tone of Weaver's mentorship. By 1961, Munro was attempting to get a book or story published in the United States, but although Weaver could muster powerful allies and relatively lucrative markets at home, his expertise in the American market was severely limited. For example, when Munro queried the American firm Appleton-Century-Crofts in the summer of 1961, Weaver urged her to give Jack McClelland first refusal on the stories instead (AMP, MsC 37.2.8.4). But then, in a November 1961 letter, he acknowledged the growing necessity of cracking the American market while revealing his less-than-expert position in this regard:

> Some time this winter if you get a story done which you feel is one of your better ones, why don't you make a concerted attempt to publish in one of the better U.S. magazines? If this idea interests you at all, I could give you a list of the magazines I'd suggest and you could change or add to it, and then simply keep the story going around to see what, if any, comment you would get on it. (AMP, MsC 37.2.8.8)

Here Weaver's limitations as an agent of Canadian culture are evident. Possibly, three months after the American "fishing expedition" of Appleton-Century-Crofts, Weaver decided to make a virtue of necessity by participating in Munro's quest for publication in the United States, acknowledging the importance of the American market and its power. However, the story that Munro sends must be new, one of her best, and all the assistance that she can expect is a list (not even an authoritative one) of magazines — as opposed to the friends and connections that he can call on in the Canadian scene. Furthermore, Weaver anticipated failure, suggesting that Munro would be lucky to get more than a form rejection letter. Barber's breezy vocabulary of matching and selling must have sounded rich with promise to Munro.

However, according to Bourdieu, "Although dealers form a protective screen between the artist and the market, they are also what link them to the market, and so provoke, by their very existence, cruel unmaskings of the truth of artistic practice" (79). Whereas in Barber's first letter the connection is personal, and Barber addresses Munro as one who understands and supports her work, her second letter unmasks the underlying economics of the author-agent relationship, and it was possibly for this reason that Munro took six months to think things over before signing on. For her, the prospect of foreign sales and possibly the economic problems of leaving her marriage eventually tipped the scales in Barber's favour. On 4 October 1976,

Barber responded to a Munro letter as follows: "Of course I want to see some stories. Send them as soon as you can." Intriguingly, she added, "Share or spare the domestic life, as you will. But if you have any whimsically ironic comments, send them — they're the get-through-the-day boost that I like" (AMP, MsC 38.2.63.2). Barber appears, in such comments, to be reforging the personal connection between two women interested in the relationship between art and women's lives. The request for tales of domestic life offers a female version of Bourdieu's characterization of author and literary marketer as *"adversaries in collusion* who each abide by the same law which demands the repression of direct manifestations of personal interest, at least in its overtly 'economic' form" (79). The Munro-Barber partnership unfolds in this vein of aesthetic association and friendship that masks the underlying exigencies of profit and loss. It is in the postscript that Barber undercuts the diffidence of her opening lines by offering Munro the information that "someone" has asked a "tentative question" about film rights (AMP, MsC 38.2.63.2).

Two weeks later, on 19 October 1976 (AMP, MsC 38.2.63.3), Barber informed Munro that she was making calls to McGraw-Hill Ryerson about the author's contracts and books in print. Barber says in this letter that she has had a call about paperback rights and explains that she wants to keep her investigation quiet because even publishers who let a book go out of print can still get fifty percent of future sales if rights are not fully reverted. She thus reinforces her position as an authority on the business end of things. She adds another enticement: *McCall's*, which published three Munro stories in the early 1970s, has phoned asking for more stories — which, obviously, Munro had not yet sent to Barber.

Two weeks after that, an exultant Barber announces in another letter that she has received the stories, that they are a "treasure," and that she has already sent "Providence" and "Royal Beatings" to the *New Yorker* — that is, within days of receiving them. It is in this letter that the author-agent relationship is confirmed; in the act of sending the stories, Munro has thrown her lot in with that of Barber, who writes:

I'm delighted to have the stories, Alice, and I hope this is the real beginning of a fine working relationship. I'm already waving banners for you down here, and that means you can roll your eyes heavenward in mild protest but no more. You also don't have to look. I feel you've turned me loose at last, and I'm ever so ready to go! Write well, enjoy, and I'll be sending these stories to all decent magazines. (AMP, MsC 38.2.63.4)

This "fine working relationship" would be characterized throughout by Barber's acknowledgement of Munro's authorial modesty, her apparent lack of interest in the economic end of writing and publishing. In a sense, Barber would write a story of their working relationship, creating the modest author who rolls her eyes at the banner waving of her cultural banker. Their working relationship would be a story that functions according to the laws of the cultural field. Bourdieu asserts that cultural bankers such as Barber "present properties close to those of . . . [the writer], and this favours the relationship of trust and belief which is the basis of an exploitation presupposing a high degree of misrecognition on each side" (40). Barber would consistently demonstrate a strong artistic appreciation of Munro's work and a mode of story making in establishing the cosiness of their friendship on the mutual grounds of art, gender, motherhood, and domestic life. This letter also establishes the counterbalancing roles of the quiet and self-effacing Canadian author trained in the ideologies of the field of restricted production[1] and the banner-waving American agent who seeks to expand Munro's symbolic and actual capital but nonetheless understands the dimensions of the field well enough to send the stories only to "decent magazines."

The deal was clinched when, on 18 November, just one week after Barber received the stories, Charles (Chip) McGrath at the *New Yorker* wrote to Munro:

> Your story "Royal Beatings" has occasioned as much excitement around here as any story I can remember. It's an extraordinary, original piece of writing, and we very much want to publish it. Everyone who has read it has been moved by the story's intelligence and sensitivity, and has marvelled at its emotional range. (AMP, MsC 37.2.30.1a)

His letter, like the previous one from Barber, abounds with generous words. The letter was doubtless sweet vindication for an author who had tried to publish in the *New Yorker* more than twenty years earlier. The *New Yorker* publication authorized Munro in a far different — broader, more lucrative, more symbolically powerful — cultural field than she was accustomed to, and ironically but not surprisingly it was the moment at which Munro felt the conflict between identity as an author and identity as a woman most keenly. On 17 November 1976, Barber wrote to Munro — the day that McGrath wrote his letter of acceptance to Barber, and the day before he wrote the good news to Munro. In her letter to Munro, Barber is strictly business: a magazine editor has called asking for stories, but they are all at the *New Yorker* at present. Barber lists a variety of familiar American magazines to which she plans to submit Munro's work and, in a handwritten marginal note, adds that "Chip says, judging by the excitement, that he's sure you're going to be one of the *New Yorker's* authors" (AMP, MsC 37.2.47.3). On the back of this letter is a doodle, described in the archive catalogue as "A. Munro's holograph annotation on verso." Various names, phone numbers, and reminders are scribbled here, but the name Alice Fremlin catches the eye. It appears that Munro, in this idle scribbling probably done while talking on the telephone, was trying on her new last name (she married Fremlin in 1976). The juxtaposition of *New Yorker* negotiations with this schoolgirl's game is intriguing: while Munro the author is making a name for herself in her new associations with Barber and the *New Yorker*, she is making a new name for herself as woman, lover, wife.

However, the conflict between these two names is elaborated powerfully on the back of another letter dating from the same period,[2] in which Barber indicates an interest in representing Marian Engel and asks Munro to "think of me if you know of writers in search of an agent" (AMP, MsC 37.2.47.1). Although only the second page of this letter is extant, it shows how Barber was also in the position of making a name for herself, and Munro's holograph annotations repeat the previous name game with some fascinating variations. The name Alice Munro appears twice. At right angles to it is the name Alice Fremlin, also repeated, the second time enclosed in a cloud. On turning the page upside down, one sees yet another name repeated, with variable spelling: Jelly Flemin, Gelly Flemlin.

The names of the author and the wife, and the nickname of the lover/husband, thus contend with each other, possibly because, at this point, Munro was claiming the masculine power of the author function. Her perception of the conflicts of female authorship is evident in an interview with Alan Twigg:

> I think it's still possible for men in public to be outrageous in ways that it's not possible for women to be. It still seems to be true that no matter what a man does, there are women who will be in love with him. It's not true the other way round. I

think achievement and ability are positively attractive qualities in men that will overcome all kinds of behavior and looks, but I don't think the same is true for women.

A falling-down-drunk poet may have great power because he has talent. But I don't think men are attracted to women for these reasons. If they are attracted to talent, it has to be combined with the traditionally attractive female qualities. If a woman comes on shouting and drinking, she won't be forgiven. (20)

Evident in this passage are many of the perceptions of the ideological tension between Munro's two subject positions — that of author, and that of woman. Whereas a man's authority adds to his attractiveness, a woman who receives offers from the *New Yorker* is in danger of not being "forgiven" for her power, of forfeiting her "traditionally attractive female qualities" — in short, of going through life unloved. Munro's idle doodlings on the back of a business letter attest to the psychic conflict; they show Munro unconsciously recognizing the bind in which her gender places her as an author.

It is not on the question of gender alone that ideological tensions are evident in the Barber correspondence, however. As the relationship between Munro and Barber established itself, issues of genre and money began to complicate and intertwine with the problem of gender and authority.

Generic bias began to complicate the picture within a year of Barber's initial contact with Munro. In fact, the first reference to genre occurs in the 17 November 1976 letter described above. In it, Barber appears relatively noncommittal:

I know that you are working on a novel. If that book comes to be, then you are much better off submitting it along with the new collection of stories (or before the collection of stories). If the novel does not come to be, then we shall work on making the story collection. (AMP, MsC 37.2.47.3)

Barber feigns a disinterestedness in terms of generic preference and here appears merely to echo previous editors that it is best to bring out a novel before a short story collection.[3] However, at this early stage, and considering her success in marketing Munro's stories, Barber did not pressure Munro.

But as time went on, the pressure increased, and Barber began subtly to push for a novel. She boasted to a publisher interested in Munro's rights that of the two stories recently placed in the *New Yorker*, "One is nearly a novella" (AMP, MsC 37.2.47.5b). In a letter to Munro in March 1977, after a long and confident opening that mentions a variety of publishing opportunities, Barber writes:

> It also occurred to me to say that the novel might prove less work for you in the end than all this revision of minor matters in stories. I never intended to suggest the novel, but I see that I'm taking up your time on the stories. We should consider two matters: aren't you getting close to having enough stories for a new collection? And would you have enough of the novel finished for you to feel comfortable in sending it to me sometime soon? Are you interested in working toward either of these projects, or are you better content just now to think only of individual stories? (AMP, MsC 37.2.47.6)

As Spender points out, any woman who holds a position of power in literary culture, whether author, editor, or agent, is handicapped by a lifetime indoctrination into the ideology of the dominant masculine culture, and a familiar refrain of the publishing world is that novels are better than stories because, among other things, they are more marketable (216). This is another point of contrast between the Weaver and Barber mentorships; Weaver's position in a small government-subsidized market allowed him to encourage Munro to "continue on in the short story" for the time being and to ignore "the novel problem" (AMP, MsC 37.2.8.8); for Barber, however, the pressures of the mass market were much more urgent. Her concerns about genre were indicative of her position in mainstream culture, in which the short story is a lesser genre, possibly even a "female" genre, and probably a "Canadian" one. Barber made the suggestions woman to woman, however, in careful, mediating tones. She suggested that the novel might be "less work" for Munro and that their present efforts to get individual stories published was "taking up" Munro's time. Disclaiming any crass motives, Barber said that she "never intended to suggest" the novel but wondered whether Munro would be "comfortable" in sending an excerpt of it "sometime soon." Was she "interested" in pursuing the book, or was she "content" to work "only" (implying a subtle negative value judgement) on individual story publications? The subtlety of Barber's approach indicated the delicacy of the negotiation.

Issues of power and empowerment, of Munro's early inculcation into the restricted field of Canadian literary culture and of her female subjection in language, comprise a long-running theme in the Barber correspondence. For example, when Barber gleefully announced Munro's first Booker nomination in 1982, Munro's humility balanced the celebration. Barber both admonished and comforted Munro: "You did get our cable and letters while you were in Australia? I'm curious. Are you so blasé — you don't think it's special to be nominated for the Booker Award? If so, relax; we can cheerlead, and did" (AMP, MsC 38.2.63.54). As it turned out, Munro had not yet heard of the nomination, but clearly Barber was comfortable with her own role as cheerleader. In a letter dated 26 January 1983, she acknowledges Munro's reticence when she invites the author to her home, possibly during the promotional tour for *The Moons of Jupiter.* Barber tells Munro that she is planning a dinner party with some old friends, one of whom bought the film rights to the story "The Turkey Season." However, Barber jokingly refers to Munro's shyness by saying, "This evening would be a relaxed one — you would not need to be 'on'. Would you like that? . . . If you would rather just hide out (with Jenny and the cats, of course — nothing is perfect), say so" (AMP, third accession, 396/87.3 Box 2 File 3).

The function of the intermediary is also evident in Barber's dealings with rejection letters. If, as Bourdieu suggests, part of the cultural businessperson's equivocal role is to act as a buffer between the artist and the harsh realities of the marketplace, then this was certainly evident in the way in which Barber stepped in to mediate the blow of a *New Yorker* rejection from Charles McGrath. He rejected "Mischief" in a 1977 letter to Barber, saying "In many ways this is the best written and most polished of all the Munro stories you sent us, but it's also the most familiar in subject*, and most people who read it here felt that it was simply too long" (AMP, MsC 37.2.47.6b). On a copy of the letter, which Barber forwarded to Munro, Barber placed an asterisk at the words "familiar in subject" (which echoed Munro's early *New Yorker* rejections of the 1950s, with their mention of her "overly familiar" themes) and added a handwritten note: "Alice, I thought it treated the subject (if he means adultery and couples) with newness — making mischief, the grief of having to forego the fantasy. I like it very much. Ginger" (AMP, MsC 37.2.47.6b). Barber, now signing off with her nickname, thus tempered with an offer of female solidarity a rejection suggesting that there is nothing new in a woman's treatment of an old subject.

Interestingly, the story was also rejected by Gordon Lish at *Esquire* for similar reasons: he said that the narrator's "escape from that assignation . . . is elided," that the flashbacks need "more graceful movement" or to be cut, and that Munro should "cut the last line after 'oldest friends she had.' What follows is too cute" (AMP, MsC 37.2.47.11). The "cute" line referred to is Rose's cynical decision to remain friends with Clifford and Jocelyn despite their betrayal, "because she needed such friends occasionally, at that stage of her life" (135). Lish seemed to be asking for a more traditional story of adultery: more sex, less speculation, historicization, and cynicism. "Mischief" was eventually published in *Viva*, a magazine of erotica for women, in April 1978.

Munro relied on Barber's support and comfort when her story was rejected by two male editors; however, in the months leading up to the problematic publication of *Who Do You Think You Are?* and beyond, the road became rougher. There were rejections and disappointments and some very costly problems with publishing rights.

Slopen asserts that Barber, in addition to securing the first *New Yorker* publications, quickly got Munro a publishing contract with Knopf. In fact, *Who Do You Think You Are?* — published in the United States as *The Beggar Maid* — first went to Norton, where editor Sherry Huber did her best to make the book into a novel. The Norton contract eventually fell through in the fall of 1978, around the time when the Canadian edition was going to press. Huber lost her job (whether or not over the failure to make Munro's story sequence a novel is unknown), and it was only then that Alfred A. Knopf picked up the book and began Munro's association with Knopf editor Ann Close. Thus, securing an American publisher was a more complicated process than Slopen indicates, and it attested to the hard work of women such as Barber, Huber, and Close in making Munro "respectable" enough by market standards to enter this male-defined literary culture.

A selection of letters between 1977 and 1982 shows the Barber-Munro relationship not only getting more personal but also inscribing generic privilege and financial tensions. Possibly, the women's emphasis on the personal served to counteract, or at least mitigate, the harder issues that they faced. In the winter of 1978, a six-month gap ensued in the Barber correspondence, though this gap may be merely an omission, either accidental or deliberate, in the archive.[4] Thus, Barber's role in the struggle over the form of *Who Do You Think You*

Are? is not documented. However, Spender's remark on the indoctrination of literary women to the ideology of a patriarchal literary culture provides a useful reminder of what Barber's position must have been: "Patriarchy is an interlocking system with its psychological and material components, and while women's consciousness may indicate the desirability and even necessity of practicing 'disagreeableness' in order to undermine patriarchy, material circumstances may prevent them from doing so" (4). Thus, though Barber applauded Munro's "disagreeableness" in psychological terms (e.g., the questioning of male literary authority), in material terms she was required to prompt Munro to produce a book that would sell. It was in June 1978 that Munro's generic difficulties with the form of *Who Do You Think You Are?* reached a crisis point, and the pressure from her American publishers to make the short story collection into a novel was intense. At this juncture, Barber's equivocal position would have been at the forefront, and, as Bourdieu points out concerning cultural businesspeople, there is a "need to possess, simultaneously, economic dispositions which, in some sectors of the field, are totally alien to the producers and also properties close to those of the producers whose work they valorize and exploit" (39). In short, the *"adversaries in collusion"* construction of the author-agent relationship created problems for both women at various points in their association.

Munro's nationality was also starting to be seen as a handicap to be overcome. Like her gender, her Canadianness was something that needed to be suppressed in order for her to achieve authority. For example, Barber confessed to disappointment at being unable to find an American publisher for one of Munro's works: "OK, we will send *Tamarack Review* 'Working for a Living,' but I'm not happy about that. The piece deserves a Universal Showcase and our failure to sell it has been a real frustration for us" (AMP, MsC 38.2.63.52). Yet Barber was also sensitive to Munro's status as a Canadian. When two publishers, one in Quebec and one in France, proposed translations of her books, Barber asked whether nationalism was an issue for Munro. The translations were ultimately published by the French Canadian company (AMP, MsC 38.2.63.25), but whether the choice was nationalistic or practical is unknown.

The publication of *Who Do You Think You Are?* presented several instances in which the ideological and practical differences between the American literary marketplace and the Canadian one were painfully evident. The most obvious was Knopf's insistence on changing the title of the book to *The Beggar Maid*. Munro says that the American publisher "felt the colloquial put-down [who do you think you are?] was not familiar to most Americans. I had to accept that, though I think it probably is in certain parts of the U.S. anyway" ("Real" 29). Her editor at Knopf addresses the "question of title" in a letter of 19 January 1979:

> We (Bob,[5] Ginger and I, plus others here) would very much like to call the book *The Beggar Maid*, with a subtitle: Stories of Flo and Rose. I'm not sure that I can quite tell you why I think that title is better for the U.S. edition, but I will try. *Who Do You Think You Are?* with that jacket [presumably, the Canadian edition with the reproduction of Ken Danby's *The Sunbather*] seems to me just right for the Canadian book. There is something a little sassy about it, and the art work is immediately known there, so I would guess that it hits just the right note of national pride and recognition. Here we need to establish you as a Canadian, yes, but mainly as a writer of distinction. *The Beggar Maid* seems to us all a more memorable title, and will hopefully remind people of the story in the *New Yorker*, which as you know from Ginger got an enormous response. (AMP, MsC 38.1.3.6a)

The letter establishes its authority by naming the group of experts "here," meaning America, as opposed to "there," meaning the far different cultural space known as Canada. The choice of *The Beggar Maid* for the title is an ironic statement of Munro's position in the American culture that she attempts to enter with the publication of this book. The American title is decidedly less "sassy" than the Canadian one, and the phrase "a Canadian yes, but mainly . . . a writer of distinction," suggests doubt about whether these two qualities are not antithetical. In another sense, the reprimand "who do you think you are?" relates to a distaste for "showing off," which Munro sees as "rather Canadian" ("Alice Munro" 104), and what could be a more profound instance of "showing off" than attempting to achieve publication and recognition in America? This wrangling over the book's title encapsulated cross-border cultural tensions; it seems that, unlike Canadians, who were in the process of building a national literature, Americans already knew *exactly* who they were. In the end, Close left the decision up to the author, but Munro's agreement is indicated in Close's next letter, of 5 February 1979, which thanks Munro for her letter and says, "I think we will go ahead with *The Beggar Maid* for the title here" (AMP, MsC 38.1.3.7).

Aside from issues of nationality and genre, a crucial issue that surfaces in the Barber-Munro correspondence and complicates the issue of gender is the financial/fiduciary aspect of the relationship. I have already noted how Barber's letter of introduction enumerated her qualifications, including a doctorate from Duke and a husband active in the publishing business. The Greenwich Avenue, New York, address on her letterhead certainly added credibility, and Barber quickly demonstrated her powerful connections in the early months of her association with Munro.

It is beyond dispute that Munro's work is permeated with an acute awareness of class differences. In the story "The Beggar Maid," for example, Rose decides to marry Patrick after all, partly because "only middle class people had choices anyway" (97). In an interview with the *Paris Review* in 1994, Munro commented that, in her early years as a writer, "I didn't realize that women didn't become writers as readily as men, and that neither did people from a lower class." This characterization of herself as a person from the lower classes is evident in her accounts of her first marriage as well. She describes her in-laws as being doubtful of her suitability as a wife for Jim Munro, partly because of her "lower caste" and her lack of "breeding" (qtd. in C. Ross 49). Munro says that, when she met her first husband, she had "never known people of this class before" ("Alice Munro" 247), and she bristled at the fact that "Life was very tightly managed as a series of permitted recreations, permitted opinions and permitted ways of being a woman. . . . I'd meet a university professor or someone, and if I knew something about what he knew, that would not be considered acceptable conversation" (252).

Barber and Munro had in common their interest in art and women's lives, and both had been bright, ambitious young women who had grown up in parochial small-town environments (Munro in south-western Ontario, Barber in the Blue Ridge mountains of Virginia). Their bond is reflected in personal information exchanged in letters, in jokes about children, and in Barber's signing off with "Love, Ginger." (In the Weaver correspondence, which covers more than twenty years, there is not a single letter signed "Love, Bob.") On the other hand, Barber had been a "university professor," had a Manhattan address, and could summon powerful New York connections. As literary agent, as "cultural banker" (Bourdieu 75), Barber was one of "these 'merchants in the temple' [who] make their living by tricking the artist or writer into taking the consequences of his or her statutory professions of disinterestedness" (40), for "only those who can come to terms with the 'economic' constraints inscribed in this bad-faith economy can reap the full 'economic' profits of their symbolic capital" (76). James L. West III, in *American Authors and the Literary Marketplace since 1900*, explains the dilemma in simpler but equally useful terms when he points out that an author is neither "professional" nor "tradesman" but a pieceworker who must enter into a fiduciary relationship with the quasi-professional classes of publishers and agents in order to find an audience and earn a living (20). Munro's fiduciary relationship with Barber at times created ironic situations. For example, on 14 March 1983, Barber wrote to Doug Gibson on Munro's behalf to request the release of $1,500 against the publisher's $3,000 reserve against returns (AMP, third accession, 396/187.3 Box 2 File 2). However, a week later, on 22 March 1983, Barber wrote to inform Munro that, though the film rights to "The Turkey Season" had been sold for $1,000, none of this money would end up in the author's hands. Barber's commission was $100, expenses amounted to $15.25, and a legal bill concerning rights to two earlier works came to $803.28. Only $81.48 remained for the author, and Barber suggested keeping that amount in the kitty toward the next legal bill.

According to West, "authors were left behind when the American middle class professionalized itself, and the business conditions under which they have worked since 1900 have been anachronistic" (20). He adds that "authorship in America has not been a profession during this century, nor has it been a trade. It has been more nearly a craft, a cottage industry. The author has crafted literary piecework at home and has carried it to the publisher, who has turned it into salable goods" (20). Like any day labourer, Munro is dependent on her agent and her publisher for marketing the goods that she produces. However, just as Barber must allow Munro the option of hiding out with her cat and her daughter to avoid a literary dinner party, Munro must likewise allow Barber her commissions in exchange for her professional handling of the products of Munro's "cottage industry."

For Munro and Barber, the tensions of their business relationship are mitigated by a strong foundation of sisterhood and friendship — a recognition of mutual ground that helps to diffuse, if not defeat, the exigencies of the literary marketplace. *Selected Stories*, published in 1996, is a retrospective of Munro's career, a selection of stories from the early years to the present. The dedication page reads:

For Virginia Barber
my essential support and
friend for twenty years

These words attest to the fact that, whatever the tensions and challenges in their business relationship, Munro still acknowledges Barber as a friend in this summation of her career. But even more important is Munro's acknowledgement of how "essential" the "support" of this cultural banker has been to the formation of her authority. In the 1996 *Morningside* interview, Munro remarked of Barber, "She got me into the *New Yorker*," to which Peter Gzowski replied, "No, Ms. Munro, you got yourself into the *New Yorker*." More likely, the joint efforts of author and agent can be credited with achieving that particular step toward the fullness of the author function. Barber and Munro have "recognized" each other as women friends, but they have also "misrecognized" their author-agent relationship to their mutual benefit.

NOTES

[1] Bourdieu differentiates between *the field of restricted production*, which is "art for art's sake" or production for other producers, and *the field of large-scale production*, which is aimed at the general public. He acknowledges that the dividing line between the fields is rarely clear cut, but the designations provide a useful mode of thinking about the difference between serious and popular art. James L. West III, in *American Authors and the Literary Marketplace since 1900*, uses William Charvat's terms of reference, opposing the "mass" author to the "public" author, the latter term describing "the serious literary artist who meant also to reach a large audience through the publishing apparatus of the time and who wanted to earn a living by writing" (5).

[2] I assign this undated fragment a date between spring 1976 and spring 1978 (i.e., during the years leading up to the publication of *Who Do You Think You Are?*) because Barber refers to Engel's *Bear*, published April 1976, and because she signs off with "Best Wishes." By June 1978, she generally signed her letters "Love, Ginger."

[3] When Theodore Purdy of Appleton-Century-Crofts rejected Munro's stories in a letter dated 26 September 1961, he praised her work, saying that "many of these stories were extremely well done and the variety of subjects covered was another encouraging factor"; but then he mentioned "the difficulty of selling volumes of collected short stories unless the author's name is already well known through other publications" (AMP, MsC 37.2.1). He also asked whether she had written or was working on a novel.

Less than three weeks later, Munro received another rejection letter, this time from Canadian publisher Jack McClelland, who likewise referred to the "age-old book trade legend" about the difficulty of marketing short story collections and asked, "But what about the novel? How is it progressing? Can we be of any help?" (AMP, MsC 37.2.22.1).

⁴ An archive or manuscript collection is a fictional construction in its own right, a text in which the "author's" deletions and oversights point to the construction of a particular kind of "story." For example, though Munro has said in her foreword to *The Anthology Anthology* that Weaver sent her detailed rejection letters (ix), not one such letter is part of her archive at the University of Calgary. Some copies of Weaver's early letters to Munro are among his papers at the National Archives of Canada, and several of these letters do contain some editorial advice and criticism. Munro's reasons for omitting certain Weaver letters from her own archive are unknown.

⁵ Bob Gottlieb, a Knopf colleague who would take over when Close left Knopf (AMP 38.1.3.5). Her position at Knopf was once again secure by spring 1979 (AMP 38.1.3.8a).

WORKS CITED

The Alice Munro Papers. Special Collections, U of Calgary Library.

Bourdieu, Pierre. *The Field of Cultural Production.* London: Columbia UP, 1993.

Buss, Helen M. *Mapping Our Selves: Canadian Women's Autobiography in English.* Montreal: McGill-Queen's UP, 1993.

Davey, Frank. "Writers and Publishers in English-Canadian Literature." *Reading Canadian Reading.* Winnipeg: Turnstone, 1988. 87–104.

Drainie, Bronwyn. *Living the Part: John Drainie and the Dilemma of Canadian Stardom.* Toronto: Macmillan, 1988.

Munro, Alice. "Alice Munro." Interview with Eleanor Wachtel. *Writers and Company.* Toronto: Knopf, 1993. 101–12.

———. "Alice Munro: The Art of Fiction CXXXVII." Interview with Jeanne McCulloch and Mona Simpson. *Paris Review* 131 (1994): 227–64.

———. Foreword. *The Anthology Anthology.* Toronto: Macmillan, 1984. ix–x.

———. Interview with Peter Gzowski. *Morningside.* CBC Radio. Oct. 1996.

———. "Material." *Something I've Been Meaning to Tell You.* 1974. New York: Signet, 1975. 20–36.

———. "Mischief." *Who Do You Think You Are?* Scarborough, ON: Signet, 1979. 100–35.

———. "The Real Material: An Interview with Alice Munro." With J.R. (Tim) Struthers. *Probable Fictions: Alice Munro's Narrative Acts.* Ed. Louis K. MacKendrick. Downsview, ON: ECW, 1983. 5–38.

———. *Selected Stories.* Toronto: McClelland, 1996.

___. "What Is." Interview with Alan Twigg. *For Openers*. Madeira Park, BC: Harbour, 1981. 13–20.

Ross, Catherine Sheldrick. *Alice Munro: A Double Life*. Toronto: ECW, 1992.

Ross, Val. "Weaving a Literary Legacy." *Globe and Mail* 27 Apr. 1994: A9–10.

Slopen, Beverley. "PW Interviews Alice Munro." *Publishers Weekly* 22 Aug. 1986: 76–77.

Spender, Dale. *Man Made Language*. 2nd ed. London: Routledge, 1985.

Stewart, Sandy. *From Coast to Coast: A Personal History of Radio in Canada*. Rev. ed. Toronto: CBC, 1985.

Weaver, Robert. Preface. *Canadian Short Stories, 5th Series*. Toronto: Oxford UP, 1991. ix–xii.

Weedon, Chris. *Feminist Practice and Poststructuralist Theory*. Oxford: Blackwell, 1987.

Weir, E. Austin. *The Struggle for National Broadcasting in Canada*. Toronto: McClelland, 1965.

West, James L. III. *American Authors and the Literary Marketplace since 1900*. Philadelphia: U of Pennsylvania P, 1988.

Machines, Readers, Gardens:
Alice Munro's "Carried Away"

ROBERT LECKER

LIKE SO MANY of the opening stories in Alice Munro's books, "Carried Away" is a frame story that focuses on two of her abiding interests: the business of writing and reading, and the implication of telling tales. As Miriam Marty Clark observes, many of Munro's stories "problematize the very mode they inhabit, undoing the illusion of transparency and advancing the reflexive, opaque, often difficult ways on [sic] the unstable worlds of narrative, memory, and writing itself" (49). Although "Carried Away" is clearly preoccupied with the process of reading, it is equally preoccupied with the ways in which reading and writing are historically conditioned acts that influence how people define themselves in relation to their community and their present. The story provides an excellent example of what John Weaver has described as Munro's attempt "to exhume and record the truth while appreciating both the material circumstances and the accidental influences on common lives in small communities" (384). Munro returns to these circumstances again and again; often they serve as markers that unify her short story collections. In *Open Secrets*, for example, she follows the fate of one small-town family — the Douds — through "Carried Away," "Spaceships Have Landed," and "Vandals."

The four sections in "Carried Away" link the creation of individual and communal identities to particular historical circumstances — the economic and social impact of two world wars and the Depression — and show how the effects of these events on material conditions forever altered the ways in which people understood themselves as social beings. On its broadest level, "Carried Away" is about a postwar, postindustrial fall that is identified with the commodification of all forms of human activity, a fall that reduces meaning (and being) to the level of what can be produced and sold. On more particular levels, the story is about losing community, losing nature, losing history and ritual and family as a result of commodification.

"Carried Away" explores — in Canadian terms — many of the tensions that Leo Marx identifies in *The Machine in the Garden: Technology and the Pastoral Idea in America*, his classic study of the impact of industrialism on the utopian ideals associated with American pastoralism. Marx argues that industrialization regimented time and space, encouraged the rise of a secular urban consciousness, and undermined the sense of community and serenity associated with "the once dominant image of an undefiled, green republic, a quiet land of forests, villages, and farms dedicated to the pursuit of happiness" (6). For Marx, the rush to embrace machine consciousness was synonymous with a cultural death drive; it created works of art and literature that depicted a suicidal "universal acquiescence" set against a vanishing rural scene. In the postbucolic landscapes of these works, Marx notes, "there is nothing in the scene capable of resisting the domination of the machine" (352).

The nostalgic impulse to recover an unspoiled rural landscape, Marx argues, accounts for the fantasy making that Freud described as "freedom from the grip of the external world" (qtd. 8), a freedom based on "an urge to withdraw from civilization's growing power and complexity" (9). Such a withdrawal involves a search for a "symbolic landscape" of the natural, the uncontaminated, the agrarian, and a simultaneous movement away from "an 'artificial' world, a world identified with 'art,'" culture, and "the cardinal metaphor of the literary mode" (9). Marx observes that, when this impulse to transcend the artificial is "unchecked, the result is a simple-minded wishfulness, a romantic perversion of thought and feeling" (10).

Much of "Carried Away" can be understood as a response to the real and metaphorical presence of the machine in the Canadian garden, enacted through the personalities of (romantically perverse?) characters who have been profoundly affected by the process of industrialization and the resulting shift in labour consciousness that took place between the two world wars. For Munro, this process is not only identified with dramatic changes in how Canadians understood concepts such as productivity, authority, progress, history, work, wealth, and personal value; she also shows that many of the benefits traditionally associated with industrialization are paradoxically negative forces that compound the destruction of a preindustrial sense of community and identity. The beauty of the story lies in its tragic revelation of this paradox.

One of the supposed benefits of postwar industrialization was an increasing emphasis on the importance of education and on developing reading skills through the public school system or through labour-oriented institutions such as the Mechanics' Institutes or the Workers' Education Association. However, as Maria Tippett observes, while the encouragement of readerly activities had its social advantages, it was also a means of instituting social control:

> To those involved in these and similar associations, cultural activity — whether one was involved in it as participant or observer — had much to offer. It allowed constructive use of the public's ever-increasing leisure time and so helped to prevent the disorderly behaviour which, many believed, was being induced by shorter working days; it served as an elevating alternative to unsuitable forms of popular culture; and it reinforced national sentiment. (52)

Munro's story shows that the postwar shift in the value associated with reading activity was by no means purely redemptive; nor was it simply a subtle means of introducing behavioural controls. More sinister is her realization that the encouragement of reading, writing, and literary appreciation also allowed people to construct their own identities as readers, to fictionalize themselves as powerful by virtue of their ability to read. But because this form of power was an illusion, it was bound to fail, and in failing it was bound to reinforce the individual reader's ultimate sense of isolation and impotence.

"Carried Away" is tragic in its revelation that there is no self beyond story, no way of living outside the constraints associated with a literary consciousness formed out of reading practices that were developed in order to improve business performance and productivity, or to reinforce the authority of institutions aligned with industry and capital. Ironically, literacy in "Carried Away" is emblematic of a central issue that Munro explores — the idea that reading does not really provide a means of "improving oneself." On the contrary, the more one reads, the more one invents multiple selves in search of a centre that can never be found.

If "Carried Away" is about a fall into machine consciousness and commodity-based systems of value, it is equally about the fall into literary consciousness that accompanied this historical transition. Reading comes to influence how the characters in the story understand themselves as gendered beings, how they inhabit their temporal and spatial contexts, how they view the natural world, how they are conditioned by the institutions and the business practices that surround them. Basically, it is about their means of self-production. In Munro's hands, Leo Marx's nostalgia for the garden is expressed as a desire for a natural, integrated self that predates literary constructions of the idea of self as a manufactured or narrated object.

Of course, the idea of an "integrated" self existing in some kind of pastoral vacuum is a sham. A crucial aspect of the story involves Munro's portrayal of how its characters discover the failure of this ideal as they confront a welter of texts: letters, book covers, library books, marriage notices, newspaper accounts, factory regulations, notes, inscriptions, paintings, popular magazines. In one way or another, each of these texts links the process of reading and writing to a literary process of self-manufacture that spells the end of agrarian consciousness. In this world, to read is to lose oneself. Or to lose one's head. Or to die.

* * *

The emphasis placed on the act of narrative commodification is immediately revealed by the epistolary mode employed in "Letters," the first part of this four-part story. The very title of the section frames the action in relation to reading and writing. Louisa, the Carstairs librarian, opens a letter that she has received from Jack Agnew, a Carstairs resident who is serving overseas with the Canadian Armed Forces during the First World War. In his letter, dated 4 January 1917, Jack reveals that he is a secret admirer of Louisa. She is quick to respond, no doubt because she is bored by the routines that define her small-town life and is searching for a partner. "She ate steak and potatoes, her usual meal," in the Commercial Hotel, where she lives. The dining room smells of oilcloth mats "wiped by a kitchen rag, and of coal fumes from the furnace, and beef gravy and dried potatoes and onions" (3).

Superficially, things here seem to be as predictable as "the bottle of brown sauce, the bottle of tomato sauce, and the pot of horseradish" that sit on every table every day (4). Yet the opening setting — the Commercial Hotel — draws our attention to the relationship between reading and commerce; the building houses many commercial travellers whose transient existence provides evidence of how wartime business practices tended to unseat people, forcing them to travel away from their homes and communities in pursuit of sales. The opening sentence of the story ties Louisa's initial reading of Jack's letter to her existence in the Commercial Hotel. Right from the start, commerce and reading are conjoined.

Louisa herself has been a commercial traveller. Even though she is a librarian, her background is in sales; she thinks in terms of business and of products that can be sold. This is why the moment that she reads Jack's letter she understands intuitively that, by responding to him, she can package her persona, commodify herself. She chooses to participate in an established literary form — the epistolary exchange — that offers its authors the ability to invent themselves as they write, and to edit their creations by choosing to emphasize certain activities over others, or to omit emotions or events that detract from the persona that the letter writer wishes to construct.

Louisa's letter writing is performative. As an epistolary act, it provides a good example of what Linda Kauffman calls "a consciously staged utterance, addressed to the absent beloved," a "self-creation" or "self-invention" that "simultaneously dramatizes his silence, the heroine's alienation, and the metonymic displacement of desire" (25). In epistolary exchanges, according to Kauffman, "Reading and writing are part of the drama enacted in the heroine's private theater" (36).

Louisa begins to invent herself and her private theatre the moment she takes up her pen to respond to Jack. This act of self-invention is complicated by the persona that Jack has also created for himself through his correspondence. In his initial letter, he admits that he has watched Louisa from a distance and fantasized about her background. Yet he doesn't remember her name. His invention of her image takes precedence over memory. He describes himself as "a lone wolf," like his father, and as "a person tending to have my own ideas always" (5), although it soon becomes clear that he and his father, Patrick, are completely different. Unlike Jack, who is a soldier and a factory worker claiming to have learned things from books, Patrick "goes out to the country fishing every chance he gets" (5). He is a gardener. He is aligned with the increasingly distant rural world that lies beyond Carstairs and its defining institution, the Doud factory. Patrick's existence is preliterate. In contrast, Jack lives in Carstairs, and Carstairs is about business. Jack haunts the Carstairs library; he frames himself as a literate. He senses the profound gulf that separates him from his father in terms of their reading practices. This is why he tells Louisa that he doubts whether his father reads the occasional letter that Jack sends to him. Unlike his father, Jack inhabits a world ruled by the factory clock. His library borrowings are metaphorically time sensitive. As objects, they are "overdue." The emphasis on timekeeping associated with "bookkeeping" (and later with Jack's very life) provides a link between factory and library, for business practice during and after the First World War was heavily invested in time management.

Craig Heron and Robert Storey observe that in this period "Many firms experimented with new, more centralized, more cost-conscious, and more authoritarian managerial systems, in order to move effective control of the labour process from the shop floor to the front office" ("On the Job" 13). Mechanization transformed almost every industry during this period, and many factories were controlled by efficiency teams inspired by the "scientific management" theories of Frederick Winslow Taylor, "whose staff invaded the shop floor armed with stop watches to measure the 'scientifically' precise time required to complete a specific task and to gather up workers' shop floor know-how, which could then be reorganized and parcelled out from the central planning and scheduling office" (Heron and Storey, "On the Job" 13).

Taylor invites a brief digression, if only because his ideas were taking hold in the period during which Jack and Louisa correspond, and because his theories probably affected the organization of the Doud-family mill that employs Jack after the war. Taylor's famous paper entitled "Shop Management" (1911) was originally intended for use by factory owners, but its "scientific" principles regarding the organization and efficiency of the workplace came to be applied in a variety of institutions, from schools to railways to navy shipyards. It is likely that, as a librarian inhabiting a factory town, Louisa has been exposed — directly or indirectly — to various forms of Taylorism, which gradually encompassed theories of time and space management that could be applied to all facets of human behaviour. In his study of Taylor's theories, C. Bertrand Thompson notes that a "characteristic feature of the Taylor system is the extensive use of classification and mnemonic symbolization" applied to "various functions of cost, administration, stores system, routing, and filing" (37). Libraries were not exempt.

With the publication of *The Principles of Scientific Management* (also 1911), Taylor became the guru of industrial organization. To get an idea of the incredible difference between his conception of the factory worker in the machine age and the depiction of the labourer in earlier models, one has only to read a description of the "variables affecting the performance of manual work" provided by Frank Gilbreth, one of Taylor's disciples:

They are classed as variables of the worker, including anatomy, brawn, contentment, creed, earning power, experience, fatigue, habits, health, mode of living, nutrition, size, skill, temperament, and training; variables of the surroundings, including appliances, clothes, color, entertainment, heating, lighting, quality of material, rewards and penalties, size of unit moved, special fatigue-eliminating devices, surroundings, tools, union rules, and weight of unit moved; variables of the motion, including acceleration, automaticity, combination with other motions, cost, direction, effectiveness, foot-pounds of work accomplished, inertia and momentum overcome, length, necessity, path, play for position, and speed. (qtd. in Thompson 35)

When Taylor visited the Bethlehem Steel Company, he was pleased to find some of his principles in place:

Dealing with every workman as a separate individual in this way involved the building of a labor office for the superintendent and clerks who were in charge of this section of the work. In this office every laborer's work was planned out well in advance, and the workmen were all moved from place to place by the clerks with elaborate diagrams or maps of the yard before them, very much as chessmen are moved on a chessboard, a telephone and messenger system having been installed for this purpose. (68)

Did the factory workers object to being classified in this way? They did. Thompson says that one objection "often urged by workingmen against scientific management" was that

they are not required to think, but merely to carry out instructions. They feel that when they receive complete instructions as to the method of performing work, it places their work upon a lower plane, transforming them from intelligent workmen into automatons. As one man has expressed it, "I like to think I think, even if I don't think." (92)

While factory workers were attempting to gain better pay and working conditions, factory owners were trying to meet Tayloresque efficiency models so as to increase productivity. Time counted. Rules counted. Safety came after time and rules. This primary emphasis on productivity is prominently displayed in the Doud factory,

where the rules are "posted beside the time clock": "ONE MINUTE
LATE IS FIFTEEN MINUTES PAY. BE PROMPT. DON'T TAKE SAFETY
FOR GRANTED. WATCH OUT FOR YOURSELF AND THE NEXT MAN"
(Munro 25).

In his letters, Jack constructs himself as the reader and observer
who appreciates the efficiency and order that Louisa has brought to
the library, her workplace. She shows all the signs of living in a world
that is dominated by commodification. She considers herself an
outsider in everything but business; when it comes to sales, she can
talk like one of the boys. Her account of her past is almost entirely
devoid of historical connections. Only the present counts. We don't
know where she was born. She seems disconnected from her childhood. All we learn is that her parents are dead, and that when they
were alive they worked for Eaton's, simply another kind of factory.
Louisa equates it directly with the Doud factory that is so central
to the economic life of Carstairs: ". . . Eaton's was our Douds" (5).
As it turns out, she has sold books at Eaton's (5). In fact, we learn
more about her "favorite authors" (Thomas Hardy and Willa Cather)
than we do about her family, friends, or personal interests (6). Louisa
defines herself as an extension of what she has sold at Eaton's and of
what she now manages as the town's librarian. She is in the business
of managing and producing fiction. What impresses Jack is not
her book recommendations or even the library holdings; it is her
managerial skills. Jack points out that Louisa has indeed made the
library more organized. Before she came, "the books were pretty
much every which way. . . ." But after her arrival, "what a change,
it was all put into sections of Fiction and Non-Fiction and History
and Travel . . ." (4).

Jack focuses on his recollection of Louisa's organizational abilities,
and on her physical appearance ("you are about of medium size or
perhaps not quite, with light brownish hair" [4]). In his mind, her
body and her organizational skills seem conjoined. Although Louisa
understands implicitly that she has been turned into a voyeur's
fantasy, she willingly participates in this construction.

Louisa immediately responds to Jack's letter in words that reveal
how much she is controlled by what she writes and by her desire to
cast herself as ordinary and unexciting, knowing all the while that
the rhetorical strategy of casting herself as mundane is far too
self-conscious for her to be perceived as truly mundane. She is, after
all, a saleswoman, and she knows how to sell herself. Louisa realizes
that her self-construction will be read ironically by Jack, who is

textually invested in eroticizing her; similarly, Jack knows that his self-construction as a person who says "you will not see me as a Brave Man" (5) invites Louisa to read him as enigmatic, invisible, and therefore powerful by virtue of his physical absence. So he has also learned a thing or two about salesmanship.

Although Louisa stresses that what she has done for the library is "nothing special," that she is "a poor person for the job" of delivering news, and that the story of her arrival in Carstairs is "no interesting story" (5), what she withholds in information — and the very act of withholding it — are as important as what she reveals. Louisa connects herself with Jack by casting herself, like him, as "an outsider" (5). She withholds narrative details about the "rumors on rumors and opinions galore" concerning the war that are circulating in Carstairs because, she says, "I am sure there is a Censor reading this who would cut my letter to ribbons" (5). Yet, at the same time, she establishes her authority by telling Jack about how "The travellers in the hotel mostly talk about how business is (it is brisk if you can get the goods) . . ." (5), and by positioning herself as someone who is entitled to share in this kind of talk. Significantly, Louisa tries to establish her credibility by invoking her acceptance into the world of commerce rather than her position as the town's librarian.

If Louisa is a good manager, then the library is her factory. As Clark says, Louisa's work in the library serves a broad ideological end. The library "functions to organize and reproduce culture and to authorize reading" (57). Within this reproduction, "books take their place wholly within capitalist modes of production and consumption. They anticipate — as the piano factory does, metaphorically — the incorporation of aesthetic production into commodity production generally" (57–58).

Louisa is in the business of managing fiction (including herself). Under her direction, the library becomes an effective point of sale, and Jack is sold. By withholding information from Jack, Louisa acts out her belief that personal power is a function of textual power. Yet she too is drawn to textual authority, to the figure that she imagines of a great panjandrum censor reading her work and withholding her stories from Jack, so as to create a doubly erotic withholding.

Textual suppression becomes a form of titillation. By engaging in and projecting this kind of suppression, Louisa assumes the role of the erotic Censor whom she imagines, the potent reader who teases other readers by denying or suppressing information, a dark masculine force "who would cut my letter[s] to ribbons," creating a text that is all the more enticing for what it is not permitted to reveal. Hovering behind Louisa and Jack's correspondence is an erotic fantasy of cutting, suppression, textual bondage, and submission, in which God becomes the biggest lover, the most powerful reader of them all — the Censor, capital C. Yet even this potent Censor who will cut her writing to ribbons must still remind Louisa of sales, since one of the things she sold on the road was . . . ribbons.

Louisa writes to the imagined Censor, and there is an imagined exchange. Don't cut my letters to ribbons. Don't cut me. Cut me. Ribbons. Don't tie me. Tie me. More than any other character in the story, she understands that textuality can be sold as sexuality, and she packages herself to this end. By refusing to reveal all that she knows, Louisa empowers herself as the erotic object of Jack's thinly disguised desire. Jack plays too. He tells her that he has watched her "putting the lights on as it was dark and raining out" and then shaking water out of her long hair (7). He casts her as an erotic performer, and she seems willing to play the part. Jack is her consumer. He reads her. Yet he only knows what she wants him to know. Her ability to control this knowing becomes a function of textual prowess.

As their correspondence continues, Louisa and Jack begin to reveal more about their own apparent addictions to reading, which for them is really a form of sublimated eroticism. I say "apparent" because it is difficult to believe that Jack is the autodidact he claims to be. He admits that some of the books he reads are "away over my head" (6). He makes grammatical errors and is prone to comma splices. He is also prone to the occasional but revealing malapropism, especially when he is at pains to convey a romantic image, but finds himself hunting for the appropriately romantic terms, as in "You went over and stood by the radiator and shook your hair on it and the water sizzled like grease in the frying pan" (7).

Have the writings of H.G. Wells or Robert Ingersoll really given Jack "a lot to think about" (7), or does he notch up these authors in order to increase his credibility in the eyes of the woman whose own credibility is so intimately linked to what she reads and writes? Is he a bigger man because he reads? He does commodify these writers, but he is not alone: every character in the story treats reading and writing as signs of personal value. It doesn't matter whether Jack read what he claims to have read. It only matters that he assigns such profound value to the act of reading itself.

In "Carried Away," literacy is equated with power and wealth. However, Munro shows that this simple equation provides a false sense of security — cheap wealth — for the ability to read does not necessarily give the reader any better means of coping with the general gloominess of his or her life. On the contrary, reading in "Carried Away" seems to provoke a skewed sense of individual value because it inevitably colours all forms of self-representation. In this case, it turns men into literary voyeurs and women into narrative objects of erotic desire. It forces them to construct their identities in relation to literary models precisely because those models form the basis of their self-understanding. Freed by story to imagine themselves, they discover that everything is narration. Everything is manufactured. The factory is everywhere. Outside it, there is nothing. Outside story, there is nothing.

In order to escape the death and destruction that surrounds him, Jack writes letters, tells stories, and tells stories about other people writing letters and telling stories. When a man dies of a heart attack, it becomes "the News of all time," and Jack realizes that he is intimately linked to this news because the man who died "was writing a letter at the time so I had better look out" (8). No matter what he does, his attempt to escape from himself through writing ends up reinforcing the death consciousness against which he wanted to write. Writing is a fall. It's the same for Louisa. She writes about children dancing behind an ice cream cart, but immediately confronts the image of the man who is pushing it, "the man who had an accident at the factory" and "lost his arm to the elbow" (8). Evidence of the destructive impact of industrialization is scattered throughout the story, right down to children and ice cream. Munro depicts one of the crucial features of wartime industrialization: "a deplorably high accident rate" (Heron and Storey, "Steel Industry" 222). A report of the Labour Department in Ottawa shows that in 1906 (the last year for which figures are available prior to the First World War) 1,107 Canadian workers were killed on the job and 2,736 were wounded (*Report* 12). During the Second World War, "the armed forces suffered fewer, though generally more severe, injuries than the industrial population" (*Law* 1). In other words, there were casualties at home, and people such as Jack and Louisa were caught in this domestic war. Irving Abella and David Millar note that, in the years between 1900 and 1918, "Many workers' earliest memories of their jobs were of some dreadful accident to a young chum, badly mangled by belts, saw-teeth, or gears, or horribly burned by a burst of steam" (4). Like so many of these young chums, Jack is eventually mangled and killed by a circular saw.

Outside the factory, many wartime factors converged to make the employment situation desperate for many people entering the job market. The period was marked by poverty, drought, dust, disease, and death. People who had been raised in rural communities were forced into the cities. They had to fight for work. The Spanish flu was rampant, killing twenty-one million people worldwide and fifty thousand Canadians between 1918 and 1919. It was "the deadliest epidemic in recorded history" (Brown). The flu took almost the same number of Canadians killed in war (sixty thousand). As a result of deaths attributed to the war and the flu, Canada lost 1.5% of its total population. On the economic front, inflation was out of control. Thousands of veterans were flooding the job market. "Prices were rising much faster than wages. Scores of thousands of returned veterans were pouring in to the labour force at the same time that jobs were becoming scarcer as war-time industries shut down" (Abella 12). Labourers were increasingly militant, and their efforts to introduce collective bargaining were ruthlessly crushed by the federal government.

In many ways, Jack Agnew is a victim of the new industrialism. The extent to which he is affected by the rise of labour consciousness is suggested by the fact that he is reading Bertrand Russell's *Bolshevism: Practice and Theory*, published in 1920 (technically, its publication postdates his service in Europe, so he could not have withdrawn the book from the library prior to his departure, as he claims). Jack keeps this book longer than any other: "The one by Lord Russell has been missing a long time," Louisa says when Arthur Doud, the factory owner, returns the dead man's books (27). Perhaps Jack was trying to understand Bolshevism because so much of Canadian labour unrest (especially the Winnipeg General Strike of 1919) was blamed on supposed Bolshevist influences.

Jack and Louisa try to write against the bleakness of life in Carstairs during the war. They try to invent themselves anew. Jack asks for a photograph of Louisa. So "She had a picture taken," and it is straightforward, showing her in her "blue silk shirt-waist" with her hair "bound . . . as usual" and with a "sterner and more foreboding" expression than she intended (10). The image is not what she really dreamed of being:

> She would have liked to wear a simple white blouse, a peasant girl's smock with the string open at the neck. She did not own a blouse of that description and in fact had only seen them in

pictures. And she would have liked to let her hair down. Or if it had to be up, she would have liked it piled very loosely and bound with strings of pearls. (10)

The passage conveys Louisa's eagerness to paint her self-portrait, to reconceive herself as an image that Jack might desire. It also demonstrates the extent to which she is an avid reader of fashion magazines about how women can construct themselves in a variety of costumes, depending on the role that they wish to play (as a saleswoman, she frequently "talked about Paris styles" [10]).

The image Louisa conveys of herself is tied to the values of the wartime fashion industry. She wants to "let her hair down" so that she more closely resembles the woman whom Jack tells her he saw in the library, a long-haired impulsive beauty. (He seems to invoke an image of her lifted from his reading of Zane Grey, probably Jane Withersteen from *Riders of the Purple Sage*, which, like "Carried Away," turns out to be a story about wealth and property.) Louisa wants to fashion herself in the image of an image, to wear a blouse that she has only seen in pictures or read about in books, a blouse that will make her into a peasant girl who can also be a rich woman, a seductive princess whose hair is adorned with pearls.

This is not the first time that Louisa has invented herself. She had an affair with a doctor when she was in the sanitorium being treated for tuberculosis. "Letters . . . played a part that time, too" (9). In that exchange, she displayed "some consciousness of herself as a heroine of love's tragedy" (9), but, if anyone asked, "She would have said love was all hocus-pocus, a deception, and she believed that" (10). Nonetheless, the proximity of romance still prompts her to feel "a hush, a flutter along the nerves, a bowing down of sense, a flagrant prostration" (10).

If Louisa imagines herself as a heroine acting out a vision of romance, it is mainly because she inhabits a world in which textuality has displaced reality, like a drug that temporarily displaces pain. When she tries "to follow the war in a more detailed way than she had done previously" (10), it turns into texts: "the maps of the war that appeared as double-page spreads in the magazines," the "colored lines" depicting military drives, an "artist's brown pictures of a horse rearing up during an air attack" (11).

The more Louisa concentrates on the war, the more theatrical it becomes. She calls reading about it an "addictive excitement" and realizes that "You could look up from your life of the moment and feel the world crackling beyond the walls" (11). So the war turns into an escape novel, a romance based on the projection of those who imagine themselves as the heroes and heroines of an ongoing play. War. Novel. Play. Dream. Fiction. Delirium. The categories get confused, begin to overlap. Jack writes: "the idea I won't ever see Carstairs again makes me think I can say anything I want. I guess it's like being sick with a fever. So I will say I love you" (11). The only problem, of course, is that Jack is already engaged to another Carstairs woman — Grace Horne. How many women is he writing to? How many women does he "love"?

Jack never thought that he would make it back from the war, so he was able to conduct his "affair" with Louisa under the assumption that no one would ever know about it. But he does make it back and is forced to cut her off when he returns home to take a job in the Doud-family factory. Louisa is devastated, particularly because she has found out about his return in a local newspaper listing rather than from him. Once again, writing displaces being. Hoping to see Jack, Louisa keeps the Carstairs Library open even though the Spanish flu is raging. But he never appears.

In the second section of the story — "Spanish Flu" — Louisa tells all this to Jim Frarey, a travelling salesman who often boards at the Commercial Hotel. For her, the story of her correspondence with Jack is "a lesson in what fools women can make of themselves" (15). Louisa is seduced by her dream of Jack, one made all the more powerful because he remains unseen. She is seduced by her reading and writing, which enable her to construct herself and Jack as objects of desire. But, far from delivering her from the daily reminders of her mortality, the construction further destabilizes her and even threatens to drive her insane. Louisa imagines her eventual encounter with Jack "so strongly she saw a shadow that she mistook for a man" (17). She imagines him "watching her, being too shy to make a move" (17). "She set herself jobs of rearranging things, else she would have gone mad" (17).

Eventually, her fictionalizing of Jack takes its final and ironic toll. Confronted by his rejection of her, "she entirely gave up on reading. The covers of books looked like coffins to her, either shabby or ornate, and what was inside them might as well have been dust" (17). Imagine her pain when she reads a short notice announcing Jack's marriage to Grace. To torture her more, Jack leaves a note on her desk in the library, confessing: "I was engaged before I went overseas" (18). Louisa never recovers from the knowledge that the man whom she has created as her lover will always remain unseen. Her tragedy is that she is condemned to fictionalize him forever. There is a crucial distinction between the ways in which she and Jack respond to stories. For Louisa, her textual encounter with Jack becomes a tragic romance that threatens her mental stability. Meanwhile, Jack is able to play with her through the mail, to lead her on, to encourage her to get carried away in her belief that he might one day return and make their textual relationship real.

To a man who perhaps sees himself as a Zane Grey cowboy or as an explorer inspired by his reading of *Sir John Franklin and the Romance of the Northwest Passage* (he's really a little boy), Louisa presents a much more romantic figure than Grace, his "resolute," thin-lipped, and wide-hipped fiancée. Jack doesn't think that he'll live to have to honour his declarations and tell Louisa so. She never sees this, but Jim does. For him (for a man?), her confusion is easily explained. She asks him, "Do you think it was all a joke on me?" And she wonders, "Do you think a man could be so diabolical?" (18).

Jim is quick to assure her that "tricks like that are far more often indulged in by the women"; Jack just "got a little carried away," he says (18). When Louisa is offended by this explanation and tries to convince Jim that she is not as "inexperienced" as he might believe (19), his thoughts reveal one of the central ways in which Munro distinguishes men and women as textual beings. For a man like Jim or Jack, letting a romantic fantasy get out of control amounts to nothing more than biting off more than one can chew, while for a woman the fictionalizing of experience becomes an addictive force, and Jim senses this: "This was it, he thought — the usual. Women after they have told one story on themselves cannot stop from telling another" (19).

Jim understands — more intuitively than intellectually — that for Louisa the act of storytelling inevitably leads to being carried away into fictions of romance. He participates in this creation through his unself-conscious muttering of bland romantic clichés and rhymes as he prepares to seduce her: "All to ourselves" (19); "It's a foggy, foggy night, and my heart is in a fright"; "All's well, all's well"; "Never climbed so close to Heaven in this place before" (20).

While Jim's words are meant to reassure Louisa, his response to her stories, and the physical surroundings in the Commercial Hotel, tell a different story. As Louisa and Jim climb the stairs to her room, "the picture of the dog on his master's grave" speaks of the cliché of loyalty, a picture of "Highland Mary singing in the field" speaks of loneliness and loss, and a picture of "the old King with his bulgy eyes, his look of indulgence and repletion," provides an image of the master, and what he has become (20). Every picture tells a story.

It is difficult to escape these images because they are so common. And for Louisa there is a certain safety in how common they are, and danger in breaking free of their hold. In the same way, she feels anchored when Jim is "pinning her down and steadying her" while they are having sex (20). But only when he is finished this pinning can she feel herself being carried off and "whirling around" in a way that unhinges her speech and allows her, finally, to tell a story that makes no sense because the "words came out with a luxurious nonchalance and could not be fitted together" (20).

Louisa may find the freedom to unfit her speech, but not for long. The story traces her inevitable return to story, an indication of how deeply she is marked by the textual scars of her social conditioning. For her, finding a man is equated with finding a story that has closure. No wonder her search for the perfect soulmate returns her again and again to images of confinement and death.

Louisa finally finds her husband, Arthur Doud, through Jack's death. The third section of the story — "Accidents" — is narrated from Arthur's point of view, which provides more information about how factory owners and labourers interacted between the wars. When Jack is decapitated at the Doud factory in 1924, Arthur visits his widow and offers to return the library books that Jack has left at home. At first, he is taken for the undertaker, allowing for a clear association between his capitalist pursuits and death. Meanwhile, in the background, a washing machine is droning away, its very presence a reminder of the growing intrusion of machines in domestic life.

As the factory owner, Arthur feels responsible for Jack's death and stained by it metaphorically and physically; it falls to him to pick up the severed head and return it to Jack's body. He stuffs his bloody clothes into the laundry hamper and scrubs "the bathroom, like a murderer" (21). Arthur is acting out the guilt that he feels about running a factory full of machines that can maim and kill men while he plays the enlightened factory owner who is supposed to function as a metaphorical father in this small Ontario town.

His fear of accidents is well founded: "There had been accidents in the factory and in fact a man had been killed when a load of lumber fell on him. That had happened before Arthur's time. And once, during the war, a man had lost an arm, or part of an arm" (26). For Arthur, it is only a matter of time before he witnesses an accident.

Desperate to control his environment, he dreams of accidents, yet is powerless to prevent them: "In his dreams of an accident there was a spreading silence, everything was shut down. Every machine in the place stopped making its customary noise and every man's voice was removed, and when Arthur looked out of the office window he understood that doom had fallen" (26). Arthur dreams the fall brought on by machines and technology. Later, when Jack is killed by a circular saw, the dream becomes reality.

With its machines and shifting product lines, the Doud factory is an example of how manufacturing had to change in order to accommodate shifts in supply and demand between 1915 and 1955. At first, it was a piano factory that made pump organs, instruments that required human action. Later, in the midst of "the glut of labor the soldiers had created when they came home" (31), Douds began to manufacture "player pianos, which Arthur believed were the hope of the future" (32). Later still, during the Second World War, the factory turned to making "outdoor bowling alleys" and "radar cases for the Navy" (47). Anything to stay afloat.

The dramatic shift in the labour force as a result of the two wars, combined with an increasing emphasis on technology and productivity, forever altered the relationship between workers and employers. Although Arthur likes to see himself as the town benefactor, like his father, he feels like an impostor who is playing an impossible role. As the owner of the factory, he is to reconcile the increasingly strident demands of the workers with the traditional assumption that his duty is to provide for them as his father did before the war, even though his father was not much more compassionate than him:

> He had operated by whims and decrees, and he had got away with it. He would go around the factory when business was slow, and say to one man and another, "Go home. Go on home now. Go home and stay there until I can use you again." And they would go. They would work in their gardens or go out shooting rabbits and run up bills for whatever they had to buy, and accept that it couldn't be otherwise. It was still a joke with them, to imitate his bark. *Go on home!* He was their hero more than Arthur could ever be, but they were not prepared to take the same treatment today. During the war, they had got used to good wages and to being always in demand. They never thought of the glut of labor the soldiers had created when they

came home, never thought about how a business like this was kept going by luck and ingenuity from one year to the next, even from one season to the next. (31)

It is difficult for Arthur to play the patron when everything tells him that time and money are what count. The entire town of Carstairs lives and breathes according to his factory whistle, which dictates "the time for many to get up, blowing at six o'clock in the morning," and then "again for work to start at seven and at twelve for dinnertime and at one in the afternoon for work to recommence, and then at five-thirty for the men to lay down their tools and go home" (25).

At one level, Arthur realizes that the factory is being run as much by machines as it is by him, and that this shift in power from man to machine has effected a corresponding shift in the loyalty of his workers: now they must respect the machines as much or more than him, because their lives depend upon their ability to safeguard themselves in a hostile mechanical world.

The accident that kills Jack is a result of the unchecked shift away from the agrarian and toward the new. In Arthur's father's time, the men who got laid off would fall back on rural pursuits, working in their gardens or shooting rabbits. But now those alternatives are vanishing, and only a few remnants of it remain connected with those Carstairs residents who are aged or eccentric. One of these residents is Jack's father, the gardener. Even on the day of Jack's funeral, his father heads out of town to go fishing. He steals corn from farmers' fields and eats the fruit of wild apple trees and grapevines. When Louisa is most distraught, she also heads for the country, where she encounters Patrick (25).

While Jack's father is clearly associated with a vanishing pastoral ideal, Jack is cut off from the country. His decapitation is symbolic of the ways in which Jack is split, even in life: part of him pursues romantic dreams of adventure, romance, exotic places; another part of him is obsessed with revolution, worker uprisings, disillusionment following the war. Clearly, he is trying to find himself through a variety of texts. The books that Arthur returns to the library show Jack following his interest in *Sir John Franklin and the Romance of the Northwest Passage* while simultaneously considering *Bolshevism: Practice and Theory*.

The narrators of "Carried Away" are obviously affected by the power of machines to alter people's lives and interested in the ways that technology is changing the behaviour of Carstairs residents. The details of Jack's accident are presented to us in gruesome detail through a news story that is also preoccupied with the mechanical aspects of his death. In fact, the story is "reprinted in the paper a week later for those who might have missed it or who wished to have an extra copy to send to friends or relations out of town" (24). In this reprint, "The misspelling of 'flange' was corrected," and "There was a note apologizing for the mistake" (24), as if the fascination for the news writer was the machinery associated with this "ghastly and tragic accident" (23) and his own technical literacy rather than the victim himself. Perhaps the reporter has not yet understood what a "flange" is, but he or she will soon find out.

Given the sensational attention that this accident receives, it is impossible for Louisa to forget about Jack, whose physical appearance remains a mystery to her. But his death allows her to meet Arthur. When Arthur enters the library, he realizes that he has not been there for years. Yet his father's picture still hangs between the two front windows, and its inscription offers Arthur a glimpse into an earlier model of the town benefactor, which he would like to emulate but will never become: "A.V. Doud, founder of the Doud Organ Factory and Patron of this Library. A Believer in Progress, Culture, and Education. A True Friend of the Town of Carstairs and of the Working Man" (28).

Of course, this description is also a fiction. His father was no true friend of the working man. But the inscription makes Arthur realize that he has failed to become involved in the very place that seems to allow these forces of progress, culture, and education to coalesce: the library. It offers patrons the opportunity to see beyond the mundane. They are surrounded by art and literature, but few take the time to transport themselves through the acts of reading and interpretation. The paintings on the wall hang there — texts available for interpretation — but they require readers in order to be understood. Only after "many hours in the Library" (28) and after several discussions with Louisa does Arthur begin to understand the historical subjects depicted in the library paintings: "the Battle of Flodden Field, . . . the funeral of the Boy King of Rome, . . . the Quarrel of Oberon and Titania" (28–29).

It also takes Arthur a long time to read the history of Carstairs in the texts that surround him, mainly because he has grown accustomed to seeing history and reading as forces divorced from his present. As his textual conversion takes place, he finds himself "pleasantly mystified by the thought of grown people coming and going here, steadily reading books. Week after week, one book after another, a whole life long" (29).

It is his growing fascination with reading that allows his relationship with Louisa to develop. Significantly, their romance is originally an interpretive one that tries to come to terms with the mechanical forces that seem to have invaded the present. Louisa and Arthur discuss the accuracy of the representation of Jack's accident, and Louisa admits that the "horrific details" in the newspaper report are warranted because "People do want to picture it. I do myself. I am very ignorant of machinery. It's hard for me to imagine what happened. Even with the paper's help" (29). In struggling to imagine what happened to Jack, Louisa is trying to add new pieces to her image of him, to complete the narrative puzzle that he has become. At the same time, she is also beginning to realize that machinery hampers interpretation, that it establishes sequences and circumstances that cannot be controlled. As she puts it, "there are no ways of protecting people" (30). Arthur tells Louisa that Jack's accident is easy to explain: "It wasn't the machine grabbing him and pulling him in, like an animal. He made a wrong move or at any rate a careless move. Then he was done for" (30).

If the inhabitants of Carstairs are being damaged and even done for, then it is partly because an increasing emphasis on mechanization and efficiency has focused their attention away from the stories that they share. In this context, communities are useless. The church has been replaced by the factory. The factory has replaced the library as a source of progress and power. Arthur senses that the library symbolizes a bygone community and its history; it provides a space in which that community can imagine itself. His understanding turns to nostalgia for a time when productivity wasn't so crucial, an era symbolically represented by the post office's "clock tower telling four different times in four different directions — and, as people liked to say, all wrong" (30–31).

For Arthur, the library becomes a site that ties him to his past, and to the guilt that he feels about his inability to support the myths of progress, culture, and education aligned with the town, its library, and its labourers. Yet he discovers that he wants to differentiate himself from his father, who "thought of himself more as a public character and benefactor" than as the public servant that Arthur wants to be (31). However, postwar conditions hamper Arthur's ambitions, because the workers are "not prepared to take the same treatment" that his father dished out, sending them home from the factory on a whim (31). "During the war, they had got used to the good wages and to being always in demand. . . . They didn't like changes — they were not happy about the switch now to player pianos, which Arthur believed were the only hope of the future" (34).

Apparently, the workers have failed to see the shift in power that Arthur represents. It is no longer the church that wields authority in this community, nor is it the municipality or the town. The money to finance things comes from the factory, and the townspeople expect "all to be provided" by the factory (32). Arthur thinks:

> Work would be provided just as the sun would rise in the mornings. And the taxes on the factory raised at the same time rates were charged for the water that used to come free. Maintenance of the access roads was now the factory's responsibility instead of the town's. The Methodist Church was requesting a hefty sum to build the new Sunday school. The town hockey team needed new uniforms. (32)

Arthur mocks the town's dependence on his enterprise. "Ask and ye shall receive" (32). Yet he believes that he has the power to deliver the community and to furnish his house with all the mechanical gadgets that he sees as the signs of his success: "some new mixing apparatus for the kitchen, also a new washing machine"; and, of course, "he had to drive a new car" (32).

Arthur's faith in player pianos points to his larger belief in the myths of progress and technology as keys to economic survival. But his embrace of a temporal world in which every second counts is undercut by his inarticulate longing for more traditional models of authority aligned with his father. Arthur thinks that his management style is "quite the opposite of his father's": "Think everything over and then think it over again. Stay in the background except when necessary. Keep your dignity. Try always to be fair" (32).

Arthur is forced to be the father figure who provides, an impostor who tries to act out his authority in the face of all those older workers who knew him as a child. Jack's false front is mirrored in "the veneer samples on his desk" that Arthur is examining so closely when Jack is killed (33). Arthur is capable of expressing little truisms ("A machine is your servant and it is an excellent servant, but it makes an imbecile master") but can't remember where the words come from ("He wondered if he had read that somewhere, or had thought it up himself") (30). He finds himself searching for the appropriate words to describe his response to Louisa: "He could no more describe the feeling he got from her than you can describe a smell. It's like the scorch of electricity. It's like burnt kernels of wheat. No, it's like a bitter orange. I give up" (40). Arthur is no author. Munro's story line may be tragic, but sometimes her humour is so refreshingly black.

The last section of the story brings us forward to the 1950s. Arthur has died. Louisa is on her way to visit a heart specialist in London, Ontario. While in the waiting room, she reads a local newspaper story about a ceremony to be held that afternoon in honour of the Tolpuddle Martyrs, who were "considered now to be among the earliest founders of the Trade Union movement"; "the Trade Unions Council, along with representatives of the Canadian Federation of Labor and the ministers of some local churches, had organized a ceremony" to commemorate them (42).

To her astonishment, Louisa reads that one of the union spokespersons is John (Jack) Agnew. Could it be that Jack never died? Would she finally get to see the man whom she has been imagining for thirty years? Could this Jack and her imagined Jack possibly be the same person? Louisa soon finds herself in Victoria Park, where the ceremony is scheduled to be held. But no sooner does she sit down than she starts "to feel a faintly sickening, familiar agitation" (43), and she leaves, heading off to the temporary bus depot, a dilapidated house that is replacing the real depot while it is being rebuilt.

The day is hot, Louisa is tired, and as she sits back to wait for her bus she nods off and starts to dream. She dreams that Jack recognized her in the park and has come searching for her. But of course she can only imagine that this is Jack, because she has never actually seen him. They discuss his family. Louisa wants to correct his version of events, to remind him that he is dead, and to admit that it is silly to spend so much time telling him about her life: "What a thing to talk to a dead man about," she says (48). Only when Jack says "Love never dies" is she brought back to reality, to her realization that "Love dies all the time, or at any rate it becomes distracted, overlaid — it might as well be dead" (48). Yet even here, in her account, Louisa constructs herself in terms of capital, making sure Jack realizes that she has made it without him, married the factory owner, lived in "a lovely house if you remember, built in three tiers like a wedding cake. Mosaic tiles in the entrance hall" (47).

In her distraction, Louisa overlays Jack Agnew with Jim Frarey and the Tolpuddle Martyrs with a group of Mennonites who are approaching the depot. The correspondence between the Martyrs and the Mennonites is important. The Martyrs consisted of a group of six men from Dorset, England, who tried to form a trade union branch and who were tried on the trumped-up charge of "administering illegal oaths" in 1834.

As Ildikó de Papp Carrington points out, the Tolpuddle Martyrs — united in their efforts to protest against worker exploitation — came from the same area as Hardy, one of Louisa's favourite writers. After being found guilty, they were "transported to Australia"; in other words, they were "carried away." So, whether consciously or not, Louisa's interest in Hardy — who was preoccupied with the effects of industrialization on rural England — demonstrates her own preoccupation with shifting labour patterns and "economic class divisions" (Carrington 555), and her attraction to Cather may indicate her interest in recapturing a more innocent, romantic past quite distant from the mechanization that surrounds her. As Robert Thacker observes, Cather eventually came to be seen as "a kind of aged literary dinosaur, charmingly still concerned with the romance of the past while American fiction had moved on to social relevance" (47–48). In this context, the Mennonites whom Louisa sees before her in London, Ontario, are equated with the Martyrs in their deliberate rejection of machinery and technological change.

Both the Martyrs and the Mennonites come to represent an agrarian ideal that has been lost, an ideal associated with community and continuity. While all of the characters in Carstairs are displaced or divorced from their family ties, the Mennonite group shows adults and children together, sharing. Louisa notices that, unlike the others in the bus depot, "these people did not look so shy or dejected. In fact they seemed quite cheerful, passing around a bag of candy, adults eating candy with the children" (50). In the conversation that she imagines having with Jack, Louisa allows him to recognize the agrarian ideal represented by the Mennonites as a version of his father's interest in the country. Jack asks Louisa if she remembers his father — with his wild walks in the country — and says, "Sometimes I think he had the right idea" (48).

As the story begins to close, temporal sequence continues to break down. The Martyrs and the Mennonites begin to meld. Louisa realizes that "She had gone under a wave, which nobody else had noticed" (50). The wave leaves her with "a beating in her ears, a cavity in her chest, and revolt in her stomach. It was anarchy she was up against — a devouring muddle" (50). Her hallucination allows her to confuse the "muddle" of the "anarchy" that she is battling with the name Mud that her son and stepdaughter give her with the "puddle" in the name of the Tolpuddle Martyrs. When she sees the Mennonites, she makes a further connection between the Mennonites and the Martyrs through rhyme: "she saw all those black clothes melt into a puddle" (49).

Louisa identifies with the Martyrs, and understands that, like them, she has been sentenced and carried away. Her original job as a travelling saleswoman only reinforces the connection between this sentence and commercial activity. In the end, as in the beginning, what defines her is factory life. Although she lives in a "lovely house," she is "always thinking about the factory, that is what fills my mind" (47).

The story's epilogue brings the reader full circle to Louisa's arrival in Carstairs and her application for the library job. "She was a traveller then for a company that sold hats, ribbons, handkerchiefs and trimmings, and ladies' underwear to retail stores" (50). She wanted to stop travelling, to settle down. Looking out over the snow-covered hills around Carstairs, seeking the country, Louisa realizes that, when the leaves cover the trees in the spring, "So much that lay open now would be concealed" (51).

The last sentence of the story finds Louisa imagining horses pulling sleighs away from the town and its factory whistle, away from the Commercial Hotel, "down the dark side roads," and "out in[to] the country," where "they would lose the sound of each other's bells" (51). Such a mysterious line. The images of fading light, fading sound, and fading connection reinforce the pervasive sense of isolation that haunts this story of love invented and love lost. But most of all they draw attention to an area that Louisa knows she cannot recover — the mysterious, disappearing "country" beyond the town where there is a different kind of time, before machines: blinkered horses, feathered hooves, darkness. Gardens. Fields. Nostalgia. A dream of being free.

WORKS CITED

Abella, Irving. *The Canadian Labour Movement, 1902–1960.* Historical Booklet 28. Ottawa: Canadian Historical Society, 1975.

Abella, Irving, and David Millar. Introduction. *The Canadian Worker in the Twentieth Century.* Ed. Abella and Millar. Toronto: Oxford UP, 1978. 1–2.

Brown, David. "It All Started in Kansas." *Washington Post Weekly Edition* 23–30 Mar. 1992.

Carrington, Ildikó de Papp. "What's in a Title? Alice Munro's 'Carried Away.'" *Studies in Short Fiction* 30 (1993): 555–64.

Clark, Miriam Marty. "Allegories of Reading in Alice Munro's 'Carried Away.'" *Contemporary Literature* 37 (1996): 49–61.

Heron, Craig, and Robert Storey, eds. *On the Job: Confronting the Labour Process in Canada.* Montreal: McGill-Queen's UP, 1986.

——. "On the Job in Canada." Heron and Storey, eds. 3–46.

——. "Work and Struggle in the Canadian Steel Industry, 1900–1950." Heron and Storey, eds. 210–44.

Kauffman, Linda S. *Discourses of Desire: Gender, Genre, and Epistolary Fictions.* Ithaca: Cornell UP, 1986.

The Law and Practice Relating to Safety in Factories. Part 1. National and International Organisation. Part 2. Legislation. Montreal: International Labour Office, 1949.

Marx, Leo. *The Machine in the Garden: Technology and the Pastoral Idea in America.* New York: Oxford UP, 1964.

Munro, Alice. "Carried Away." *Open Secrets.* Toronto: McClelland, 1994. 3–51.

Report of the Commission on Labour Accidents. Montreal: Queen's Printer, 1908.

Taylor, Frederick Winslow. *The Principles of Scientific Management.* 1911. New York: Harper, 1913.

Thacker, Robert. "Alice Munro's Willa Cather." *Canadian Literature* 134 (1992): 42–57.

Thompson, C. Bertrand. "The Literature of Scientific Management." *Scientific Management: A Collection of the Most Significant Articles Describing the Taylor System of Management.* Ed. Clarence Bertrand Thompson. Harvard Business Studies. Vol. 1. Cambridge: Harvard UP, 1914. 3–48.

Tippett, Maria. *Making Culture: English-Canadian Institutions and the Arts before the Massey Commission.* Toronto: U of Toronto P, 1990.

Weaver, John. "Society and Culture in Rural and Small-Town Ontario: Alice Munro's Testimony on the Last Forty Years." *Patterns of the Past: Interpreting Ontario's History.* Ed. Roger Hall, William Westfall, and Laurel Sefton MacDowell. Toronto: Dundurn, 1988. 381–402.

Alice Munro as Small-Town Historian: "Spaceships Have Landed"

W.R. MARTIN AND WARREN U. OBER

IN AN INTERVIEW with Eleanor Wachtel a few years before the appearance of *Open Secrets* (1994), Alice Munro said, "One of the things that interest me so much in writing, and in observing people, is that things keep changing. Cherished beliefs change. Ways of dealing with life change. The importance of certain things in life changes. All this seems to me endlessly interesting. I think that is the thing that doesn't change" ("Interview" 292). Her observation is worth pondering.

In "Society and Culture in Rural and Small-Town Ontario: Alice Munro's Testimony on the Last Forty Years," John Weaver shows how Munro's work has been a comprehensive record of the enduring conditions and details of the small town. At first glance, then, it might seem strange for Munro to put such emphasis on change, and indeed much of her work is a record of the seemingly unchanging life that she knew as a child and young adult. But the strangeness of her statement is only superficial. In *Lives of Girls and Women*, Del, the protagonist, tries to cram into what she writes the sorts of objective detail that Uncle Craig, the diligent amateur historian, has collected, but she comes to realize that "no list could hold what I wanted, for what I wanted was every last thing, every layer of speech and thought, stroke of light on bark or walls, every smell, pothole, pain, crack, delusion, held still and held together — radiant, everlasting" (210). In the end, Munro not only uses a much finer mesh than Uncle Craig but also, by capturing the "emotional" dimensions and intensities of that life through the magic of art, far transcends what he strives for.

As early as *Lives of Girls and Women*, then, as Weaver has shown, Munro identifies "two poles of historical inquiry" (381). At one pole is "the historian as a collector," who, like Uncle Craig, "reifies facts and artifacts without ordering their meaning"; at the other is "the creative soul," such as Del, who strives to "record the concrete but also the passions." The "artist's vision" possessed by this kind of historian involves "an aspiration to total history" (382). The passion and insight conveyed by what Weaver calls total history must go together with, and in part derive from, an awareness of the unique and delicate balance, as well as the transience, of the world of experience that the artist is driven to record and preserve, as it were, in amber. It is the artist-historian's way of arresting change, of preserving what is loved.

Hence, one can see why for Munro, as for many other artists, change is "endlessly interesting." Change is in fact Janus-faced: fascinating, in that the movement and the process involved in it transfix us; dreaded, in that it places at risk "cherished" beliefs and values. Munro's sensitivity to this ambivalence takes many forms: often in the study of a family through three generations, as in *Lives of Girls and Women* and "The Progress of Love" (*Progress* 3–31); prominently in the relation between mothers — and grandmothers — and daughters in *Lives of Girls and Women*, in "Marrakesh," "Winter Wind," and "The Ottawa Valley" (*Something* 156–74, 192–206, 227–46), and in the later stories "Friend of My Youth" and "Goodness and Mercy" (*Friend* 3–26, 156–79), a volume dedicated "To the memory of my mother"; and, in "Meneseteung" (*Friend* 50–73), the portrait of an individual set back in time: Almeda Roth, a poet living a lonely life in Huron County in the second half of the nineteenth century but far ahead of her time and place.

In "The Stone in the Field" (*Moons* 19–35), the protagonist's family visits her father's aunts, the Flemings, who live in otherworldly simplicity and remoteness; as the protagonist says,

> I could never get them straight. They looked too much alike. There must have been a twelve- or fifteen-year age span, but to me they all looked about fifty, older than my parents but not really old. They were all lean and fine-boned, and might at one time have been fairly tall, but were stooped now, with hard work and deference. (25)

Although she "didn't know it at the time and wouldn't have wanted to," "they looked a good deal like me" (25). This story is paired in *The Moons of Jupiter* with "Connection" (1–18), in which the same protagonist meets four visiting Chaddeley "cousins" — really her mother's cousins. "Old maids was too thin a term, it would not cover them" (1). When they arrive in "Dalgleish in Huron County," "population, 2,000," Cousin Iris, "heaving herself out of the driver's seat," announces, "Now there's two thousand and four" (2). The visiting cousins, from Philadelphia, Des Moines, Winnipeg, and Edmonton, provide various amusing but at times disconcerting diversions. The protagonist, then, stands not only between Chaddeleys and Flemings but also, like Del in *Lives of Girls and Women* and some other Munro protagonists, between the big town and a rural past not quite out of reach.

Munro's interest in change extends far back beyond individuals and society into the eons of prehistory. In "Walker Brothers Cowboy" (*Dance* 1–18), a father enthrals his young daughter with his graphic account of Lake Huron in the ice age; in an uncollected story, "Characters," the word *drumlin* becomes a point of fascination, and, more recently — in "What Do You Want to Know For?" — Munro gives an account of her fondness for driving through the countryside of western Ontario with her husband, a retired geographer and the editor of *The National Atlas of Canada* (Catherine Ross 78), and observing the "record of ancient events," the landscape "formed by the advancing, stationary, and retreating ice that has staged its conquests and retreats here several times, withdrawing for the last time about fifteen thousand years ago" ("What" 204). This alternating, backward and forward, movement might remind readers of "The Progress of Love" (*Progress* 3–31), in which "progress" is seen not as advance or betterment but — as in a tour or circuit — as change and recurrence on a microcosmic social scale, in contrast to macrocosmic geological processes.

The town of Carstairs, which resembles Wingham, Munro's home town, is the scene of most of the stories in *Open Secrets*; in "Spaceships Have Landed" (226–60), it assumes mythical and archetypal status. The Douds, the first family of Carstairs, with their piano factory, are classic exemplars of the small-town adage "Shirtsleeves to shirtsleeves in three generations." In the opening story of the collection, "Carried Away " (3–51), Louisa, the Carstairs librarian and the story's central consciousness, becomes the second wife of the widowed Arthur Doud, son of the founder of Douds Factory. The final two stories take the Doud narrative to its end. In the penultimate story, "Spaceships Have Landed," Billy Doud, Arthur and Louisa's son, sells the piano factory after his mother's death and converts the family mansion into "a home for old people and disabled people" after his half-sister Bea's death (260). In "Vandals" (261–94), the final story, Bea, Louisa's alcoholic stepdaughter, is involved in an obsessive relationship with a pedophile, the true vandal of the story.

The Douds and their Carstairs factory also figure briefly in two other stories: Millicent, in "A Real Life" (52–80), readers are told, has "set her sights high" in the vain hope that "Mrs. Doud," Louisa, will become her "best friend" (56); in "Open Secrets" (129–60), Mary Johnstone, leader of the church hike in which one of the girls disappears and is presumably murdered, has "a job in the office at Douds Factory" (133), and in the same story the senile Mr. Siddicup, a suspect, "used to be the piano tuner at Douds" (146).

The Doud family, then, with its piano factory and its varying fortunes, serves as a sort of anchor for *Open Secrets*, a reminder that the stories have firm roots in the life of a small town, and its social and economic history, in "the country to the east of Lake Huron" ("Introduction" xv). Even "The Albanian Virgin" (81–128), requiring a university in its setting, involves London, Ontario (110), which is the metropolis of so many of the small towns in Munro's stories, notably Jubilee (Wingham) in *Dance of the Happy Shades* — "Postcard" and "The Peace of Utrecht" (128–46, 190–210) — and throughout *Lives of Girls and Women*. Toronto, where Uncle Benny gets lost (*Lives* 20–22), is an almost legendary city and in "White Slavers" the source of scary stories by Flo, Rose's stepmother, about white slavers and the police (*Who* 55), who'd "be the first ones to diddle you!" (56).

Sharing a Carstairs locale with the Doud stories, though placed earlier and with a broader geographic scope, "A Wilderness Station" (*Open Secrets* 190–225) deals in a fairly straightforward way with social history and with change and recurrence in the lives of Huron County dwellers from the rough pioneer existence of the 1850s to the developed communities of the twentieth century.

Although there are strange twists and ironies in the story, both genre and method are familiar. By means of contemporary letters and reports, readers are given — from 1851 to 1959 — slices of the history of Carstairs and Walley (Munro's version of Goderich, the seat of Huron County) "from the raw days of clearing bogs and woods and making dirt roads to the era of modern infrastructures and industries" (Martin and Ober, "Misreading" 27). These changes are given sharp focus by the juxtaposition of two Huron County women, Annie Herron and Christena Mullen. When "Simon Herron, the elder of two brothers who have started to clear their parcel of Crown land" near what is to become Carstairs, "writes to the matron of an orphanage in early Victorian Toronto applying for a suitable wife" (27), she eventually dispatches eighteen-year-old Annie, who "has a waywardness about one eye but it does not interfere with her vision and her sewing is excellent" (Munro, "Wilderness" 191). Annie, as the wife and later the widow of Simon Herron,

> then experiences every sort of hardship, neglect, and discrimination known to poor women of her time and place, including cruel ingratitude and savage mistreatment by the two brothers she joins, but by her own character, toughness, and integrity she eventually establishes herself as a valued servant of a wealthy, well-established family in Walley. (Martin and Ober, "Misreading" 27)

Into this family Christena is born to status and affluence: she wears a ball gown made by "Old Annie" when the governor general and Lady Minto visit Walley (Munro, "Wilderness" 217), and on her twenty-fifth birthday, in 1907, she buys a Stanley Steamer, which costs twelve hundred dollars, "that being part of my inheritance from my grandfather . . . who was an early Clerk of the Peace in Walley" (216).

The last part of the story is told in a letter from Christena, written in 1959 (when she is about seventy-seven), in reply to an enquiry from a Queen's University history researcher who is writing a biography of Treece Herron, grandson of Annie's brother-in-law, George Herron. Christena tells how Old Annie, with her now-respected status in the Mullen family, asked Christena to take her in her car to Carstairs to see the Herron family (218). There they met Treece, a "mannerly young man" (221), and his family, all of them polite and apparently newly prosperous. Treece, a divinity student, later became an eminent, "colorful politician," apparently a Liberal; Christena never voted for him, she explains, "since I am a Conservative" (216).

Munro, in her "evocative chronicles of rural and small-town Ontario," as Weaver observes, works tirelessly "to exhume and record the truth while appreciating both the material circumstances and the accidental influences on common lives in small communities" (381, 384). "A Wilderness Station" links the lives of two Huron County women and involves a conspicuous irony. Christena and Old Annie are very different, not only because they are separated by about forty years in age, but also because the former's circumstances, unlike the latter's, have brought Christena wealth, education, and freedom from all the social and other constraints that hedged Annie in: she drinks a martini — her "late-afternoon pleasure" — and the "good rule" that she follows is "to get as much pleasure as you could out of things even when you weren't likely to be happy" (224). But she has had "love-troubles," and despite her good looks, her other advantages, and her attraction to the opposite sex — she admits that she "wasn't above flirting with" young Treece during her visit (224) — she has never married. The irony is that, for all the striking differences between Old Annie's disadvantages and hardships, on the one hand, and the liberation, education, and inherited status and wealth of Christena, on the other, neither has found fulfilment in love and marriage. Here, in Huron County, where pioneer conditions so recently seemed to impose a common rural simplicity on its inhabitants, Munro presents her readers with a surprising recurrence and convergence of opposites.

Her statement to Wachtel ends with "I think that [change] is the thing that doesn't change." Her interest in human affairs is not only with change but also with what is unchanging — or recurrent — within history. Although "Spaceships Have Landed" seems at first to be one more story about Carstairs, it is much more than a socio-economic study or history. Readers must keep in mind what Munro recently wrote in her "Introduction to the Vintage Edition" of *Selected Stories*: "I don't think I'm writing just *about* this life [in "the country to the east of Lake Huron"]. I hope to be writing about and *through* it" (xv). "Spaceships Have Landed" has firm roots in myth and allegory that make it rare and strange in her oeuvre — even "risky," to adopt the term that Munro used for some of the stories in *Open Secrets* when she was interviewed by Peter Gzowski on *Morningside* on 30 September 1994.

"Spaceships Have Landed" is unlike any other story that Munro has written, but intertextuality is nothing new in her work. In "Alice Munro and James Joyce," W.R. Martin points out similarities between Munro's *Dance of the Happy Shades* and Joyce's *Dubliners*, especially those between the last stories in the two volumes, both of which give their titles to their volumes. And in "Reality and Ordering: The Growth of a Young Artist in *Lives of Girls and Women*," J.R. (Tim) Struthers draws attention to parallels between Munro's book and Joyce's *A Portrait of the Artist as a Young Man*. The influence on Munro by Southern writers such as William Faulkner, Eudora Welty, Flannery O'Connor, and Carson McCullers has been acknowledged and widely discussed (for example, by Nora Robson in "Alice Munro and the White American South: The Quest").

In "Alice Munro's Willa Cather," Robert Thacker, in an examination of the two published versions of "Dulse," those in the *New Yorker* (1980) and *The Moons of Jupiter* (1982), as well as the drafts in the University of Calgary Library, delves deeply into the compatibility between Cather and Munro, whose fiction derives "from protracted and intimate knowledge of their respective rural small towns" (43) and both of whom — as well as Lydia, the protagonist in "Dulse," and Mr. Stanley, an admirer of Cather whom Lydia meets while escaping from a midlife crisis — faced problems of self-absorption. Cather "serves as a precise object lesson for Lydia, though the matters [raised] are not resolved, only intimated and essayed" (53). In "Bardon Bus," also in *The Moons of Jupiter* (110–28), a quotation from Sir Walter Raleigh's "Epitaph" — "and in the dark and silent grave, shuts up the story of our days" (*Moons* 122) — achieves an intensification of resonance and a widening of implication.

In *Friend of My Youth*, there are several striking examples of Munro's use of allusion. In "Goodness and Mercy" (156–79), the twenty-third Psalm, quoted not only in the title but also at length in the text (169), and references to an aria from *Don Giovanni* (158, 168–69), help to elucidate and amplify another complex and ambivalent relationship between mother and daughter. "Oh, What Avails" (180–215) takes its title from Walter Savage Landor's poem "Rose Aylmer," which also provides a theme for the story (215). In "Hold Me Fast, Don't Let Me Pass" (74–105), the protagonist, an intelligent and observant woman from Huron County, visits the Scottish border country, and the story relates to a border ballad, "Tam Lin." In most of the earlier stories, interestingly, Munro uses writers such as Joyce indirectly, parallel to her texts, whereas later she deals with "Tam Lin" specifically and in detail. (For a discussion of the effects achieved by the way in which Munro turns the plot of "Tam Lin" upside down, see Martin and Ober, "Alice Munro's 'Hold Me Fast, Don't Let Me Pass' and 'Tam Lin.'")

Still later, in the title story of *Open Secrets* (129–60), Munro develops her own example of a "folk" ballad in stark counterpoint to the ambiguities and complexities of the story's plotline:

> And maybe some man did meet her there
> That was carrying a gun or a knife
> He met her there and he didn't care
> He took that young girl's life.
> . . . .
> And nobody knows the end. (140)

In "The Jack Randa Hotel," also in *Open Secrets* (161–89), there is an apparently incidental mention (165) of Thornton Wilder's *The Skin of Our Teeth*. This mention is more significant than it seems at first: the leading character, Gail, is invited by Will, her lover to be, to help him with the costumes for his Walley High School production of the play. This situation is ironic because Gail and Will have been, as it were, in a "play" of their own, playing games with their lives, avoiding real commitment to each other and deep knowledge of themselves. The main characters in Wilder's play are Mr. Antrobus, who "invented the alphabet and the wheel, and . . . a lot of things" (Wilder 135), and his wife; together they represent humankind. Mr. Antrobus, having just survived two wars, not to mention many other crises, has lost "the desire to begin again, to start building" (133), but at the end of the play, remembering "some of the words in . . . books" — and Spinoza — (136), he pulls himself together to resume life's struggle. Munro's story is about the way in which Gail and Will, in the end, after tacking and veering and avoiding reality, also come to grips with their lives and, after separation, come together, finally and decisively.

In one of Munro's recent stories, "Jakarta," Kath and Sonje, in the midst of reading the short stories of D.H. Lawrence and Katherine Mansfield, discuss at some length the young woman, March, and the soldier in Lawrence's "The Fox" and Stanley Burnell in Mansfield in ways that bear on their own situations and problems (46, 48–49). Similarly, in Munro's recently published story, "Save the Reaper," the title points to Alfred, Lord Tennyson's *The Lady of Shalott*, imperfectly remembered by Eve, the story's significantly named protagonist. Munro's title perhaps becomes a prayer for a release from the exigent present and for a recovery of the past, simple and idyllic as Eve recalls it, in light of the awkwardness and disaffection in her family relationships and a life that now seems sordid and spoiled. "Save the Reaper" is a notable study of change and the futility of nostalgic longing.

Thus, Munro's stories gain in resonance and significance because they are written in the context of a wide range of literature in English and in the classical tradition. Her allusions show small-town Ontario to be part of the wider world. But, as Miriam Marty Clark argues in "Allegories of Reading in Alice Munro's 'Carried Away,'" the word *allusion* "does not adequately describe" Munro's "lodgings at the intersection[s] of many texts" (50); recently, Munro's fiction "foregrounds and thematizes its own plurality, addressing itself directly to prior texts and other discourses" (53). "Spaceships Have Landed" provides a clear example of this intertextuality. Just how groundbreaking it is in Munro's work — assuming that her use of the ballad "Tam Lin" in "Hold Me Fast, Don't Let Me Pass" is a proleptic special case — is indicated by the fact that, only a short time before the story appeared, James Carscallen wrote, in his comprehensive study *The Other Country: Patterns in the Writing of Alice Munro*, that "Her work offers us the great human myths, but as half-concealed — both from the characters themselves and from the reader — behind a surface ordinariness that seems anything but mythical" (viii). In "Spaceships Have Landed," though ordinariness is maintained, the mythological analogue is hardly concealed from the reader.

"Spaceships Have Landed" is the most ambitious of Munro's stories about the history of small-town Huron County. It is ironic that but for editorial intervention it would be more difficult to see just how brilliant her conception and its execution are. The story first appeared in the *Paris Review* in 1994, but without the opening passage of six pages concluding with "A call of nature, then, all right, a call of nature" — the discussion in Monk's speakeasy — that occurs in *Open Secrets* (226–32). Munro, it seems, was persuaded by the editor of *Paris Review* to cut the six pages; in their place, after the short paragraph "Wayne's sister's selfishness had made Lucille break out in hives" (*Open Secrets* 244), she substituted a passage of one page that doesn't appear until the twelfth page of the thirty-page *Paris Review* version. As Munro told Gzowski in the *Morningside* interview, the speakeasy passage is very significant, and she duly restored it in *Open Secrets*.

Nonetheless, with the caveat that it seems inferior to the book version because it discloses the scope of the story and Rhea's part in it too baldly, the passage that Munro substituted in the *Paris Review* and then omitted in *Open Secrets* is worth quoting at length:

> Something had changed in Rhea since she . . . had been . . . shown what respect was owing to her by becoming Billy Doud's girl. It was a matter of getting *inside*, of being entirely and gratefully normal, of living within the life of the town. Rhea used to see the town of Carstairs from outside, as if it had a mysterious personality hidden from all the other people who lived inside it. For instance, one day in winter, looking by chance out the back window of the library in the town hall, she saw a team of horses pulling a load of grain sacks on the

municipal weigh scales. Snow was falling. . . . The big grain sacks, the heavy obedient animals, the snow, made Rhea think suddenly that the town was muffled in great distances, in snow-choked air, and that the life in it was a timeless ritual. . . . These feelings or visions didn't come so much from what she could see before her as they did from books that she had got to read from that same library — Russian stories and *Winesburg, Ohio*. (276–77)

In this single passage, Munro took a shortcut to what is achieved in the opening six pages of the *Open Secrets* version, making two significant points while exploring Rhea's mind. The first point is that, for Rhea, becoming the girlfriend of Billy, who was with her at the bootlegger's, is "a matter of getting *inside*" Carstairs, from which she has felt "cut off" (277). But now the feelings and the visions that came first from literature come from her own apocalyptic insights. This is a turning point in her life: Rhea has realized her calling, which is to accept and live out within the community the physical-sexual life of the body that will propagate the race. It is on the same night that Eunie, Rhea's erstwhile closest friend, disappears and moves into her very different, indeed opposite, calling to the life of the spirit, in which the life of this world interacts with the life of the other world in sexless union. Thus, both Rhea and Eunie (as we will suggest in detail shortly) decisively abandon their old selves and embrace their new callings. In a small-town Ontario speakeasy and its immediate environs is to be found the whole range of human experience, and these two women, Rhea and Eunie, come to represent its opposite poles.

The other significant, and related, thought that Rhea "suddenly" has in the *Paris Review* meditation is that life in Carstairs is "a timeless ritual" and is thus *real* and meaningful (276). In her introduction to *Selected Stories*, Munro reveals that Rhea's epiphany involving the snowy day, the horses, the sleigh, the grain sacks, and the weigh scales was in fact her own, experienced at the age of fifteen. (She does not mention the parallel passage in "Spaceships Have Landed," which is not included in *Selected Stories*.) Munro says that she, *in propria persona*, saw the horses moving onto the scales, not as "framed and removed," but as "alive and potent, and it gave me something like a blow to the chest" (xvi). This experience is the archetype of what is at the centre of so many Munro stories: a turning point, an epiphany, a realization of something "for the first time" (*Progress* 103) — a change, whether tragic or triumphant, after which everything is different and life begins anew. The moment is sometimes dramatized, or directly related, as in the *Paris Review* version of "Spaceships Have Landed," but more often it is conveyed from a distance, as in "Carried Away" when Louisa tells Jim Frarey about finding the short note from Jack Agnew on her desk ("I was engaged before I went overseas" [*Open Secrets* 18]), and sometimes it comes, just as effectively, by implication, as it does in the speakeasy scenes in the book version of "Spaceships Have Landed."

In "Walker Brothers Cowboy," the first story in Munro's first volume, *Dance of the Happy Shades*, the girl narrator's life changes momentously with her father's visit to Nora, and at the end of the story the narrator feels "my father's life flowing back from our car in the last of the afternoon, darkening and turning strange, like a landscape that has an enchantment on it" (18). In a similar manner, at the end of the last story in that first volume, "Dance of the Happy Shades," the narrator realizes that the handicapped girl's playing of the Gluck piece has been a "communiqué from the other country where she lives" (224): everything has changed, and a different life begins. In her introduction to *Selected Stories*, Munro seems to suggest that this scene with horses, grain sacks, and scales, viewed from a rural, small-town, Huron County library, was a turning point in her own life, as it is in Rhea's.

These two points, Rhea's commitment to the physical-sexual aspect of human experience and her epiphanic sense of life in Carstairs as a timeless ritual, which are directly related in the *Paris Review* version of "Spaceships Have Landed," are conveyed in the six speakeasy pages in *Open Secrets* in an artistically suggestive rather than a baldly direct manner. For instance, the reference in the *Paris Review* to Sherwood Anderson's *Winesburg, Ohio*, the classic portrait in fiction of a North American small town, is an obvious shortcut to the sort of effect that Munro wants to achieve. Rhea, though still a girl, feels at home in the heterogeneous but representative group gossiping and arguing at Monk's, and the reader senses that this aimless chatting is just what has been an unchanging element of human cave dwellings, settlements, and villages for millennia — one of the timeless rituals of Homo sapiens.

Carstairs, at the centre of "Spaceships Have Landed," is in Huron County, but it is also an immemorial and universal human settlement. It is, if not the eternal city, at least the abiding town; throughout its history, despite all its changes, it has remained essentially the same.

Although it is not really old, its present configuration has been through archetypal phases:

> On the river flats lay the old fairgrounds, some grandstands abandoned since before the war, when the fair here was taken over by the big fair at Walley. The racetrack oval was still marked out in the grass.
>
> This was where the town set out to be, over a hundred years ago. Mills and hostelries were here. But the river floods persuaded people to move to higher ground. House-plots remained on the map, and roads laid out, but only the one row of houses where people lived was still there, people who were too poor or in some way too stubborn to change. (234)

Fairgrounds, grandstands, racetrack oval, mills, hostelries, floods, house plots — all are timeless features of human communal life; there are no garages, drive-ins, or strip malls to suggest organic discontinuity. When readers are told that Carstairs had its beginnings "over a hundred years ago," its roots are placed in the realm of "once upon a time"; with the loss of its fair to the county seat, it also becomes an image of human history in which, to compare the small and obscure with the large and famous, its eclipse by Walley is parallel to that of Babylon by Baghdad. At the end of the story, the eclipse seems complete: "The river houses all gone. The Morgans' house, the Monks' house — everything gone of that first mistaken settlement" (259). But Carstairs, though it undergoes changes, remains the archetypal town.

By holding a mirror up to unchanging aspects of human nature, the story's opening scene at the bootlegger's house effectively introduces the theme. Unlike the *Paris Review* passage, the restored narrative doesn't *tell* the reader about a timeless ritual; the ritual is enacted in the quotidian setting of the scene at the bootlegger's, a scene that is — to appropriate one of Munro's own phrases — both "touchable and mysterious" ("Everything").

Rhea, underage and the only female person in the scene apart from the bootlegger's wife, is present with her date, Billy, and his friend Wayne (whose surname is never mentioned). The group gathered in the speakeasy is representative of the community. Rhea knows many of them by sight: Mr. Monk, the bootlegger, who presides over the gathering; the enigmatic Mrs. Monk, whom Rhea rightly or wrongly imagines to be the local whore; a snow-shoveller; a salesman of pots and pans and former teacher; a dry cleaner; an undertaker; and two students — Billy, scion of one of the local first families (the Douds of the piano factory), and Wayne, the United Church minister's son. Class differences in this cross-section of society are conveyed not only by differing economic circumstances but also by changes in the behaviour of the young in the presence of their elders and in that of men in the presence of women.

One member of the group is known to readers only as the teller of a wonderful tale, purportedly true, about how a man, "Away up north in the Province of Quebec" (227), in answering "a call of nature" and looking for something "to come in handy" (226), finds "stuff" "Laying all over, in sheets"; "And on the spot they developed the biggest asbestos mine in the entire world. And from that mine came a fortune!" (227). (The true story of the discovery, though interesting, is more prosaic: in 1876, during "the building of the line of the Quebec Central Railway . . . at Thetford and Coleraine, . . . the accidental knocking off of a fragment of rock . . . and the consequent exposure of a vein of chrysotile signalized the beginning of the asbestos industry in Canada" [Mendels 16–17].) Asbestos has been known and used since ancient times. The Romans are said to have used it for cremation cloths — "the funeral dress of kings" — and for lamp wicks (James Ross 3), and Marco Polo was shown asbestos cloth during his travels in what is now Siberia (3–4). The asbestos story told at the bootlegger's is a tall tale, which indeed has a slender basis in fact, is "extravagant, outlandish or highly improbable," belongs to "the same family as fantasy and fairy tale" (Cuddon 684), and flourishes as lore "especially in rural areas" (685) or "on the . . . frontier" (Brunvand 65). The story diverges from its point and is interrupted by misunderstandings, irrelevancies, non sequiturs, and even a discussion of which expressions are appropriate in the presence of women: for example, "a call of nature" is finally substituted for "something about a crap" in deference to Rhea and Mrs. Monk (226). Munro's handling of the episode suggests a community activity that has been repeated since the rise of Homo sapiens and the timeless ritual of storytelling around a campfire; it brings to mind David Helwig's inspired description of Munro's writing as "gossip informed by genius" (qtd. in Turbide 47). Munro's story may be set in southwestern Ontario, but its bearing is universal and timeless.

In this opening scene, Rhea begins to play the prominent role that her name boldly suggests. The Graeco-Roman goddess Rhea is an avatar of the Neolithic Great Mother goddess, "the earth mother and the corn mother, and the protector and multiplier of flocks and herds" (Mackenzie 172) — she has, in Robert Graves's poem "Rhea," a "mother-mind" (197). There also seems to have been an earlier pre-Hellenic and Cretan Rhea who "was at once Gaia, Demeter, Artemis, and . . . Aphrodite" (Mackenzie 173–74). Munro's Rhea is, like her namesake, passionately heterosexual and certainly philoprogenitive. She imagines Mrs. Monk going up to a bed and arranging herself "without the least hesitation or enthusiasm" for "a quick and driven and bought and paid-for encounter," "shamefully exciting" to Rhea, and she entertains the thought of being approached in the same manner, "To be so flattened and used and hardly to know who was doing it to you, to take it all in with that secret capability, over and over again" (232). Rhea possesses the mothering instinct; it would be unkind to describe her as promiscuous, but she embodies the kind of Shavian life force on which human continuity depends. She is conscious of her community and aware of the past, conceiving common processes as perpetually reenacted throughout the cycles of human life.

"Spaceships Have Landed" is in part an allegory on the nature of love, an allegory in which Rhea and Eunie are opposite yet complementary poles. If Rhea embodies a love that is sexual and fecund, then Eunie represents a love that is Platonic. If Rhea's love is existential, then Eunie's is mystical. If Rhea is *eros*, then Eunie is *agape*.

Eunie, as her name implies, is the embodiment of unique characteristics. Her given name may be Eunice, the name of the mother of St. Paul's beloved disciple, Timothy, whom Paul compliments on his "unfeigned faith," "which dwelt first in . . . thy mother Eunice" (2 Tim. 1.5, KJV), a Jewish woman married to a Greek man (Acts 16.1). Readers are possibly intended to make such a connection, for within the allegory Eunie seems to represent the Judaeo-Christian mystical heritage, whereas Billy Doud, who becomes her husband, seems to embody the Greek, and especially the Platonic, tradition.

Although Eunie is not present at the bootlegger's, her importance in the story is suggested by the first sentence of the story: "On the night of Eunie Morgan's disappearance, Rhea was sitting in the bootlegger's house at Carstairs" (226). Despite their striking differences in temperament and symbolic significance, Eunie and Rhea converged in early girlhood to become the inseparable "Two Toms," playing games that were "the most serious part of their lives" (235) and in which there was an "intense and daily collaboration" (237). It is later, in maturity, that they become distinctively and consciously separate, though clearly complementary; this strange, almost symbiotic, relationship in youth between later opposites points to an archetypal structure in the story. Whereas Rhea looks to the past and "is of the earth, earthy" (1 Cor. 15.47, KJV), Eunie seeks to transcend space and time. Unlike everyone else in Carstairs, she is imaginative, playful, and original; moreover, "Eunie never seemed subject to her parents, or even connected to them, in the way of other children. Rhea was struck by the way she ruled her own life . . ." (237). It is Eunie who has the vision of the spaceship landing; she seems attuned to the supernatural and the ideal. The extraterrestrials from the spaceship, three children,

> took her to their tent. But it seemed to her that she never saw
> that tent once from the outside. She was just suddenly inside
> it, and she saw that it was white, very high and white, and
> shivering like the sails on a boat. Also it was lit up, and again
> she had no idea where the light was coming from. (255–56)

This play on the words *outside* and *inside* might remind readers of the significance of the same words in the passage quoted from the *Paris Review*.

Upon Eunie's return home the next morning, her father summons Billy, as the available representative of a first family of Carstairs: "Mr. Doud . . . was always sent for in an emergency" (254). Before the episode at the Monks' house the night before, Billy was for some time Rhea's boyfriend, but, although he "brought her honor" and some importance (240), Rhea found little satisfaction in the affair. His necking always seemed like teasing and unimpassioned (242); "he himself might have been carved from soap," being "tall and pale, cool and clean" (240). In short, Billy comes across not as impotent but as somehow asexual. However, he is "enchanted" by Eunie and the account of her adventure, and "His love — Billy's kind of love — could spring up to meet a need that Eunie wouldn't know she had" (257).

Readers are told in the windup of the story that Billy eventually turns the Doud-family mansion into "a home for old people and disabled people," "a place where they could get comfort and kindness," and then asks Eunie to marry him; "'I wouldn't want for there to be anything going on, or anything,' Eunie said" (260). Eunie, then, in her fulfilling if sexless marriage with Billy, exemplifies an emotional disposition certainly different from Rhea's, and she finds what she has been unaware of lacking. Their marriage seems to be founded on something like the love described by Plato, a love that transcends the world of concrete objects and becomes the selfless love of an ideal (203–07). When Billy devotes himself and his resources to serving humanity, Eunie brings to their partnership a visionary imagination that, in contrast to Rhea's, can fully respond to "Billy's kind of love."

Munro further suggests the whole range of human diversity by placing between the socially conscious and philoprogenitive Rhea and the individualistic, imaginative, and promethean Eunie, distant opposite edges of the human psyche, a third girl, Lucille, who is colourless and unremarkable, fascinated by "the vagaries of her body," which she treats as though it were "a troublesome but valuable pet" (243). She is much concerned about "the conflict that was raging round her wedding, about whether the bridesmaids should wear picture hats or wreaths of rosebuds" (244).

After the memorable scene at the bootlegger's house, however, Wayne, Lucille's fiancé, leaves her virtually at the altar to elope to Calgary with Rhea. It is on the same night that, by a fine structural stroke, Munro brings the story to its climax: not only does Eunie walk out of her house in the middle of the night and have her vision, but also Rhea has the experience that changes her life and brings her to herself. Although her date is Billy, Wayne "caught Rhea's eye, and from then on . . . watched her, with a slight, tight, persistent smile" (228); this flirting leads, after a few too many drinks, to the sudden coming together of Rhea and Wayne: "Up against the wall of the house, she and Wayne were pushing and grabbing and kissing each other" (248). But their passionate lovemaking is interrupted by the Monks' dog, Rhea's attack of vomiting, and Mrs. Monk herself — who imperturbably drives the very sick Rhea home.

The next morning, as Rhea's real life begins, she sees Eunie, at the beginning of *her* new life, returning from her encounter with the children from the spaceship. Wayne intends to marry Lucille, but Rhea persuades him to leave immediately for his job in Calgary and to drop her off on the way in Toronto or Winnipeg or wherever. For Wayne too, of course, this is a sudden breaking out into a different life.

Soon after they got to Calgary, Rhea and Wayne were married. You had to be married then, to get an apartment together — at least in Calgary — and they had discovered that they did not want to live separately. That would continue to be the way they felt most of the time, though they would discuss it — living separately — and threaten it, and give it a couple of brief tries. (258)

This is as close as Rhea and Wayne — and Munro — come to saying that they love each other. But in the story's conclusion, readers are told that

> Rhea and Wayne have lived together for far more than half their lives. They have had three children, and between them, counting everything, five times as many lovers [here one might remember Mr. and Mrs. Antrobus in Wilder's play]. And now abruptly, surprisingly, all this turbulence and fruitfulness and uncertain but lively expectation has receded and she [Rhea] knows they are beginning to be old. There in the cemetery she says out loud, "I can't get used to it." (259)

She belongs to *this* world, to *this* life.

In her introduction to *Selected Stories*, Munro says that she writes so often about "the country to the east of Lake Huron," with its "almost flat fields," "swamps," "hardwood bush lots," "brick houses," "falling-down barns," "burdensome old churches," et cetera, because she loves it. When she writes "about something happening in this setting," she says, "I don't think that I'm choosing to be confined. Quite the opposite." Munro is not simply writing *"about"* rural Ontario but also writing *"through"* it (xv).

Always concerned with change and its patterns of recurrence and permanence, Munro as the artist-historian of small-town Ontario, under a surface of ordinariness, repeatedly makes effective use of traditional genres and structures and of archetypal images, figures, and themes from the range of Western literature and myth, nowhere more conspicuously than in "Spaceships Have Landed." It is extraordinary in its daring and scope, a story in which are represented the span of human history and myth and the range of the human psyche — and all this neatly contained in and made compatible with the familiar realities of a portrait of a small town in remote, rural Ontario. Alice Munro is not confined to any view of history that ignores feelings and visions; she transfigures daily life and gives her readers universal experience.

Brunvand, Jan Harold. *Folklore: A Study and Research Guide*. New York: St. Martin's, 1976.

Carscallen, James. *The Other Country: Patterns in the Writing of Alice Munro*. Toronto: ECW, 1993.

Clark, Miriam Marty. "Allegories of Reading in Alice Munro's 'Carried Away.'" *Contemporary Literature* 37.1 (1996): 49–61.

Cuddon, J.A. *A Dictionary of Literary Terms*. Rev. ed. Harmondsworth, Eng.: Penguin, 1982.

Graves, Robert. "Rhea." *Poems Selected by Himself*. Harmondsworth, Eng.: Penguin, 1961. 197.

Mackenzie, Donald A. *Myths of Crete and Pre-Hellenic Europe*. London: Gresham, n.d.

Martin, W.R. "Alice Munro and James Joyce." *Journal of Canadian Fiction* 24 (1979): 120–26.

Martin, W.R., and Warren U. Ober. "Alice Munro's 'Hold Me Fast, Don't Let Me Pass' and 'Tam Lin.'" *ANQ: A Quarterly Journal of Short Articles, Notes, and Reviews*: forthcoming.

———. "A Misreading Corrected." *Canadian Notes and Queries* 53.1 (1998): 26–29.

Mendels, M.M. *The Asbestos Industry of Canada*. McGill University Economic Studies 14: National Problems of Canada. Orillia: Packet-Times Press, 1930.

Munro, Alice. "Characters." *Ploughshares* 4.3 (1978): 72–82.

———. *Dance of the Happy Shades*. Toronto: McGraw, 1968.

———. "Everything Here Is Touchable and Mysterious." *Weekend Magazine* 11 May 1974: 33.

———. *Friend of My Youth*. New York: Knopf, 1990.

———. Interview. With Peter Gzowski. *Morningside*. CBC Radio, 30 Sept. 1994.

———. "An Interview with Alice Munro." With Eleanor Wachtel. *The Brick Reader*. Ed. Linda Spalding and Michael Ondaatje. Toronto: Coach House, 1991. 288–94.

———. "Introduction to the Vintage Edition." *Selected Stories*. By Alice Munro. Vintage Contemporaries. New York: Vintage, 1997. xiii–xxi.

———. "Jakarta." *Saturday Night* Feb. 1998: 45–60.

———. *Lives of Girls and Women*. 1971. New York: New American Library, 1983.

———. *The Moons of Jupiter*. 1982. Harmondsworth, Eng.: Penguin, 1984.

———. *Open Secrets*. Toronto: McClelland, 1994.

———. *The Progress of Love*. New York: Knopf, 1986.

———. "Save the Reaper." *New Yorker* 22 and 29 June 1998: 120–35.

———. *Something I've Been Meaning to Tell You*. 1974. New York: New American Library, 1984.

___. "Spaceships Have Landed." *Paris Review* 131 (1994): 265–94.

___. "What Do You Want to Know For?" *Writing Away*. Ed. Constance Rooke. Toronto: McClelland, 1994. 203–20.

___. *Who Do You Think You Are?* Toronto: Macmillan, 1978.

Plato. *Lysis; Symposium; Gorgias*. Trans. W.R.M. Lamb. 1925. Loeb Classical Library. Cambridge: Harvard UP, 1961.

Robson, Nora. "Alice Munro and the White American South: The Quest." *The Art of Alice Munro: Saying the Unsayable*. Ed. Judith Miller. Waterloo: U of Waterloo P, 1984. 73–84.

Ross, Catherine Sheldrick. *Alice Munro: A Double Life*. Toronto: ECW, 1992.

Ross, James Gordon. *Chrysotile Asbestos in Canada*. Canada: Department of Mines (Mines Branch) 707. Ottawa: Acland, 1931.

Struthers, J.R. (Tim). "Reality and Ordering: The Growth of a Young Artist in *Lives of Girls and Women*." *Essays on Canadian Writing* 3 (1975): 32–46.

Thacker, Robert. "Alice Munro's Willa Cather." *Canadian Literature* 134 (1992): 42–57.

Turbide, Diane. "The Incomparable Storyteller." Rev. of *Open Secrets*, by Alice Munro. *Maclean's* 17 Oct. 1994: 46–49.

Weaver, John. "Society and Culture in Rural and Small-Town Ontario: Alice Munro's Testimony on the Last Forty Years." *Patterns of the Past: Interpreting Ontario's History*. Ed. Roger Hall, William Westfall, and Laurel Sefton MacDowell. Toronto: Dundurn, 1988. 381–403.

Wilder, Thornton. *The Skin of Our Teeth*. *Three Plays*. By Wilder. New York: Bantam, 1958. 65–137.

"Darkness Collecting": Reading "Vandals" as a Coda to *Open Secrets*

NATHALIE FOY

IT IS DIFFICULT not to rhapsodize about the stories collected in Alice Munro's *Open Secrets*. "Magical" is the word that Peter Gzowski so enthusiastically used to describe them in his 1994 *Morningside* interview with Munro (see Munro, interview), and both new and magical they are. There is a shift away from her previous work with this collection, as she explores narrative in a way that seems more celebratory, less caustic, than before. In an interview for the *Paris Review*, conducted the year that *Open Secrets* was published (1994), Munro attributes the shift to a simple need for new material: "I'm doing less personal writing now than I used to for a very simple obvious reason. You use up your childhood. . . . Maybe it's advisable to move on to writing those stories which are more observation" ("Alice Munro" 244). These are finely observed stories written with Munro's signature use of realism, but the shift to "more observation" is not all that accounts for their newness. Munro has combined her realism with an entirely new plane of narration. As she mentioned to Gzowski, *Open Secrets* is "riskier" than any of her previous works:

> I want to move away from what happened to the possibility of this happening or that happening and a kind of idea that life is not just made up of the facts, the things that happen, . . . but all the things that happen in fantasy, that might have happened, the . . . alternate life that can almost seem to be accompanying what we call our real lives.

It is this sense of parallel narratives, of the layering of narratives, on which I will focus as I read the many-layered "Vandals" as a coda to *Open Secrets*. "Vandals" brings together the elements of magic, romance, memory, and writing woven throughout the collection. Before I begin that reading, however, I want to flesh out my sense of the newness of these stories.

147

What struck me most forcibly about *Open Secrets* was the complexity of the stories, the striking similarities between them, and the sense I had of Munro's veneration for fiction. The stories have such multiple narrative threads, such richness and density, that it is not surprising that they overlap and intersect in places. The similarities are not enough to constitute an overall pattern in the collection, but they are striking enough to encourage juxtaposed readings. There is a way in which, when the stories intersect in their similarities, they shed light as well as shadow on each other. The intersections may give us new perspectives on the stories, but they also reveal that our understanding may still be limited and our view obscured.

In discussing "An Ounce of Cure," Munro talks about her early approach to writing: "When I started to write . . . I made the glorious leap from being a victim of my own ineptness and self-conscious miseries to being a godlike arranger of patterns and destinies" ("Author's Commentary" 125). This may have been her early approach to writing, as a "godlike arranger," but curiously she combined this role with a caustic sense of the limits of fiction, its inability to ever achieve godlike organization. In an excellent analysis of Munro's fiction before *Open Secrets*, Ajay Heble notes that Munro's writing operates "as both an instance and a criticism of narrative," and, "while Munro clearly remains attracted to language because of the possibility the words can reflect meanings which already exist 'out there' in the world, she is also painfully aware of the fact that writing can never simply be an unquestioned means for 'getting at' real life" (4, 5–6; see also Mayberry). With *Open Secrets*, however, there seems to be a departure from the self-consciousness of fiction, and the question has shifted from writing's ability to represent "real life" to the very notion that there is a "real life." There is no interrogation of fiction and language in this collection, of the clash between realist narrative and epistemological uncertainty. There is a move away from concern about the limits of representation and toward respect for inspiration, for the endless possibilities of story, the resilience of narrative, and the magic of half-perceived stories.

"Magical" is indeed an apt description of these stories because it captures the sense that here Munro is both celebratory and reverential in her stance toward fiction. Magic has a dark side, an intricacy, and an exclusivity, features that command reverence and that Munro grants to fiction. The power of magic lies in the gap between what is revealed and what is hidden, so, although there is a dreadful clarity in these stories, at times there is also a stubborn opacity to them. We are shown just as much as we need to see and no more, and the characters are often shown or allowed to remember even less. I do not mean to suggest that this is Munro in her guise as "godlike arranger," however, or that she is an all-knowing magician. Instead, she is reproducing her sense of fiction making. As she mentioned to McCulloch and Simpson, "I don't think I have this overwhelming thing that comes in and dictates to me. I only seem to get a grasp on what I want to write about with the greatest difficulty. And barely" ("Alice Munro" 240). It is as if Munro glimpses perfect stories existing in a parallel world and must flesh out those glimpses while writing: as she mentioned to Gzowski, "I do think of the story as happening, not of me making up the story. The story is happening, and I'm finding out about it. . . . It's as if I'm doing justice to something somewhere." If the stories in *Open Secrets* are magical, then it is because Munro has realized them so wonderfully.

They are also magical because they are so intricate, so many–layered, combining reality and fantasy. Each one has more than "just . . . a single thread" (Munro, interview). At the end of "Carried Away," for example, Louisa has what seems like a real encounter with Jack Agnew, but it can only be fantasy because she has never seen him and because he is dead (40). She meets the man that he became in a parallel story in which he was not decapitated, but she meets the ghost of a lover whose face she has never seen. There are incredible convolutions to this encounter, and they lead to her vertiginous "devouring muddle": "Sudden holes and impromptu tricks and radiant vanishing consolations" (56). Throughout the collection, there are instances similar to Louisa's when narratives splinter, unravel, proliferate, thereby creating parallel stories. The vertiginous moments occur when characters glimpse one of the parallel narratives. The story does not collapse when the thread unravels; it just diverges and then continues in parallel lines. A critic for the Montreal *Gazette* observed, and Munro agreed, that all the stories in *Open Secrets* are instances of "Sudden holes and impromptu tricks and radiant vanishing consolations" (qtd. in Munro, interview).

If it is possible to read all the stories as such, then there is also a way in which "Vandals" can be read as a coda to the collection. Like the rest of the stories, "Vandals" is many–layered, and it contains many of the narrative threads of the collection. The story's characters, each with significant aspects of his or her narrative unknown to the other characters, unwittingly inhabit and reenact each other's narrative as well as the narratives of characters from earlier in the collection. "Vandals" completes the text by picking up threads from earlier narratives, but, as the darkest story in *Open Secrets*, it has its own dark layers. It acts, then, as its own last note: it is "darkness collecting" (344). What follows is a reading of "Vandals" that examines both the similarities between its narrative layers and the similarities between it and the preceding stories in order to understand the actions of the eponymous vandals and Munro's reasons for ending the collection in this way.

A seemingly minor similarity between stories is the interest that Jack Agnew and Ladner have in history and Bea Doud's curiosity in their books. In "Carried Away," Bea sees Jack's books on the floor of her father's car, a moment at which narratives diverge and layer. Her asking about them reminds Arthur Doud that he must return the books to the library, so the significance of the books to Arthur is that they connect him to Louisa and to the narrative thread of their romance. The books link Louisa, Jack, and Arthur, though only Louisa and the reader know the full significance of that triangle and of the double significance of the books to her. They connect her to Arthur, but they also point to Jack's never-observed proximity, his life led parallel but invisible to her own. Finally, the books become the source of an amusing anecdote that Bea likes to tell, but she does not "mention that the books were connected with the man who had had the accident. That would have made the story less amusing. Perhaps she had really forgotten" (29). In her mind, the link to Jack is erased by the repetition of an anecdote that excludes him. The intervening years have severed her from the story that we know to be there, a story on which she only has the most tenuous grasp (I will return to this issue of memory and intervening narratives). Nonetheless, Bea's noticing Jack's books highlights the multiple layers of the story and our privileged vantage over those layers.

When Bea notices Ladner's books in "Vandals," layers are also highlighted:

> Bea thought of his long evenings in the winter — his orderly solitude, his systematic reading and barren contentment. . . .
> Here is this man, she was thinking, not so strange a man after all. Nothing so very mysterious about him, maybe nothing even so very interesting. The layers of information. (319)

The irony, of course, is that the layers of information invisible or inaccessible to her are anything but "orderly," "systematic," or "barren." What Bea does not know then, and what she never learns, is that Ladner is a pedophile. His abuse of Liza and Kenny is a parallel narrative to her own troubled romance with him, but it is one that she never glimpses. Unlike her forgetting Jack's link to her anecdote in "Carried Away," her ignorance of this parallel story is complete. Bea is naïve, but by juxtaposing these similarities we are able to absolve her of the blame for the abuse, blame that Liza eventually transfers to her. We know that Bea is capable of forgetting unpleasant associations, and, although she is deeply wrapped up in her own relationship with Ladner in a way that probably limits her ability to see his relationship with Liza for what it is, she is free of complicity in Liza's abuse and the silence around it.

Another similarity between the stories in *Open Secrets* is the female protagonist's fondness for drink, which is associated with storytelling. In "Vandals," as Bea writes the letter that she neither finishes nor sends, she sits happily with her bottle of red wine (308), just as Christena Mullen writes her letter in "A Wilderness Station" under the effects of a martini, her "late-afternoon pleasure" (261). In "Carried Away," Louisa also drinks, though she states gravely that "It is for my health" (1). Before she gets carried away with Jim Frarey, however, she drinks a little too much, a fact that does not escape his notice: "She was drinking whiskey, now, too, though she would not try it without drowning it in water. It used to be only a glass of wine" (13). The drink loosens her tongue, just as it makes Christena and Bea more communicative, if only on paper. Frarey thinks that "Women after they have told one story on themselves cannot stop from telling another. Drink upsets them in a radical way, prudence is out the window" (19). This is a perspective that I think we are asked to question, however. It is not the alcohol but their loneliness or their need to reminisce that prompts the storytellers. It all depends on one's point of view, and readers have a clearer view than the observers within the stories: "In her big, neglected house in Carstairs, she [Bea] had entered a period of musing and drinking, of what looked to everybody else like a slow decline, but to her seemed, after all, sadly pleasurable, like a convalescence" (308). The drinking and the unsent letters are part of a process of grief, of "convalescence," a process that necessarily includes loneliness and reminiscence. By linking Bea's drinking to Louisa's and Christena's, instead of reinforcing the importance of the alcohol in the characters' storytelling, Munro asks us not to see the telling of these stories as imprudent, as Frarey does. Rather, she gives us more power than we would have if the stories were to slip out from the drink-loosened lips of imprudent story-tellers. She gives us a privileged vantage point from which to receive the stories. No character ever receives Bea's letter, after all, and we know much more than either Jim Frarey or Leopold Henry does about his storyteller's narrative.

We are not always at an advantage, however. There are notable examples of mysteries, potential layers of narrative in the collection, that are brought to our attention but never fleshed out. What was it, for example, that brought Ladner to Canada? "He had not left England immediately [after the Second World War] but had worked for years there, in a museum, until something happened — Bea never knew what — that soured him on the job and the country" (311). What was it, in "The Albanian Virgin," that prompted the assault on the notary public? "He was not dead but he might be blinded. Robbery? Or an act of revenge, outrage, connected with a layer of his life that I hadn't guessed at?" (145). For Claire, robbery and revenge are certainly possibilities, because she has heard Lottar's story, but this is more than Claire's subconscious linking in action. Munro deliberately entices us only to thwart our attempts to solve these mysteries. These unexplored and unexplorable layers are like uncut gatherings in the book, rich with possibilities but inaccessible. We have a sense that the story is *there*, that Munro knows exactly what happened, but we have no way to access it.

Similarly, stories are often told only to be cancelled and rewritten. Peter Parr's gossip-informed and erroneous history of Ladner is given to us (and Bea) in full but then corrected: "He was a man who had been wounded and disillusioned in the worst way and had withdrawn from the world, yet gave all he could back to it in his attention to nature. Much of this was untrue or only partly true, as Bea discovered" (311). This cancellation highlights the existence of parallel narratives about Ladner and the fact that what Bea later discovers is also only partially true. Perhaps her experience of discovering "truer" layers that replace Peter's gossip should alert her to the possibility that her absorption in her narrative of romance obscures other truths, that her narrative with Ladner is still incomplete. But this is not about the limits of narrative itself; it is about its endless possibilities, its protean and proliferating meanings.

Munro stated to McCulloch and Simpson, "I have all these discon-nected realities in my own life, and I see them in other people's lives. That was one of the problems — why I couldn't write novels, I never saw things hanging together . . . well" ("Alice Munro" 257). The stories in *Open Secrets* hang together precisely because they are not continuous but layered. Some layers remain forever parallel, and some intersect in the weird geometry of this collection. The shape of the collection is not linear or horizontal; its momentum is not teleological. Again, my sense of this shape derives from Munro's writing process itself: "I don't take up a story and follow it as if it were a road, taking me somewhere, with views and neat divisions along the way. I go into it, and move back and forth and settle here and there, stay in it for a while" (Munro, "What Is Real?" 825). Similar elements ricochet in time and in narrative layers, and links are made vertically through layers of palimpsest as similarities are reworked.

Ildikó de Papp Carrington quotes Munro's discussion of the genesis of "Carried Away" and her sense of parallel stories:

> Munro says that originally she "had a pretty realistic story going," but "all the time [she] felt a parallel story going, in which the accident never happened and another reality developed. . . ." She "didn't want the point to be the 'ghost' . . . but something interchangeable, some way in which events, even drastic ones, do, and don't, matter." ("What's" 561)

Munro's ambivalence about the significance of events raises troublesome questions about the morality of these parallel stories, which "do, and don't, matter," questions to which I will return, but Munro's sense of a parallel and equally valid story that accompanies each person's "real" life is present both thematically and structurally in *Open Secrets*.

Thematically, characters are sometimes aware of a parallel story that cannot be told. Sometimes they are unaware of parallel narratives, and we must then make links between the layers of narrative. In "Open Secrets," Maureen has a vision that brings together three layers of the story, but she is unaware of the significance of the parallel story that she daydreams, and then she forgets it. Her husband demeans her with his demands for sex, and "right through her husband's rampage she thought of the fingers moving in the feathers, the wife's hand laid on top of the husband's, pressing down" (182). The hands are those of Theo and Marian Hubbert, who have just been to see lawyer Stephens with information about the disappearance of Heather Bell. Immediately after her husband's "rampage," Maureen has a daydream, she sees a parallel story, but her story intersects with those of the Hubberts and Heather:

She sees one of those thick-fingered hands that pressed into her tablecloth and that had worked among the feathers, and it is pressed down, unresistingly, but by somebody else's will — it is pressed down on the open burner of the stove where she is stirring the custard in the double boiler, and held there just for a second or two, just long enough to scorch the flesh on the red coil, to scorch but not to maim. In silence this is done, and by agreement — a brief and barbaric and necessary act. So it seems. (184)

Carrington reads this scene as "an image of Marian punishing Theo for doing something to Heather" ("Talking Dirty" 603). It may be the Hubberts' arms that Maureen sees, but I think that this is a moment of intersecting layers in which *she* is pushing down Theo's hand because she links her husband's rampage with Theo's. She is punishing both men for their violence. She is unaware that this is the significance of the vision, however, and the intersection is one of the many vertiginous moments in *Open Secrets*. Much later in life, when Maureen stands stirring custard again

In kitchens hundreds and thousands of miles away, she'll watch the soft skin form on the back of a wooden spoon and her memory will twitch, but it will not quite reveal to her this moment when she seems to be looking into an open secret, something not startling until you think of trying to tell it. (186)

Time and narrative seem to have folded over on themselves, and we see Maureen at the stove again years later, but the fold has obscured for her the layer underneath. As Carrington states, we use Maureen's hallucination to help solve the mystery of Heather's disappearance by making the evidence speak to us in our participation in fiction making:

Although she is willing to "talk dirty" for her husband in private, she is unable to talk dirty *about* him, for then she would be talking dirty about both of them in public. So, in spite of witnessing Theo's punished hand in her hallucination, she is as voiceless as the allegedly crazy Mr. Siddicup, the original witness of what that hand did. Therefore, to decode and interpret the secret language of what they saw, the reader must turn detective and talk dirty for both of them and for Munro. ("Talking Dirty" 605)

Ultimately, it is less important that Maureen understand and utter the unutterable than that we do. She has clearly had enough talking to do. The parallel stories that she glimpses do "matter," but her remembering them does not because we make the stories matter by forging links between them.

In "Carried Away," Louisa also has a parallel narrative, her epistolary love affair with Jack, but she is aware that she can never tell Arthur her own open secret about her interest in Jack's appearance. Her curiosity comes across as a morbid interest in his severed head:

> "I should not have asked you," she said. "I should not have mentioned it. I can never explain to you why I did. I would just like to ask you, if you can help it, never to think that that is the kind of person I am."
>
> Arthur heard the word "never." She could never explain to him. He was never to think. . . . [H]e picked up this suggestion, that their conversations were to continue, and perhaps on a less haphazard basis. (42)

It is at this point that Arthur's and Jack's narrative paths cross, and Arthur trips into Jack's role as the romantic lead. Their conversations do indeed continue, and Arthur becomes what Jack once promised to be: Louisa's husband. In order for Arthur to take over the romantic plot, however, he can never be aware of whom he replaces or why he does so. The secret is "open" in this case because Louisa has told Frarey, but it is also unutterable, perhaps because she is able to envision a future with Arthur that she did not with Frarey.

The light that both of these stories shed on Liza's revenge in "Vandals" combines the elements of skipping from one plot line into another and the question of complicitous knowledge. When Warren asks Liza why she vandalizes Bea and Ladner's house, Liza oddly responds: "I already told you what she did to me. She sent me to college!" (332). The blame for Ladner's abuse is deflected onto Bea, whose gesture came far too late to save Liza from the abuse. For Liza, the story of the abuse and the territory on which it occurs are part of a dark fairy-tale narrative to which Bea is oblivious. Bea and Liza simultaneously occupy entirely different spaces on Ladner's property and in his narrative life. Whereas Bea looks to Ladner to offer her a dangerous romance, "an insanity that could contain" her, it is Liza who must cope with the darkest manifestations of his insanity (314). In the space that Liza occupies, the dark fairy-tale world, Ladner's madness disrupts all normal rules of morality and narrative. Fairy tales are morality tales, but Ladner strips all that is good or moral from Liza's fairy tale so that it does not and cannot conform to the standard format.

Linda Lamont-Stewart points to what I see in this story as Munro's particular fairy-tale style: Munro's

> technique is comparable to that of "magic realist" painters, in whose works a precise, almost photographic depiction of an ordinary scene is startlingly disrupted by the presence of something strangely out of place in the context. The texture of reality . . . includes the irrational, [and] the grotesque absurdity and horror are never far below the deceptively calm surface of everyday life. (114)

Beneath the surfaces of the romanticized gossip about Ladner and Bea's romantic plot with him lies the irrational fairy-tale world of his monstrous abuse. Liza's dark fairy tale refuses to complete itself according to form or to cast itself with characters in correct roles. When Bea arrives, Liza sees her as the fairy godmother who will dispel Ladner's dark power: "By the time Bea had been at Ladner's place for a week, Liza could not stand the thought of her ever going away" (333). Presumably, for that first week, the abuse stopped, so Liza comes to see Bea as her protector: "But this did not mean that Liza's love for Bea was easy or restful — her love was one of expectation, but she did not know what it was that she expected" (336). Bea is unaware both of the weight of expectation that has been placed on her and of the fairy-tale plot or role that she has to step into, so the fairy tale cannot end or be cast according to Liza's needs:

> Bea could spread safety, if she wanted to. Surely she could. All that is needed is for her to turn herself into a different sort of woman, a hard-and-fast, draw-the-line sort, clean-sweeping, energetic, and intolerant. *None of that. Not allowed. Be good.* The woman who could rescue them — who could make them all, keep them all, good.
>
> What Bea has been sent to do, she doesn't see.
>
> Only Liza sees. (343)

Like a magician, Ladner obscures what Liza alone sees, and Bea cannot transform either herself or those whom she is meant to rescue. Despite Bea's failure to step into the role of fairy godmother, plots do intersect and overlap, but they do so in ways that only we see.

Perhaps because Ladner's world is so densely forested and so densely layered with narratives, secret and spoken, Liza's perspective is constantly narrowed: "they had got so far into the trees that Liza was not sure of the way out" (333). Only we can see how the plots overlap. On her side of the road, she can see clearly:

> No divisions over here, no secret places — everything is bare and simple.
> But when you cross the road . . . into Ladner's territory, it's like coming into a world of different and distinct countries. . . . A sense there of tropical threats and complications. . . . Here are the scenes of serious instruction where Ladner taught them how to tell a hickory tree from a butternut and a star from a planet, and places also where they have run and hollered and hung from branches and performed all sorts of rash stunts. And places where Liza thinks there is a bruise on the ground, a tickling and shame in the grass. (340–41)

Just as Liza deflects the blame for her abuse from Ladner to Bea, so too the pain of the abuse is relocated to a bruised ground. In Ladner's territory, cause and effect are disjointed in another instance of the disruption of normal rules.

Ladner's forest can be linked to the one that Maureen in "Open Secrets" sees from her husband's window and to the complicated nexus of tangled plots that she envisions and then forgets (162). The echo recalls and therefore prepares us for an impending crossing of plots in "Vandals." Instead of the plots crossing only in Maureen's head, however, all the narratives about Ladner coexist simultaneously in the "real" world. To some, he is a "pacifist" and a nature lover (311). Bea and the children know him as a taxidermist, someone who specializes in deceptive exteriors and shape-shifting, changing an inanimate fur into a lifelike object: "Ladner fitted the skin around a body in which nothing was real" (334). Liza and Kenny also know him as a shape-shifter in his own right, the monstrous Mr. Hyde to what Bea sees as the mysterious Dr. Jekyll:

> Bea did not understand about Ladner. And how could she? Liza herself couldn't have described to anybody what he was like. In the secret life she had with him, what was terrible was always

funny, badness was mixed with silliness. . . . You couldn't get out of it, or even want to, any more than you could stop an invasion of pins and needles. (339)

Ladner's dark world is amoral, and it has the power to allow crossed plots to coexist.

When Liza and Warren revisit this world, it is described again as a different dimension: "The change of noise for silence and speed for stillness made it seem as if they had dropped out of streaming clouds into something solid. They were stuck in the solid middle of the winter day" (324). In this tumultuous visit to the house, in which Liza enacts revenge for Ladner's rampages by having one of her own, she, Warren, and we cross into a different world, where regular rules of linearity and causality do not apply. Liza and Warren bring their mutually exclusive pasts into this world, but when they get there they act out parts of narratives to which they do not belong.

When Liza begins her vandalism, she first empties the desk drawers: "she started pulling the drawers all the way out and dumping them and their contents on the floor. She made a funny noise — an admiring cluck of her tongue, as if the drawers had done this on their own" (326). Her first act of revenge is a reenactment of Ladner's technique of making the children feel responsible for their abuse. After raping her,

> he collapsed heavily, like the pelt of an animal flung loose from its flesh and bones. . . .
> He *clucked his tongue* faintly and his eyes shone out of ambush, hard and round as the animals' glass eyes.
> *Bad-bad-bad.* (341–42; first emphasis added)

Now Liza fights back against this monster that he was, but in doing so she trips into a reenactment of *Warren's* past, about which she does not know. Warren has trashed a house before (330), but this time he trips into her past when he attempts to stop her rampage by ignoring it: "He was trying to be like a grownup who won't watch. Ignore her and she'll quit. . . . Warren wouldn't turn. His whole body felt as if it was humming, with the effort to be still and make this be over" (327–28). This description, ironically, makes him not like a grownup but like the young Liza, who tried to control Ladner by ignoring him: when he tried to "grab at her, to get her between the legs[,] . . . Liza pretended not to notice" (337–38). When Liza phones

Bea from the vandalized house, she again takes Ladner's role by mocking her, "setting her lips blubbering as she listened to the voice on the other end of the phone" (331), just as Ladner mocked her behind her back in the pond (336).

This is a world of crossed narratives in which characters unknowingly enact roles from other characters' lives. It is as if the strength of these narratives combined with the dark magic of Ladner's territory is such that the narratives will not disappear and must be reenacted. Even after the rampage is over, Liza plays Ladner's role. She walks down to the forest to see if "the bear was still in there" (344). The bear is Ladner, whom she has just defied in his house and whom she now confronts on his forested territory. She also recuperates the good in Ladner, however, by taking over his instructive narrative and teaching Warren how to identify different trees: "There's a cedar. There's a wild cherry. Down there's birch. The white ones. And that one with the bark like gray skin? That's a beech. See, it had letters carved on it, but they've spread out, they just look like any old blotches now" (344). The letters, P.D.P., are those whose dual significance is mentioned earlier. They point to Ladner's role as an instructor ("proceed down path") and as an abuser ("pull down pants") (338). Because Liza has taken over his role as instructor and defied him as abuser, the letters are blurred. They may "look like any old blotches now" to Liza, but we know what they meant, and they are not entirely erased. The letters are like Bea's lingering sense of Ladner's physical presence in her bed, like a ghost limb (308), or like Dorrie's house in "A Real Life," where walnuts continue to fall each year but go uncounted because Dorrie is no longer there (92). Something continues despite an important absence. Millicent can no more knock down Dorrie's ramshackle house than Bea can burn down Ladner's vandalized house. The physical obstinacy of the houses and the obscured letters parallel a kind of obstinacy of narrative here, a refusal of erasure, despite Liza's misremembering and her misrepresentation of the reason for the vandalism. In the end, I think, Liza does succeed in dispelling the darkness, but for Warren, with night falling, the shadows in the trees, the darkness of their recent vandalism, and the mute, dark space around Liza's reason for it, the darkness is just collecting. His sense of the potential of an imminent danger (rather than one just dispelled) is another of the endless possibilities of narrative.

When characters do bump up against parallel, unerased narratives, they experience a kind of vertigo. In "Carried Away," when her imagination summons Jack, Louisa becomes "dizzy and humiliated" (55):

> She had gone under [a wave] and through it and was left with a cold sheen on her skin, a beating in her ears, a cavity in her chest, and revolt in her stomach. It was anarchy she was up against — a devouring muddle. Sudden holes and impromptu tricks and radiant vanishing consolations. (56)

In "Vandals," though, there are no "radiant . . . consolations" for Liza, whose submergence under waves is an attempt to block out memory, to erase story. Warren notes that,

> when they started to dance, it was Liza who slid under. . . . There was Liza, dancing, and the only thing he could do was wait it out while she tore her way through the music, supplicated and curled around it, kicked loose, and blinded herself to everything around her.
> That's what she's got in her, he felt like saying to them all. (328)

Whereas Louisa experiences vertigo in a process of accessing a narrative that diverged from actual events in her past, Liza wants to forget her past, to blind herself. Like Maureen, she cannot cope with an accurate memory of the past. Blinding herself is a method of self-protection, and "what she's got in her," like Maureen's open secret, never comes out whole.

That so many open secrets in this collection remain unutterable does not point to the limits of language or to the ephemerality of narrative; rather, Munro depicts the often self-imposed limits of knowledge and the vagaries and self-protection of human memory, its inability or reluctance to capture stories whole. Without exception, we know more about each story than do the characters who inhabit it. Even in "The Albanian Virgin," there is the sense that we get a more detailed version of Lottar's story than does Claire, the first-person narrator. Heble writes about Munro that "recovery of the past in her fiction is . . . repeatedly complicated either by the fact of language itself or by signifying practices through which characters are able to suppress or exclude certain areas of meaning" (185). Recovering the past in *Open Secrets*, however, is complicated by intervening narratives, by the intrusion of other plotlines that the characters' memories favour, or by the simple passage of time.

For Maureen in "Open Secrets," the "life ahead of her" (the death of her husband and her remarriage), in which narrative folds over on itself, erases that near realization to which her hallucination points (186). Her memory manages to catch only a corner of the narrative sheet on which her open secret is inscribed, and there is an implicit condoning of that erasure because, unlike Mary Johnstone, Maureen is open to narratives other than her own. Frances comments that the girls almost did not go hiking that day: "Because of the downpour Saturday morning. They were waiting half an hour in the United Church basement and she [Miss Johnstone] says, Oh, it'll stop — my hikes are never rained out! And now I bet she wishes it had've been. Then it would've been a whole other story" (150). Of course, it is a whole other story for Maureen. Her forgetting her vision is condoned because, unlike Mary, she is not so deeply focused on her own narrative that she is closed to other narratives. Mary, though, is depicted as being in multiple narrative ruts, all of which obscure other narrative possibilities. Her annual hikes have become dreaded and predictable, and her "'plain talk' about boys and urges" is mocked (183). Mary also gets into a rut on this last hike when she stubbornly refuses to believe anything but her own explanation for Heather's disappearance: that Heather is simply an attention seeker who needs to be cajoled out of hiding. Her refusal to allow other explanations delays the search for Heather, and it presumably leads to town censure. Mary writes letters to the editor "explaining why she behaved as she did, why in all good sense and good faith she behaved as she did that Sunday" (186). She writes so often, though, again in a rut, that the editor finally has to tell her that "Heather Bell is old news" and that "the story can't be rehashed forever," a callous if necessary remark (186).

I think that we are asked to steer between these two extremes. Both the editor and Mary are wrong: we can neither be too absorbed in our own narratives nor afford to allow tragedies to become stale news. There is a danger that either extreme means missing or devaluing parallel narratives. Maureen, when she hallucinates and when her memory twitches, stands between those extremes, as do we, but we have a much clearer perspective.

Whereas Maureen forgets her hallucinatory vision of parallel narratives almost entirely, Liza in "Vandals" seems to be unable to forget her abuse. I think that a part of Liza is afraid of forgetting it. She is certainly disapproving of what she sees as Bea's ready ability to forgive or forget Ladner's humiliating her: "She had forgiven Ladner, after all, or made a bargain not to remember" (343). Again, this humiliation went on without Bea ever knowing about it, so Liza is encumbered with memories of Bea's humiliation as well as her own. Liza may not forget her abuse, but she misremembers it if she blames Bea. Perhaps this is a result of her inability to cope with the truth or of Ladner's censoring effect on her. Ladner makes the children feel guilty for the abuse, and, in the same way that Maureen cannot tell her open secret, Liza fears telling hers because she would become blameworthy in others' minds. By enunciating her anger in such an indirect way as to blame Bea for sending her to college, Liza is able to vent her anger without revealing or facing its true cause.

Ladner exercises a similar but distinct silencing effect on both Bea and Liza. The silence changes Liza:

Not all the information they had was about dead things. . . . Soon they knew much more. At least Liza did. She knew birds, trees, mushrooms, fossils, the solar system. She knew where certain rocks came from and that the swelling on a goldenrod stem contains a little white worm that can live nowhere else in the world.
She knew not to talk so much about all she knew. (334–35)

As the silenced victim of abuse, Liza sees Ladner as the one who has the power to open secrets, but it is not exercised:

He was imitating Bea. He was doing what she was doing but in a sillier, ugly way. He was most intentionally and insistently making a fool of her. . . .
This was thrilling and shocking. . . . Part of her [Liza] wanted to make Ladner stop, to stop at once, before the damage was done, and part of her longed for that very damage, the damage Ladner could do, the ripping open, the final delight of it. (337)

Liza is afraid because she does not want to lose her fairy godmother, but she wants Ladner to implicate himself so that the ugly truth about him can spill out. Immediately after this passage, Liza swims over to Ladner, but when he grabs her she realizes that she needs to keep Bea around to protect her. Rather than speaking, Liza offers her the fraudulent, compensatory gift of a rhinestone earring (342). The gift fails to keep Bea in her role as protector, however, and Liza eventually goes away to college and meets Warren, becoming what Bea calls a born-again Christian, symbolically a new person: "She never drank alcohol now, she never even ate sugar. . . . She did the laundry every Wednesday night and counted the strokes when she brushed her teeth and got up early in the morning to do knee bends and read Bible verses" (323). Munro states in her interview with Eleanor Wachtel that

> It's not uncommon now to go from . . . being one sort of person to being an entirely different kind of person. So you've got all these rooms in your head that you've shut off but that you can remember. I think some people don't really bother much with remembering; it seems a useless activity. But most writers are addicted to it. I suppose I am, too. ("Alice Munro" 110)

The characters in *Open Secrets* are unable to remember correctly, and Munro makes bothering to remember our addiction and responsibility. Liza cannot remember correctly because Ladner imposed silences on her that now limit her ability to do so. What makes this story real is that Liza misremembers; remembering would be too painful.

With Bea, Ladner's own silences silence her. When she looks back on their relationship, she sees her second visit to his property as their "real beginning" (320):

> She had a couple of friends then, to whom she wrote and actually sent letters that tried to investigate and explain this turn in her life. She wrote that she would hate to think she had gone after Ladner because he was rude and testy and slightly savage, with the splotch on the side of his face that shone like metal in the sunlight coming through the trees. She would hate to think so, because wasn't that the way in all the dreary romances — some brute gets the woman tingling and then it's goodbye to Mr. Fine-and-Decent? (313–14)

It is exactly Ladner's turning out to be that hard-hearted brute that silences Bea: "Now she wrote letters only in her head" (315). For the remainder of the text, the italicized passages are her unsent letters. She writes letters only in her head because she finds that the dreary romance is more than a cliché: it is humiliating. Like Maureen's, her sexual needs are ignored by a man who wants to control when and how they have sex, and she is humiliated by her pitiful, lustful wants (315):

It seemed that she had to be cured of all her froth and vanity and all her old notions of love.

One night I got into his bed and he did not take his eyes from his book or move or speak a word to me even when I crawled out and returned to my own bed, where I fell asleep almost at once because I think I could not bear the shame of being awake. In the morning he got into my bed and all went as usual. (320–21)

Bea is the extreme and ultimately silenced version of many women in this collection. Their narratives are romantic plots of not-quite-requited love, which makes them feel chastised for their notions of love and even of themselves. Like Claire in "The Albanian Virgin" ("I did not want him to think that I drew some sort of comfort from this mishmash of love and despair and treachery and self-dramatizing" [130]) and Gail in "The Jack Randa Hotel" ("Was she a person who believed that somebody had to have the upper hand?" [194]), Bea in "Vandals" does not want to believe that she is attracted to the "brute" in the "dreary romances," but they all are. Her love for Ladner closes her into his world, and it ultimately cuts off all her communication with the outside world as she goes into an uncommunicative decline after his death. His death freezes the silences that Bea and Liza have maintained, and they must move laterally, skirting the silences, in order to move ahead. Both move in destructive ways, Bea drinking, Liza vandalizing, but Liza does triumph in the end. She does dispel the darkness around her.

Lamont-Stewart notes that Munro's protagonists are frequently humiliated by their inability to understand and control their lives (114). With *Open Secrets*, though, I think that many of the women are humiliated by the impact that love has on them. None of the characters experiences a love that is "easy or restful" (336). Love is invariably accompanied by darkness, pain, humiliation, or the threat of danger. Like Gail in "The Jack Randa Hotel," the women's love for their partners becomes "all that could pain or appease . . . [them], in the world" (210). Like Louisa, Bea seems to see love as a humbling process. In "Carried Away," Louisa puts Jack's failure to make contact with her down to her own failing: "what was it in my case but vanity, which deserves to be slapped down!" (18–19). Louisa also has a hauntingly similar sensation that accompanies the first hint of romance: "She would have said love was all hocus-pocus, a deception, and she believed that. But at the prospect she still felt a hush, a flutter along the nerves, a bowing down of sense, a flagrant prostration" (8).

I have struggled to determine why so many of the women in *Open Secrets* do prostrate themselves to love, why Munro seems to insist on showing us that love is not a frothy notion. It is much more than her giving us an accurate anatomy of love. Again, the answer that I found has to do with narrative and with her writing process. I do not see Munro's anatomy of love as a lesson to women about the dangers of becoming absorbed in fictional romantic plots. Munro herself points away from this danger. The doctor in "A Wilderness Station" diagnoses a "delusion peculiar to females":

> They may imagine themselves possessed by the forces of evil, to have committed various and hideous crimes, and so forth. Sometimes they may report that they have taken numerous lovers, but these lovers will be all imaginary and the woman who thinks herself a prodigy of vice will in fact be quite chaste and untouched. For all this he — the doctor — lays the blame on the sort of reading that is available to these females. . . . (239–40)

We know this not to have been the case in Annie's madness, and in "Carried Away" even Louisa, who surrenders to a romantic narrative in which Jack comes back to thank her for her influence on his successful political life, has the right outlook on the rhetoric of romance. The parallel Jack says that "'Love never dies.' She felt impatient to the point of taking offence. This is what all the speech-making turns you into, she thought, a person who can say things like that. Love dies all the time, or at any rate it becomes distracted, overlaid — it might as well be dead" (54). Ironically, the very character in her romantic daydream iterates the cliché that she rejects.

I think that the nature of these women's love is analogous to Munro's relationship to fiction. In her interview with McCulloch and Simpson, Munro described writing as a kind of romance: "It's sort of like a love affair" ("Alice Munro" 239): "It's something I never would have been able to think of losing twenty years ago: the faith, the desire. . . . The vigilance has to be there all the time" (262). Munro remains ever vigilant in her writing, ever afraid of forgetting why she does it:

> these days I'm a little panicked at the idea of stopping — as if, if I stopped, I could be stopped for good. . . . There's a kind of

excitement and faith that I can't work without. There was a time when I never lost that, when it was just inexhaustible. . . . This may be the beast that's lurking in the closet in old age — the loss of the feeling that things are worth doing. (261–62)

Munro herself has a not-quite-requited love with fiction and memory. She romances narrative (she puts the romance of unrequited love in her fiction and courts fiction), assiduously striving for identity with the story "out there" that somehow spurns her attempts to capture it completely: "Every final draft, every published story, is still only an attempt, an approach to the story" ("What Is Real?" 826).

Her courting fiction also accounts for why Munro writes dark stories, darkness implying both shaded, inarticulated patches and cheerlessness:

[One] of the questions most frequently asked . . . is, "Why do you write about things that are so depressing?" . . . I don't do it to show anything. I put this story at the heart of my story because I need it there and it belongs there. It is the black room at the centre of the house with all the other rooms leading to and away from it. That is all. A strange defence. ("What Is Real?" 826–27)

Munro has no choice but to put ingredients into the story or the collection in the places that they themselves demand; as she mentioned to Gzowski, she knows that the story "needs something," and, even though that something is unpleasant, she reserves the right to include it (interview).

The darkness collecting throughout *Open Secrets* is similar to the theory about the Dark Ages that Cleata in "The Jack Randa Hotel" gleans from reading *The Anglo-Saxon Chronicle*:

She said that the reason the Dark Ages were dark was not that we couldn't learn anything about them but that we could not remember anything we did learn, and that was because of the names.

"Caedwalla," she said. "Egfrith. These are just not names on the tip of your tongue anymore." (191)

The characters' open secrets are not on the tips of their tongues in this collection but buried deep beneath narrative layers. Explanation, enunciation, is sometimes beside the point. Munro states:

I feel that all life becomes even *more* mysterious and difficult. And the whole act of writing is more an attempt at recognition than of understanding, because I don't understand many things. I feel a kind of satisfaction in just approaching something that is mysterious and important. Then writing is the art of approach and recognition. I believe that we don't solve these things — in fact our explanations take us farther away. (qtd. in Thacker 54)

The mute spaces in the collection, the unarticulated layers, the uncut gatherings, the unspoken secrets — all remain darkened so that we may approximate Munro's sense of her work, that it is mysterious and difficult. The dark powers of magic, romance, memory, and writing are linked. Munro's own open secret is that, although these are lovely things in their pure, well-lit forms, they become seductive and dangerous when they are turned into the more complex, less lit versions of themselves. It is a secret that many people know, but few are willing to acknowledge it. By ending the collection with the image of darkness collecting, Munro requires us to examine that open secret.

I have struggled to find a metaphor that describes the narrative threads in this collection (threads of wool, palimpsest, folded paper — all inadequate), but its resistance to being reduced to a metaphor attests to its brilliance. W.R. Martin writes that the objects named in the titles of Munro's stories in *The Moons of Jupiter*, such as dulse, stone, and moons, "contain meanings that defy complete definition: they name objects that are symbols" (131). In *Open Secrets*, the opposite is true. Symbols themselves are inadequate to capture the meanings of the stories, but "darkness collecting" is an abstract image that represents the collection and a stunningly articulated image with which to end it.

WORKS CITED

Carrington, Ildikó de Papp. "Talking Dirty: Alice Munro's 'Open Secrets' and John Steinbeck's *Of Mice and Men*." *Studies in Short Fiction* 31 (1994): 595–606.

___. "What's in a Title? Alice Munro's 'Carried Away.'" *Studies in Short Fiction* 30 (1993): 555–64.

Heble, Ajay. *The Tumble of Reason: Alice Munro's Discourse of Absence*. Toronto: U of Toronto P, 1994.

Lamont-Stewart, Linda. "Order from Chaos: Writing as Self-Defense in the

Fiction of Alice Munro and Clark Blaise." *The Art of Alice Munro*. Ed. Judith Miller. Waterloo: U of Waterloo P, 1984. 113–21.

Martin, W.R. *Alice Munro: Paradox and Parallel*. Edmonton: U of Alberta P, 1987.

Mayberry, Katherine J. "'Every Last Thing . . . Everlasting': Alice Munro and the Limits of Narrative." *Studies in Short Fiction* 29 (1992): 531–41.

Munro, Alice. "Alice Munro." Interview with Eleanor Wachtel. *Writers and Company*. Toronto: Knopf, 1993. 101–12.

___. "Alice Munro: The Art of Fiction CXXXVII." Interview with Jeanne McCulloch and Mona Simpson. *Paris Review* 131 (1994): 226–64.

___. "Author's Commentary." *Sixteen by Twelve: Short Stories by Canadian Writers*. Ed. John Metcalf. Toronto: Ryerson, 1970. 125–26.

___. Interview with Peter Gzowski. *Morningside*. CBC Radio, 30 Sept. 1994.

___. *Open Secrets*. 1994. Toronto: Penguin, 1995.

___. "What Is Real?" *The Art of Short Fiction*. Ed. Gary Geddes. Toronto: Harper-Collins, 1993. 824–27.

Thacker, Robert. "'Clear Jelly': Alice Munro's Narrative Dialectics." *Probable Fictions: Alice Munro's Narrative Acts*. Ed. Louis K. MacKendrick. Downsview, ON: ECW, 1983. 37–60.

"A Dark Sort of Mirror": "The Love of a Good Woman" as Pauline Poetic

DENNIS DUFFY

Poetic: [a.] and [sb.] 2. sing. and pl. That part of literary criticism which treats of poetry; also, a treatise on poetry: applied esp. to that of Aristotle. Also in extended senses.

— *Oxford English Dictionary*

The sudden switch from sex to murder to marital cooperation seemed to me one of those marvelous, unlikely, acrobatic pieces of human behaviour.

— Alice Munro, "Contributors' Notes" (443)

[S]o the story falls apart.

— Alice Munro, "Changing Places"

"THE LOVE OF A GOOD WOMAN" is now the title story of Alice Munro's latest collection (1998; 3–78). From its first appearance in the *New Yorker* (23 and 30 December 1996) with the subtitle "A Murder, a Mystery, a Romance," it seemed to be one of her richest works.[1] It struck me then as something more as well: a pivotal work in the structure of her fiction, and the capstone of the temporal arch that her narrative arc has been spanning over the history of Sowesto (a popular term for *South*western Ontario). At least since the appearance of "The Moon in the Orange Street Skating Rink" (*Progress*), and moving on to stories such as "Meneseteung" (*Friend*) and "A Wilderness Station" (*Open Secrets*), Munro's fiction has exploited material remote in time in addition to material that could conceivably appear experiential. Accounts of roughly contemporary experience, such as "The Moons of Jupiter" and "The Progress of Love" (to mention but two tales that entitled collections), no longer furnished the typical time frame for a Munro fiction.

The period shortly before the death of Robert Laidlaw, Munro's father, in 1976 — the temporal setting for "The Moons of Jupiter"

— saw him revising an earlier draft of *The McGregors: A Novel of an Ontario Pioneer Family*. This loosely knit sequence of pioneer narratives — set within an era that he himself never experienced — appeared posthumously in 1979 (Ross 79–80). Before seven years had passed, Munro was following in his footsteps. The recent electronic publication of Laidlaw's memoir of 1912 (written in 1975) — an account of two boys frightened and disoriented by coming across a gas bubble while exploring a swamp — fits the new footprint even more closely into the old, for the memoir concludes with a reflection upon the visionary quality of the experience. The narrator acknowledges the power of the gothic staples of fright and awe to fuse a new view of experience: "It seemed to me that there could be things existing perhaps not in our world but along side it." That is, the father's memoir seems to fit what I describe below as a poetic: an account of experience that redefines the nature of experience itself. "The Love of a Good Woman," the daughter's pivotal fiction, concludes with a mysterious, near-visionary moment along the tangled banks of a river. Like the heroine in "Walker Brothers Cowboy," the opening story of her first collection, Munro has been about her father's business.

The 1951 setting of "The Love of a Good Woman" comes from Munro's own time, the year following her first appearance in print as a fiction writer, the year when Alice Laidlaw married James Munro. As Professor Robert Thacker pointed out to me, Jeanette Quinn, one of the major characters, dies on Alice Munro's birthday (10 July). In a brief commentary on the story, Munro uses the actual name for the river in the story (Maitland) rather than her own designation, "Peregrine" (Sir Peregrine Maitland governed Upper Canada from 1818 to 1828). Yet she transferred the incident that triggered the story from its British Columbia location to a Sowesto setting, taking care to omit the ponderously symbolic location (Desolation Sound) because it seemed "a bit too much for a story" ("Contributors' Notes" 443). She would, however, employ Desolation Sound as a remote location in the story "Cortes Island" (*Love* 117–45). Whatever the year's personal significance, however slippery the edge between history and imagination, the time in which the story is set adds another piece to the puzzle, developing a northern Yoknapatawpha, a fictional world bearing a considerable resemblance to the historical world, whether experienced actually or vicariously.

As is often the case with Munro, this project of regional reimagining can be tricky. Del Jordan in *Lives of Girls and Women* imaginatively awakens when she dismisses the opportunity to grind out a local antiquarian miscellany. An early passage in "Something I've Been Meaning to Tell You" skewers the tourism-driven local lore — instant ruins and buried treasure — that communities generate and exploit (*Something* 1–2). Rose concludes "Royal Beatings" with a Flo-like mockery of Hat Nettleton's old-timer anecdotage and a metropolitan broadcaster's showcasing of it (*Who* 21–22). Munro emphatically distances her own observations from those of local history and tourism marketing, enterprises recalling Wade's fake fort in Jack Hodgins's *The Invention of the World*. Yet Munro's oeuvre imaginatively corrals a fair portion of the historical time frame of the Sowesto region that she has made her own.

However significant the role of "The Love of a Good Woman" in supplying that broad coverage, my chief interest is in a complementary function of the story: its role as what I call a *poetic*, a piece of writing about the kind of writing that the author has been engaged in over a period of time.[2] A number of Romantic examples of this subgenre, this "extended" meaning of the OED definition quoted above, spring to mind: Wordsworth's "Michael," Shelley's "Mont Blanc," Keats's "Ode on a Grecian Urn." In English Canadian literature, Rudy Wiebe's "The Naming of Albert Johnson" (1974) and Robert Kroetsch's *Seed Catalogue* (1977) go beyond the telling of their own stories. They seem to speak also of the kind of representation, the kind of artifact, that their authors characteristically produce. Writers within a classical tradition produce an explicit *ars poetica* (Horace's poem of that title, Milton's "Lycidas," Pope's "Essay on Criticism"); later writers offer works that resonate within an entire oeuvre. "This," we say in hindsight, "*this* is where the writer has been headed all along." The term "poetic" helps to define and justify our response to what we see as a touchstone work.

Modernists and postmodernists can always play the metafictional card as a means of underlining the role that a project plays in their work, but Munro's use of the metafictional has often been troubled. For example, "The Ottawa Valley" concludes *Something I've Been Meaning to Tell You*, published in 1974. Its well-known final paragraph, typographically distanced from the rest of the story, implicitly disclaims omniscient authorial control over the material, a caveat that we now understand as a typical gesture of metafictional writers. The same year saw the appearance of the uncollected "Home," which uses metafictional interventions to display the author's unease with the moral aspects of her rapportage. Yet five years later Munro excluded the writerly Janet stories from *Who Do You Think You Are?* at the last minute, later explaining that this metafictional venture seemed "just too fancy" (qtd. in Ross 82). Helen Hoy's impressive article on the rewriting of the collection that later emerged as *Who Do You Think You Are?* indicates just how wary Munro is of *overt* metafictional devices, and how cautious she is in the face of a threat to her "aesthetic of indirection" ("Rose" 78–79). However ambivalent her attitude toward the metafictional, Munro has also recently gone about constructing her own canon, as the inclusions and arrangements of her 1996 *Selected Stories* indicate.[3]

"The Love of a Good Woman"'s claims to be a representative or keystone text involve its many parallels — both thematically and stylistically — to other texts within the Munro oeuvre and upon its summative handling of desire and the body.[4] A cull of the story's echoes of motifs, characters, and images from her earlier work reveals a few of the numerous ways in which this piece forms a coda to her fiction.

- Death by drowning, and the associations between immersion and sexuality, have occurred, variously, in "Baptizing" (*Lives*), "Walking on Water" (*Something*), and "Miles City, Montana" (*Progress*), a motif more fully discussed by Ildikó de Papp Carrington (see *Controlling* 211–13, 215–16; and "Don't Tell").

- The man with the hatchet who ends this story appeared long ago in "Images" (*Dance*).

- The complicit joint reading of written texts by Enid and Rupert recalls a similar exercise by Rose and Ralph Gillespie in the title story of *Who Do You Think You Are?* (see 189–95).

- Jeanette's savage cynicism, as it claws away at Enid's innocence during the deathbed revelation, recalls similar processes throughout *Who Do You Think You Are?*, especially the bizarre instance of Flo's accuracy in predicting Rose's sexual molestation in "Wild Swans" (55–56).

- Most importantly, the ritual, surreal, profound ambiguity of domestic violence caught so memorably in "Royal Beatings" — "That is not to say he is pretending, that he is acting, and does not mean it. He is acting, and he means it" (*Who* 16) — is echoed in "The Love of a Good Woman": "Then if Cece looked back at him . . . his father was apt to start showing his teeth and acting like a dog. It would have been ridiculous — it was ridiculous — except that he meant business" (*Love* 16; NY 110).

Carrington demonstrates that if Nietzsche's philosophy speaks of an eternal return, then Munro's fiction revels in it (*Controlling* 4–11, 71–98). Since no motif remains beached in a single Munro story, what is special about "The Love of a Good Woman"? Consider the use of two complicit readers in *Who* with that in "Love." The first instance permeates the remainder of a story and the rest of the collection, while the second develops a formal equivalent to the process of bonding that the passage depicts, as if Munro has abandoned statement for drama.

Rose and Ralph in "Who Do You Think You Are?" close the first sinister circle of interpretation when they share a schoolkids' giggle: Ralph substitutes "Milton" for the penultimate name in the title of Keats's "On First Looking into Chapman's Homer." He thus invokes the name of the town idiot, Milton Homer, who supposedly delights in exposing himself in movie queues. His very mention is always good for a laugh in Hanratty, Ontario, as is the idea of "looking into" the coat that he opens up to reveal his member. We readers widen the circle of complicity when we recognize the send-up of high culture in the association of two major epic poets — Milton and Homer — with this classroom nonsense. The mockery also twits Rose's classroom teacher, Milton Homer's aunt, who represents that high cultural tradition; she flings Rose the question that furnishes the title of both the story and the collection. Miss Hattie Milton herself recalls another cultural priestess whom Rose exploits and mocks: Dr. Henshawe of "The Beggar Maid."

Yet even as we relax into the smugness of witnessing cultural destruction (the sort of satisfaction that comes from watching Groucho abuse the Margaret Dupont character), a further complexity emerges. Rose and Ralph are accomplished mimics: she goes on to become an actress, and he a kind of grown-up class clown whose miming of Milton Homer becomes a party trick. The flasher himself was a mimic; his unauthorized appearances at Orange Day parades and at christenings included a large dollop of mimicry/mockery of the attendant solemnities. Interestingly, his participation in both sacred and secular rites became legitimated, even solemnized, like the incorporation of the Feast of Fools within the mediaeval Christian liturgy. Milton Homer is a carnivalesque deflator of our ceremonial existence; he is Lear's Fool to the town of Hanratty.

Rose and Ralph then seem no longer distant from the Milton Homer whom they mock. Ralph's party trick palls, as newcomers no longer realize whom Ralph imitates. The mocker himself is mocked. His fate is melancholy: he dies a pathetic, crippled drunkard when he mistakes one door for another and tumbles down a set of basement stairs at the legion hall. Rose, who comes across his fatal fall in a chance perusal of the local news sheet, reacts with shocked self-recognition rather than distanced observation: "What could she say about herself and Ralph Gillespie, except that she felt his life, close, closer than the lives of men she's loved, one slot over from her own?" (*Who* 206).

Rose, that bright but sloppy student, has finally mastered the lesson that Ralph's mastery of Milton Homer's manners teaches: nobody is exempt from mockery. Ralph then becomes one of a demonic trinity of mockers in Rose's life. In "Wild Swans," the possibly false clergyman, another mimic, who fingers Rose on the train, extends his partly welcome presence to all her subsequent sexual encounters (*Who* 63–64). In "The Begger Maid," her ex-husband, Patrick, who freezes her when he makes a horrid face at her during a chance airport encounter, is the last of the demon lovers/mockers (*Who* 96–97). Both "Wild Swans" and "The Beggar Maid" conclude with acts of mimicry: the first story with the recounting of the anecdote of Flo's friend Mavis, who poses as a film actress; the second with the face that Patrick makes, "the sudden, hallucinatory appearance of your true enemy" (*Who* 100). This unholy trinity in turn recalls the progenitor of them all, the contested father whom the women in his life bully into his kingly role in "Royal Beatings," who fuses acting with meaning it, who mocks the townsfolk when they confuse the planet Venus with the mimicry of it by a purported American dirigible (*Who* 20).

Paolo and Francesca lapse into adultery when they peruse a set of romances (Alighieri, Canto V, ll. 89–142). The altered school reader gives Rose and Ralph their first contact with a node of parody that conducts them to the rest of their experiences recounted in *Who Do You Think You Are?*. Enid and Rupert in "The Love of a Good Woman" read/recount the contents of a newspaper in a passage that first registers the sexual charge between them. Too lengthy for detailed discussion, the scene is set within the most hackneyed of domestic situations: one partner reading and commenting aloud on a newspaper to the other (*Love* 44–49; NY 124–26). One association leads to another in the structuring of this moment. Rupert brings a new fan for the sickroom along with a newspaper for Enid; the front page mentions the heat wave; their whispered conversation (so as not to disturb the patient) reminds her of similar soft-spoken chats in high school. She initiated those asides to Rupert back then in her wish to palliate her and her friends' merciless teasing of the awkward boy. The pair exchanged information, the kind of random facts taught at school that also appear in a newspaper. Our culture calls it "general knowledge." The reverie is interrupted by another look at the newspaper in present time, a look that also involves assembling random facts: Enid begins the crossword puzzle. Again she recalls high school, this time at a later stage: "What kind of life did they think they were preparing for? What kind of people did they think they were going to be?" (*Love* 48; NY 125–26). Then more random facts appear. This time they originate in a high-school history text. As Enid ponders the forgotten meaning of the Edict of Nantes, the crossword intrudes. Rupert supplies her with "cassava," the seven-letter word for "Bread of the Amazon" (*Love* 48; NY 126).

Recurrence drives the passage. Back and forth the couple volley their command of general knowledge in an approach to carnal knowledge. Enid guesses the first crossword clue, Rupert the second. Her classroom asides to him were a pendulum swing from her public teasing. She fixes him a cup of tea in the knowledge that his "not to bother . . . might as well be yes in country speech" (*Love* 48; NY 125). We know what is happening in the present: they are domesticating their relationship. They are now the old married couple, with the wife in her sickroom the excluded third. A few pages later, we find Rupert watching Enid admiringly as she maintains the orderliness of her two notebooks. The first resembles a ship's log: "a record of what was eaten, vomited, excreted"; the other holds "many of the same things, though perhaps not so exactly" (*Love* 55; NY 128). Rupert is "pleased" when Enid writes down something that one of his daughters has said (*Love* 55; NY 128). The pair are writing themselves into romance, and Enid's books are no less the work of panders than those that Paolo and Francesca read together. This habitualization progresses obliquely, through shifts and seemingly random recurrences. Yet these banal actions are part of the forging of their new identities in answer to the existential questions that I have cited. What kind of people are they going to be? They are going to be people who perform "marvelous, unlikely, acrobatic pieces of human behavior." They have come together as part of a random assemblage: she happens to be a practical nurse, he happens to have a dying wife, they happen to have attended the same school. Their present situation has resulted from a series of accidents, just like the museum's accession of the case of medical instruments whose cataloguing opens the story.

Even so, coherent histories of the world can emerge from connecting the dots formed by random facts: matching the Tyrrhenian Sea (one of those earlier recollections) with the Edict of Nantes presents a set of European historical and geographical references that can be imposed upon a grid. If, as a character in an earlier, uncollected story notes, there is a "landscape under the one you see. . . . The lakes and shores we map and name but never saw," then the map of Europe sits atop the chart for an erotic voyage ("Characters" 73). Unless the voyage at the story's end leads to death. What is this overlay of erotic interest with displays of geographical/historical trivia but another moment in a chain of accidents that began when Enid sat in the school desk in front of an awkward boy whose sexuality she viewed nervously? Now she sits beside Rupert, but she is still nervous about his sexuality. The boat, Munro tells us, still waits by the bank of the Maitland River ("Contributors' Notes" 443). Ripeness is all. Experience is incremental. Fate, like Oedipus, takes small steps.

Inside the cover of Enid's history text that dealt with the Edict of Nantes "were written all the names of the previous owners, some of whom were middle-aged housewives or merchants around the town," boys and girls thrust into adult habits of authority (*Love* 48; NY 125). These boys are new versions of the inflated boys whose later masculine authority Rose views with wonder and disbelief in "Who Do You Think You Are?" (*Who* 204). The density of that earlier story's scene of complicit reading springs from the confluence of associations and the recurrence of events and topoi. The density of the complicit reading in "The Love of a Good Woman," on the other hand, is a matter of establishing through narrative shift a formal equivalent to emotional valence. The couple whet their mutual interest and curiosity through a mimicry of domestic ritual, not through a passionate encounter. This domesticity contrasts sharply with the gothic expectations and suspense at the end of the story. The gothic leaps to an inevitable climax; the quotidian plods and meanders to a similar conjunction: Enid and Rupert begin cohabiting.

From this brief survey of two instances of readerly complicity, let us shift our attention to a second strategy that underpins this story, one that also parallels earlier Munro usages: that jaggedness of experience caught in Cece's terrorized response to his father's absurd antics. The paradoxical nature of experience, a familiar Munro motif, emerges through three incidents: the equivocality of the story's ending, the puzzling nature of its opening (both of these are matters of content), and the role assigned to the three boys who discover the drowned optometrist (this last a matter of narrative structure).

"In my end is my beginning" could serve as the story's epigraph. Judith McCombs pointed out to me in conversation that the story's opening presents the most useful clue for answering the riddle of its conclusion. Whatever we make of the ending, and of Jeanette's account of the death of Willens, we lack certainty about the fate of the imperilled gothic heroine Enid. A man who has every reason for wishing her mute approaches her in a secluded spot along a river. He carries a hatchet. They are about to embark in a rowboat. Surely something is at hand. We have seen the asexual Enid getting hooked on this man, whose unwashed odour, "the smell of a body so distinctly not in her power or under her care," has placed a "welcome" hold on her. The stink is "something new and invasive" (*Love* 77; NY 140–41), recalling the invasion and welcome with which the United Church minister initiates Rose in "Wild Swans." Curiosity rather than lust, the narrator of "Wild Swans" tells us, the itch *"To see what will happen"* leads Rose to her role as "[v]ictim and accomplice" (*Who* 62–63).

Enid is curious about Rupert: "She hadn't asked him yet, she hadn't spoken" (*Love* 75; NY 140). So the boat's "slight and secretive motion" rocks her into a state resembling sexual reverie that makes her "feel as if everything for a long way around had gone quiet" (*Love* 78; NY 141). What revelation is at hand? We are never told the nature of the rough beast who has come slouching toward Enid. Sexuality and death are not that dissimilar in their hold over her. She comes, after all, from a Christian society. Her culture licenses her involvement with death; its folklore whispers pruriently of a nurse's preoccupation with sex. Her father sexualizes her job when he warns her of the window that it offers into intimate matters, "the familiarity nurses had with men's bodies" (*Love* 40; NY 121). If men's bodies reek of sex, then women's (in the person of Jeanette Quinn) reek of death. The Pauline duality prevails even as bizarre parallels emerge: Willens was Jeanette's sexual partner; he was Enid's bridge partner.

Both sex and death are bathed in falsehood. Having once spied her father sucking at the breast of one of his clients, Enid now realizes that her mother's abrupt dismissal of the childish account of the scene was another in a series of lies. When Enid was a child, she spoke as a child. Now that she has put away childish things, she has become a nurse. Was her father nursing when she spotted him with the woman? By becoming a nurse, Enid thwarts her father's will. By becoming a nurse, she replicates his parody of nursing.[5] What engine of fate then drives her to Rupert? Is she his mother, his nurse, or her own father? Is she an Atwood heroine about to marry the hangman? Is she giving herself to Bluebeard? What's the difference anyway?

To this welter of questions, add the uncertainty over Enid's final lot. The opening of the story, its detailed, sensuous description of the tools of D.M. Willens, may imply her fate. Somebody has donated those tools to the Walley museum. Would Rupert have done so on his own, risking an explanation of how those objects came his way? Might not Enid have done so, as part of a housecleaning after Rupert's death? After all, she has noticed from the beginning how desperately the house needs a cleaning, just as she will later discover what she notes at this time: the reason behind that sloppy brown paint job on the front-room floor (*Love* 53, 61; NY 127, 132). Her disgust with Jeanette and the story of the killing may lead her to withhold compassion and comfort from the dying woman. It does not stop Enid from bathing the girls then. She is nothing if not tidy, and tidiness is power. A glance at a messy shed leads her to resolve to "make this house" without "secrets from her and [a place] where all order was as she had decreed" (*Love* 77; NY 140). Of course she will eventually donate the box of instruments to the museum! That is, assuming that Rupert dies before she does, that he does not kill her at the river, and that she does not actualize her fantasy of turning him in after turning him on. Does the title indicate that the killer Rupert is redeemed, in Harlequin Romance fashion, by "the love of a good woman"? Shortly after fantasizing about handing Rupert over to the law, Enid wonders if the dead Jeanette told the truth about the killing of Willens. Is anybody telling the truth here?[6] Can anybody be trusted? Can any *body* be trusted? Will we ever find out the provenance of those visionary tools? What can they help us to see?

"So the story falls apart" (Munro, "Changing Places")? Or does it hint at "the landscape under the one you see," "the one that nobody ever saw" (Munro, "Characters" 73)? How appropriate, in view of what Hoy has seen as a metaphysic of Munro's fictional world ("Dull"), to frame in supposition a story such as "The Love of a Good Woman"! It might seem ridiculous — it is ridiculous — except that it means business.

That phrase — describing Cece Ferns's menacing of his namesake son — plunges us into another curious aspect of the story: the attention paid to the home lives of the three boys who find Willens's waterlogged body. We are told far more about their lives at home than the plot demands. Their mechanical function is to spy the drowned body, play a prank on one of Walley's dim elders, and disappear. Yet *Fifth Business* has accustomed us to the possible reverberations of events involving three small-town boys.[7] The boys, their discovery, the account of their homes: they add up to more than a third of the story. Yet we never meet Cece Ferns, Bud Salter, or Jimmy Box again. Why?

Perhaps they are there as a result of the author's imaginative richness. Munro's stories often resemble add-water-and-stir novels. They condense a wealth of implication and detail within a minute space that a lesser writer inflates into a novel. Her motifs, like small stones thrown with great force, spread out to lap the whole pond. Consider, for example, the Romantic nomenclature of "The Albanian Virgin" in *Open Secrets*. The narrator's thesis subject is Mary Shelley's later novels; the narrator bears the first name of Claire Clairmont, a mistress who bore Lord Byron a child who later died. Claire breaks up an earlier union to marry Nelson, whose first name is the surname of the admiral who was the Romantic era's most heroic public adulterer. Claire Clairmont changed her name from Jane; the virgin switches genders to avoid forced marriage, and her original name of Charlotte becomes Lottar while in Albania. The feral sexuality of the former priest Gjurdhi, who falls for the virgin, magnetizes Claire. His name is a form of George, Byron's first name; Byron's omnivorous sexual appetite was a byword in his own day. Finally, one of the best-known of the many portraits of Byron shows him in Albanian dress. It graces the cover of the Penguin *Byron: Selected Prose*. Albania and its affairs occupied his life and art alike, though he was never an Albanian virgin. Surely we can read this Romantic motif as a significant subtext, but many readers may choose to ignore it. Could the tale of the three boys provide an instance of a similar authorial exuberance?

Munro offers a second reason for the boys' inclusion when she comments that the boys got into the story even before her insistent heroine took it over ("Contributors' Notes" 443). That may explain how the boys got there, but what led her to keep them and their homes there? The prominence given to the boys despite their abrupt exit — along with Munro's comment — provokes the suspicion that the current story may be the product of the splicing of two earlier ones. If this is so, then the splicing is seamless. As in *King Lear*, with its mysteriously exiting Fool, plot and subplot cohere around a set of thematic and symbolic concerns.

The boys' stories first offer three versions of family: Cece Ferns is the abused child of a violent, alcoholic, ne'er-do-well father and a passive, hypochondriac mother. He will never escape Walley or his proletarian origins. Jimmy Box lives in an impoverished, overcrowded household maintained by a crippled father and an industrious mother (whose public display of affection embarrasses Jimmy), a household marked by kindness, forbearance, optimism, and mutual support. Bud Salter plays bratty little brother to a pair of spoiled, termagant sisters. His mother cannot control them; his father can only bellow in the style of Archie Andrews's father. Each of these families, unhappy in its own fashion, foreshadows the two unhappy families — the Quinns and Enid's — to come.

All three boys pay close attention to bodies. Cece must defend himself against his father's assaults, while his mother takes refuge in illness in a manner that parodies the act of nursing, "*cradling* a pain" as she prepares a greasy dish of stodge (*Love* 15; NY 108; emphasis added). The crippling of Jimmy's father by polio determines his family's economic status. Because his father can do no more than run a bike shop, the family lives with relatives, his mother works in Honeker's department store, and family members shrink themselves and their personalities in order to fit into the crowded quarters. Bud's face has been marked by the claws of one of his sisters; Bud squelches the other's teasing with a jeer about a menstrual disaster that she suffered.

The boys endure a subordination to all grown-ups, relatives or strangers, that might seem incredible to anyone who did not grow up at the time when this story is set. Because they are unwilling to run the gauntlet of interrogation, and possible blame, that their discovery of the drowned body will provoke, the boys tell their story to a deaf town watchman (*Love* 27; NY 116).[8] When Captain Tervitt finally gets around to inserting his hearing aid in order to understand their story, they scream at him that his fly is open and run away. "The jolt of freedom, the joy of outrage, the uttermost trespass": thus does the narrator catalogue their emotions (NY 117). Munro omits these phrases from the later version. Could they also describe the emotions of anyone relating a story with a trick ending, a story containing a rather devastating picture of "family values"? Those feelings — the triumph of sticking out your tongue at a teacher and *getting away with it* — certainly match Rose's in her toying with sexuality in "Wild Swans." Could such feelings also explain Enid's attraction to a presumed killer?

What are those boys finally up to in "The Love of a Good Woman"? Any number of things.

- They perform a diminutive parody — a Canadian version — of canonical works such as Poe's "The Imp of the Perverse," Diderot's *Rameau's Nephew*, and Dostoyevsky's *Notes from Underground*, studies of the sheer joy that transgression within a repressive society entails. Rupert's killing of the optometrist, Jeanette's outrageous couplings with him, Enid's possible union with a killer: what are these actions but the sort of joyously annihilating gestures that mark Flo's speech throughout *Who Do You Think You Are?* or the sort of savage mockery that Rose's ex flips her way at the end of "The Beggar Maid"?

- They intensify the portrait of a hierarchical society, a pecking order headed by mature males, descending to married females, to old men, to children, all held beneath a vow of silence and denial. Call it "open secrets." The boys fear telling the grown-ups of their discovery; Enid denies what she witnessed between her father and his client. We never quite discover the inner meaning of this closed secret that begins and ends the story. Everything stays in its ordered place, even the reader.

- They figure forth in their swiftly but tellingly described home lives the sense of an ornately conceived, meticulously realized social structure that is ever ready to spill over the story's frame. If the narrator only wanted to, what tales she could tell. "And there are also many other things which Jesus did, the which, if they should be written every one, I suppose that even the world itself could not contain the books that should be written" (John 21.25, KJV).

Here ends the Gospel of John. Is that the kind of book, bigger than the world, that Alice Munro wants to write? Is that the something that she has been meaning to tell us? "And no list could hold what I wanted, for what I wanted was every last thing, every layer of speech and thought, stroke of light on bark or walls, every smell, pothole, pain, crack, delusion, held still and held together — radiant, everlasting" (*Lives* 248). Here ends the symbolic autobiography of her early years. Munro is delivering now what she promised then. But the news is not good; if Enid's little notebook jottings present us with the image of a writer, then it is no self-flattering one for the author. No radiance in these parts.

"The Love of a Good Woman" — through its density of detail, thematic repetition, and structural amplitude — sums up much of what we may view as the Munro Project. Still, another aspect, a tonal one, merits attention. The very notion of the canonical originated in religious and critical practitioners' drives to select and validate the texts forming Judaeo-Christian scripture. Fittingly, this canonical story's treatment of the body resembles the posture found in the writings ascribed to Saint Paul, especially in his first letter to the Corinthians.

"The Love of a Good Woman" uses a setting — a Sowesto rural slum — that Munro has been making her own at least since "Executioners" (*Something*). Its viewpoint is unsparing, and follows Swift and Orwell in its obsession with smells. The world of the sleazy, back-concession, blind pig in which "Spaceships Have Landed" (*Open Secrets*) is set appears here without letup. "The Love of a Good Woman" reeks of semiwashed bodies, of the dead and the dying, of soiled stockings, of greasy frying pans, of sour milk and stale food, of dried semen and feverish sweat. The body here is indeed sown in corruption.[9] "The smell rising from the body seemed to be changing, losing its ammoniac sharpness. Changing into the common odor of death" (*Love* 65; NY 135). The genteel Enid, the little girls whom she lets paddle in washtubs, and the drowned optometrist are the only characters not in need of a bath. As the equivocal ending shows, the problem is that water is not only dangerous but also sexy. Like women.

The dying Jeanette is bitter, vicious, indifferent to husband and children; there is a hint that her fatal illness originated in a reaction to the drugs that she swallowed in order to abort a foetus planted in her by the optometrist whom her husband killed (*Love* 32; NY 118).[10] Enid is celibate, sex obsessed, naïve, fussy, a master of casuistry, and as in love with death as any gothic heroine. Her dreams tattle on her: "In the dreams that came to her now she would be copulating or trying to copulate . . . with utterly forbidden and unthinkable partners" (*Love* 51; NY 127). The dying body — the smell, the discoloration, the "malignant" nipples, the "ferretlike" teeth — over which she presides strikes her "as the sign of a willed corruption" (*Love* 38; NY 120), echoing 1 Corinthians 15.42. Nightmare sex and actual death have thrown her body and her mind out of sync ("Moving her body shook up the information that she was trying to arrange in her head and get used to" [*Love* 63; NY 133–34]). The ending depicts an almost gleeful Enid dicing with her own life in order to assert her power over the hatchet man: "Through her silence, her collaboration in a silence, what benefits could bloom" (*Love* 76; NY 140).[11] We are in Rocky Horrorland, where we shriek out a warning to the oblivious gothic heroine lurching toward disaster.

The graphics accompanying the story's original *New Yorker*

appearance underlined the irony apparent in the clichéd title. The lurid, pulp-fiction cover (a version of it is repeated in the 1997 fiction issue, again featuring a Munro story), and the "ALICE MUNRO Sex! Adultery! Murder!" come-on featured on the supercover attached to the original, were reinforced by the illustrative photograph that appeared in the body of the story. It is a picture of a white nightgown, a coded image for gothic romance (Gilbert and Gubar 581–650). The photo's caption cites a passage on the lurid nature of Enid's present dream life. Story and packaging alike emphasize that we are back in the gothic Sowesto that Munro has never left, the Sowesto that John Richardson originated and that James Reaney dramatically maps.[12]

Gothic traps its characters in vast machines, whether they are the laboratory tools that vivify Frankenstein's creature or the webs of deception that enmesh the heroine of *The Woman in White*. Whether urban (*Metropolis, Blade Runner*) or pastoral (*Roughing It in the Bush, Absalom, Absalom!*), fictional or nonfictional, the mode of representation demands a setting of threatening complexity. The setting is often of a technological nature, like the technologies of warfare and pioneering in the latter two works, and/or of a mechanistic nature, as in "The Love of a Good Woman." We begin with an entanglement in the tools that Willens employed. The passage proleptically emphasizes the scratched spot on the optometrist's dark mirror that rubbing has produced. The cool functionality of this set of tools later yields to the rubbing and twitching, the prodding and ejaculation, that Jeanette looks forward to during the frequent visits of "Doctor" Willens. Sex offers its own version of repressed gothic memory. Sex flips time back to childhood: the brutal friction climaxing in Willens's death seems like a grown-up version of playing at "doctor"; Jeanette's ritual query of how much she owes the eye man, the signal for him to whip out his blowtorch-sized "dingey," illustrates that fore*play* is both dramatic and ludic (*Love* 62; NY 132).

The oddest associations appear, all of them serving to degrade the body: Willens's head is slammed against the bedroom floor until he dribbles "pink stuff" like the froth that "comes up when you were boiling the strawberries to make jam" (*Love* 58; NY 130). Recall the syrup that drips from the grape *mosto* in "Meneseteung," reminding Almeda Roth of the menstrual cycle, whose implications she prefers to ignore (*Friend*). Both jam sessions reel with disgust at the body's excretions and exertions.

The opening survey of the optometrist's equipment concludes with a Pauline echo: "The flat face [of the retinoscope] is made of glass and is a dark sort of mirror" (*Love* 4; NY 102).[13] As is the story. For it oozes a Pauline revulsion both at the release of the body into pleasure and at what the body releases. Bodies not only stink here but also bloat, decay, shrink, and disgorge nicotine during a feverish sweat. During Enid's witnessing of her father at play, the woman's pointed breasts resemble the bases of ice-cream cones. No wonder sex is a matter of a man thumping a woman "like an old billy goat. Right on the bare floor to *knock her up* and down and try to bash her into pieces" (*Love* 62; NY 132; emphasis added).[14] We have come a long way from the randy, pathetic exuberance of Rose's half-sought orgasm in "Wild Swans"; we have returned to the reddened snow (recall Anne Hébert's *Kamouraska*) that follows the public beating of the suspected abusive father in "Royal Beatings."

Who shall deliver us from this body of death? Is there no way of seeing through a glass clearly? Munro's fiction has long marked the indignities that a masculinist culture offers women, yet beyond the tortures of male attention, constriction, and violent abuse lies the incurable process of ageing that haunts Munro's characters. It can surface almost as an aside in a story such as "Five Points" (*Friend*), with the youthful lover's nasty observations on his girlfriend's sagging butt; it can underlie virtually every moment within "Wigtime," in the same collection, in which three girls (and later women) allow their lives to revolve around an exploitative man whom we never even meet. (He is back in "My Mother's Dream," also in *The Love of a Good Woman*.) In one way or another, whether in fact or in fantasy, Enid is on the verge of embracing a demon lover. She is about to set out on a boat ride with the killer. Is the boat his "dingey"? Like the clueless gothic heroine, we tremble on the verge of a revelation — "as if everything for a long way round had gone quiet" — that never quite arrives, unless we want to return to the (chronologically later) county museum appearance of Willens's tools and spot a revelation there.

"The Love of a Good Woman" establishes itself as a Munro poetic both in the pervasiveness of its usage of earlier themes and motifs and in its tonality of what I call a Pauline gothic, a melodramatic representation of bodily decay and disaster without any hint of "incorruption" at the end. It accomplishes, if you will, the necessary Protestant-ization of the Catholic *weltanschaung* on which the gothic depends for its atmosphere. This is why Enid wonders whether a Catholic would have to confess the torrid dreams that she has had (*Love* 51; NY 127). Thus, Webster's *The Duchess of Malfi* extracts considerable frisson from a common stock of Jacobean images of

Catholicism that lend the play a richness of allusion and decor that an austere religion could never supply. In early gothic fiction, the monks and monasteries, the witches and castles, of mediaeval Europe whose survival oppresses the beleaguered heroine yield to the light of reason. Reason destroys the popish-driven plot. In later gothic fiction (*Jane Eyre*, for example), a set of restrictions chiefly moral in nature, but no less grotesque, threatens the heroine. Camp gothic is strewn with Catholic vestiges, those crumbs of the Host that the *Anglo*-Irish Bram Stoker's spiritualist/scientist Van Helsing strews about the set of *Dracula*.

The gothic of "The Love of a Good Woman" obtrudes an almost Manichean distaste for the body. Like the incidence of anorexia in our era, Pauline gothic indicates that a consumer culture of sexual liberation in fact rests upon a profound unease with the flesh that loops a postmodern culture back to the most discomforting of its Judaeo-Christian origins. Munro furnishes us with a hint of this sexual disgust and bewilderment in "Lichen" (*Progress*). There male fetishizing of the female pudenda is matched by the woman's initial failure to recognize just what his photo fetishizes. "Vandals," the final story in *Open Secrets*, expands this theme of sexual revulsion when it treats the anger that sexual abuse provokes in its victims.

A story such as "The Love of a Good Woman," lengthier and more complex than any story in *Open Secrets*, and far more engrossing than the rest of the latest collection, a work appearing soon after the epochal publication of *Selected Stories*, acquires an immediate landmark status. Some of the reasons for this status I have outlined. The message is clear: whatever one spoke, thought, or understood as a child, whatever one sees through this dark sort of mirror, will soon be seen face to face. Call it death.

ACKNOWLEDGEMENTS

Professor Robert Thacker not only heartened me in the writing of this piece but also provided editorial advice, critical insight, and scholarly assistance in abundance. Professor Coral Ann Howells's generous sharing of her thoughts from what was then her forthcoming book on Munro directed my attention to a question that I had overlooked. Ms. Judith McCombs caught my errors without gloating. Generosity also marked Professor Ildikó de Papp Carrington's willingness to provide me with a copy of her forthcoming article. Ms. Jessica Harris supplied me with information on white nightgowns. The Cornell Group permitted me to quote from Robert Laidlaw's memoir. Mr. Dallas Harrison improved my style.

¹ Despite the author's note that "Stories included in this collection that were previously published in the *New Yorker* appeared there in very different form," the differences between the periodical and hardback versions seem relatively slight. No paragraph has been shifted in its location, and only minor stylistic alterations have been made. (A list of these changes follows in the appendix.) For readers' convenience, my citations supply hardback page references first, followed by NY and its page numbers.

² Note the title's reductive, ironic resemblance to that other defining narrative, *Lives of Girls and Women*: from archetype to cliché!

³ For example, Munro settles the question (a matter of considerable critical commentary) of whether she reads *Lives of Girls and Women* as a long fiction or as a collection of stories in favour of the former alternative by excluding it from *Selected Stories*. On the other hand, she resolves the same query about *Who Do You Think You Are?* in the opposite direction by including four of its stories within *Selected Stories*.

⁴ Here is a summary of events in the story. On 10 July 1951, Mrs. Rupert (Jeanette) Quinn dies of "heart failure due to uremia" (67). Born in Montreal in 1924, and raised in an orphanage there, Jeanette's marriage to the Walley, Ontario, farmer Rupert Quinn has produced two daughters, Sylvie and Lois. Nursed at home throughout her final illness by a local caregiver named Enid (whose last name we never learn), Jeanette recounts to her on 9 July her version of the role that she and Rupert played in the supposedly accidental death by drowning in the Peregrine River (in a backwater formed by a onetime mill pond known as Jutland) of Mr. D.M. Willens, a local optometrist who made house calls and whom Rupert caught in a compromising situation with Jeanette. Three local boys discover his body floating in his partially submerged car. The museum in Walley now displays the fitted case holding his intricate tools. The story opens with this display. It closes with Enid alone on a riverbank with Rupert, uncertain of what the result will be of her planned disclosure to him of what she has heard from Jeanette.

⁵ "My Mother's Dream," the final story in *The Love of a Good Woman*, deals with the thin line between the "false" and the "true" mother, as revealed in the domestic politics of nursing.

⁶ I take issue with Coral Ann Howells's interrogation of the reliability of Jeanette's admittedly questionable account of the death of Willens. Howells argues for the recurrence of an abiding Munrovian preoccupation with women's gothic fantasies. Enid's dream life turns lewd, an index to her prurient eagerness to accept her dying patient's false and lubricious account of Willens's murder (149-53). However cogent and well supported, the argument is unconvincing for the following reasons:

Any argument of this nature always comes up against the "How far can you go?" question that bedevils, for example, critical interpretations of "The Turn of the Screw." Once all narrative reliability is dethroned, can anything in the story be saved? What else may be delusional? In "The Love of a Good Woman," someone or something put Dr. Willens in that car and that car in the river. Jeanette's deathbed version of that process is extremely detailed. Her account may be a lie, but it nonetheless has the ring of truth.

Munro has clothed truth in clichéd gothic apparel before: Flo's stereotypical warnings in "Wild Swans" about sexual molesters on trains at first seem no worthier of belief than her tale of the horny undertaker in the love-bug hearse. Yet, like the battlefield object in Timothy Findley's *The Wars*, "that thing they had thought was a ski pole" that turns out in fact to be a ski pole (122), Flo's fantasy of fake clergymen sex fiends on trains turns out to be bang on.

In the story's final section, entitled "Lies," Enid recalls Jeanette saying, at her life's end, *"Lies. I bet it's all lies"*). The "it" remains undefined; we are only told that Enid remembers this sentence "out of all the words that Mrs. Quinn said in that room" (*Love* 74; NY 138). The passage that follows fails to state, however, that Jeanette's account itself is a lie; rather, it minutely describes Enid's witnessing of her father's groping of a client. Enid's mother discounts as a dream her child's hesitant description of the scene. This dismissal Enid describes as *"Lies"* in a one-word paragraph in the hardback version (*Love* 75; NY 140). Thus, "lies" could refer at once to everything, to nothing, or to something in between.

As Howells notes, the story's conclusion emphasizes the mist-laden river setting and Enid's fantasies and apprehensions in the midst of it. Could this closing demonstrate that Jeanette's account itself was fantastic? Perhaps. Yet when we consider that Munro's commentary on the story adopts the indicative rather than conditional mode ("Contributors' Notes" 443), I think that we are wrestling with an aporia; Occam's principle urges me to adopt the less complicated interpretation.

Ildikó de Papp Carrington's impressive forthcoming article "Don't Tell (on) Daddy: Narrative Complexity in Alice Munro's 'The Love of a Good Woman'" came to my attention after I had nearly completed my article. While Carrington's essay adopts a nuanced view of the veracity of Jeanette's murder story, it nonetheless endorses its basic authenticity. The essay also provides an authoritative account of some of the narratological reasons behind Munro's inclusion of the material on the three boys who discover the partially sunken car, and offers valuable suggestions about the echoes from Theodore Dreiser's *An American Tragedy* resonating in Munro's story.

[7] Cece Athelstan, you will recall, is one of Deptford's leading Dirty Old Men in *Fifth Business*.

[8] Interestingly, the "country" version of the term — "gantlet" — appears in the *New Yorker* but is altered to fit standard English in the later version. Yet "Drowned" (NY 117) is colloquialized into "Drownded" (*Love* 29). The

usage of "yokes" when it is egg "yolks" that are being described remains in both versions (*Love* 15; *NY* 108).

9 "It is sown in corruption; it is raised in incorruption" (1 Cor. 15.42, KJV).

10 "I can't help it, she said, pulling a long face, / It's them pills I took to bring it off, she said" (Eliot 158-59). The drowned figure, the boat ride that may be an undoing, the cultural fragments represented by the optometry tools, the "early spring" setting (the cruellest month?) in which the floods reveal the presence of death: what are they but taking out the centrepiece of high modernism, itself a parodic inversion of the epic tradition, for a bit of slumming?

11 We have encountered this degree of complicity before, in "Wild Swans": "She [Rose] thought it would be an especially fine thing, to manage a transformation like that. To dare it; to get away with it, to enter on preposterous adventures in your own, but newly named, skin" (*Who* 64).

12 See Duffy 130-32. The hardback jacket cover makes do with a soft-porn painting (Paul Peel's *Le Repos*) of a woman in après-sex disorder with a partially exposed right breast.

13 "For now we see through a glass, darkly" (1 Cor. 13.12, KJV).

14 The play here on the colloquial term for getting a woman pregnant reinforces the hypothesis that Jeanette may have once conceived a child by Willens.

APPENDIX

Following are the textual variants between the periodical (NY) and the hardback (HB) versions.

HB lacks NY's subtitle ("A Murder, a Mystery, a Romance") and running titles.

HB 7 omits opening word in "First, they had to come across the bridge . . ." (NY 104).

HB 11 omits "exactly" in "They had something close in front of them . . . which was exactly the thing most adults seemed to have" (NY 107).

HB 25 contains the misprint "chil-dren."

NY 116 reads "Run the gantlet"; HB 27 reads "Run the gauntlet."

NY 117 reads "Drowned"; HB 29 reads "Drownded."

HB 29 omits "The jolt of freedom, the joy of outrage, the uttermost trespass" (NY 117).

NY 118 reads "She lived on a farm a few miles away, out on the highway, and every few days she came and took the sheets and towels and nightdresses away to wash"; HB 31–32 reads ". . . home to wash."

NY 121 reads "'I suppose it's all mixed up. . . . [G]et married,' he mother said"; HB 40 reads ". . . her mother said."

HB 47 omits "dark" in "her dark thick hair" (NY 125).

NY 127 reads "But there was a good house . . ."; HB 53 reads "But this was. . . ."

NY 128 reads "Rupert arrived late some nights . . ."; HB 55 reads "Rupert arrived so late. . . ."

NY 130 reads "He was out of the wind and he just set the chair right side up . . ."; HB 57 reads "He was out of the wind and he just set the chair up. . . ."

NY 130 reads "It was pink stuff . . . when the froth comes up when you were boiling . . ."; HB 58 reads "But it was pink stuff . . . when the froth comes up when you're boiling. . . ."

NY 134 reads "You know. You know"; HB 64 reads *"You know. You know"* (a blank line follows).

NY 136 reads "I forgot about that snappy little car"; HB 69 reads "Her and her snappy little car."

NY 140 reads "Lies"; HB 75 reads *"Lies."*

WORKS CITED

Carrington, Ildikó de Papp. *Controlling the Uncontrollable: The Fiction of Alice Munro*. De Kalb: Northern Illinois UP, 1989.

___. "Don't Tell (on) Daddy: Narrative Complexity in Alice Munro's 'The Love of a Good Woman.'" *Studies in Short Fiction* 34.2 (1997): forthcoming.

Eliot, T.S. *The Waste Land. Complete Poems and Plays 1909–1950*. New York: Harcourt, 1952. 37–55.

Findley, Timothy. *The Wars*. Toronto: Clarke, 1977.

Gilbert, Sandra M., and Susan Gubar. *The Madwoman in the Attic: The Woman Writer and the Nineteenth Century*. New Haven: Yale UP, 1979.

Howells, Coral Ann. *Alice Munro*. Manchester: U of Manchester P, 1998.

Hoy, Helen. "'Dull, Simple, Amazing and Unfathomable': Paradox and Double Vision in Alice Munro's Fiction." *Studies in Canadian Literature* 5 (1980): 100–15.

___. "'Rose and Janet': Alice Munro's Metafiction." *Canadian Literature* 121 (1989): 59–83.

Laidlaw, Robert. *Boyhood Summer 1912*. Published by the Cornell Group. http://www.odyssey.on.ca/~jjamieson/boyhood.htm (retrieved 14 Oct. 1998).

McCombs, Judith. Conversation. 20 Nov. 1997.

Munro, Alice. "Changing Places." *Writing Home: A PEN Canada Anthology*. Toronto: McClelland, 1997. 206.

___. "Characters." *Ploughshares* 4.3 (1978): 72–82.

___. "Contributors' Notes." *Prize Stories 1997: The O. Henry Awards*. Ed. Larry Dark. New York: Anchor/Doubleday, 1997. 442–43.

___. *Dance of the Happy Shades.* Toronto: McGraw-Hill, 1968.

___. *Friend of My Youth.* Toronto: McClelland, 1990.

___. "Home." *74: New Canadian Stories.* Ed. David Helwig and Joan Harcourt. Ottawa: Oberon, 1974. 133–53.

___. *Lives of Girls and Women.* Toronto: Ryerson, 1971.

___. "The Love of a Good Woman: A Murder, a Mystery, a Romance." *New Yorker* 23 and 30 Dec. 1996: 102–41.

___. *The Love of a Good Woman.* Toronto: McClelland, 1998.

___. *The Moons of Jupiter.* Toronto: McClelland, 1982.

___. *Open Secrets.* Toronto: McClelland, 1994.

___. *The Progress of Love.* Toronto: McClelland, 1986.

___. *Something I've Been Meaning to Tell You.* Toronto: McGraw-Hill, 1974.

___. *Who Do You Think You Are?* Toronto: Macmillan, 1978.

"Poetic." *Oxford English Dictionary.* 2nd ed. http://www.chass.utoronto.ca:8080/oed/oed.html

Ross, Catherine Sheldrick. *Alice Munro: A Double Life.* Toronto: ECW, 1992.

Thacker, Robert. Letter to the author. 31 May 1998.

Recasting the Orpheus Myth: Alice Munro's "The Children Stay" and Jean Anouilh's *Eurydice*

ILDIKÓ DE PAPP CARRINGTON

THE CLASSICAL MYTH of Orpheus and Eurydice tells the story of the young lovers' marriage, Eurydice's accidental death, and Orpheus's grief-stricken descent into the underworld to bring his beloved wife back into the world of the living. A poet and a musician, Orpheus sings so beautifully that he charms Hades into allowing him to take her back. But the Lord of the Dead imposes one condition: Orpheus must not look at her until they have completed their ascent to the upper world. Just as they reach it, however, he turns to see whether she is following him, and she is lost to him again and forever (Graves 111–12).

Alice Munro's first reference to this myth is a brief but climactic musical allusion to *Orfeo ed Euridice*, Christoph Gluck's eighteenth-century opera, in the title story of *Dance of the Happy Shades* (211–24), her first collection. When a handicapped girl, an unexpected performer in a children's piano recital, plays "The Dance of the Happy Shades," "something fragile, courtly and gay, that carries with it the freedom of a great unemotional happiness," the snobbish mothers in the audience do not know how to react to her indisputable talent (222). Although the piano teacher mentions the French title of the piece, *Danse des ombres heureuses*, nobody recognizes it as part of the opera based on the Orpheus myth (223). But through the contrast between the mothers' world and Gluck's otherworldly music, Munro emphasizes the unexpected effect of art on life.

In her second use of the Orpheus myth, Munro devotes an entire story to developing this powerful effect in an ironic intertextualization of Jean Anouilh's *Eurydice (Legend of Lovers)*, a dramatic retelling of the Orpheus and Eurydice myth in modern France.[1] In "The Children Stay," one of Munro's revised *New Yorker* stories in *The Love of a Good Woman* (181–214), her latest collection, Pauline Keating is a disturbingly beautiful young mother rehearsing for the title role in an amateur Canadian production of Anouilh's play. With her husband, Brian, and his parents, Pauline discusses Anouilh's plot, quoting and paraphrasing the dialogue and analysing both the characters and the director's unexpected casting of the various roles. "What he sees in us is something only he can see," Pauline explains (196). But she carefully conceals the central fact: after the weekly Sunday rehearsal in downtown Victoria, British Columbia, she and the director, Jeffrey Toom, make love in the locked rehearsal room. When the Keatings' summer vacation on Vancouver Island in 1967 interrupts this exciting secret schedule, Jeffrey pursues Pauline out of the city, takes her to a motel in Campbell River, and forces her to phone Brian to announce that she and her lover are going to Washington State, where he has "a one-year appointment" in a college drama department (185). In response to this announcement, Brian imposes a condition: "The children stay" (212). Pauline's painfully reluctant acceptance of this condition not only gives Munro the title of her story but also structures her ironic intertextualization of Anouilh's drama.

In discussing Anouilh's use of the Orpheus myth in *Eurydice*, Leonard Cabell Pronko defines "[o]ne kind of aesthetic pleasure afforded . . . by any modern treatment of a well-known tale" as the process of "discovering the parallels that the author establishes with his sources" (199). Applied to Munro's use of Anouilh's play, this process of discovery not only reveals many parallels between his drama and her story but also, much more importantly, highlights the differences against the background of these parallels. In the original *New Yorker* version of the story, Pauline's comment on the director's casting, "What he sees in us is something different from the obvious," is Munro's clearly self-reflexive comment on her own casting (95). Munro thus indicates that she is using ironic intertextuality for the double purpose defined by Linda Hutcheon: to "mark . . . a *rupture* with, or at least a subversion or critique of, the [original] text" and, at the same time, to "establish . . . a community of discourse among readers and thus [to] mark . . . a kind of interpretive *continuity*" (96). The continuity results in "the elitist pleasure of irony," closely parallel to the aesthetic pleasure that Pronko defines, because both depend on recognizing the parallels (96), but the irony subverts the legend of the French lovers. By recasting the roles of the Anouilh characters, complicating, combining, and multiplying them into "something different from the obvious," Munro makes these differences dramatically physical in order to define the multiple meanings of her title and to reject Anouilh's conception of love.

The lovers in *Eurydice* meet in a provincial railway-station restaurant, each accompanied by an embarrassing parent. Because both Orphée and Eurydice are very young, their love affair is part of their struggle to achieve individualization and disconnection by freeing themselves from their parents and their pasts. Orphée and his father are poor travelling musicians, but, unlike Orphée, his clingingly dependent and "rather ridiculous" old father plays so "abominably" that he would starve without his son (Anouilh 80, 58). Eurydice, her vain mother, and her mother's posturing lover are all members of a "tenth-rate [touring] company that plays in flea-pits" (79). Instantly falling in love and just as instantly agreeing that Eurydice's mother and her lover are "[h]orrible and stupid" (68), Orphée and Eurydice go off together to consummate their love in a dirty, badly furnished hotel room in Marseilles where, a waiter informs them, many other disgusting guests have done the same in the same bed, "All using their saliva to say 'our love'" (89). In contrast to these guests' repellent behaviour, the young couple's lovemaking is a confusing mixture of nervous fright, shame, and awkward tenderness.

Eurydice's shame is a reaction against her past, which contains not only a mother but also two recent lovers, Mathias, so desperately in love with Eurydice that he throws himself under a train as soon as she rejects him for Orphée, and Alfredo Dulac, the middle-aged impresario of the touring company. When Dulac, who for a year has been forcing Eurydice to submit to him, follows her and sends her a note at the hotel, she is so ashamed of her past that just before he arrives she runs away. Taking a bus out of the city, she dies when the bus crashes into a truck.

Orphée's attempt to get Eurydice back is engineered by a symbolic character, a young man who plays a double role in the drama. When Mathias commits suicide, the mysterious young man, in the background until this moment, calmly assures the appalled lovers that "It never hurts to die" (82). Then, just as Eurydice leaves the hotel, he reappears, introduces himself to Orphée as M. Henri, and makes a significant comment about the lovers' first meeting in the station: "These moments when we catch a glimpse of Fate laying her snares are very exciting, aren't they?" (95). After Eurydice's death, M. Henri returns a grief-stricken and completely disoriented Orphée to the same dreamlike station at night. When Orphée insists, "I want to know where we are," M. Henri identifies the place as "the doors of death" (101, 103). On the platform, a living Eurydice is "standing on the same spot where [Orphée] saw her … for the first time" (104).

Like Hades, M. Henri has the power to return Eurydice to Orphée but imposes the same condition: to keep her alive, Orphée must not look at her until dawn. This power, coupled with an excited awareness of the snares of fate, makes M. Henri not only the messenger of death but also the director of the play. "To a large extent, he is pulling the strings of the drama" (Pronko 189).

However, because Orphée has not actually entered "the doors of death" and because Eurydice is already alive again, his violation of M. Henri's condition shows that his youth makes him incapable of accepting reality. This inability is revealed by his obsession with male hands and their defiling touch. In the first act of *Eurydice*, when his questions force Eurydice to admit not only that she and Mathias have been lovers but also that she has had an earlier lover, Orphée replies, "I'll try never to think of . . . their hands touching you" (Anouilh 74). In the hotel room in the second act, he reveals the belief behind this obsession. Insisting that every experience, "good" or "evil," leaves a permanent mark on the remembering body, he convinces Eurydice, who has concealed her relationship with Dulac, that "all the hands that have ever touched you are still sticking to your flesh . . ." (86, 87). It is this conviction, confirmed by Dulac's note, that shames her into running away. When Dulac arrives at the hotel to tell Orphée that Eurydice, whom he calls "the child," has been his mistress for a year, Orphée accuses him of lying. Dulac's calmly patronizing reply, "You're a child, too, my boy," dismisses Orphée's insistence — "I love Eurydice and she loves me" — as irrelevant and immature (97). The man is talking about sex, the boy, about a young love that is frightened and disgusted by his beloved's sexuality. In the third act, when Eurydice is restored to Orphée and pleads, "Don't look at me. Let me live," he deliberately looks at her to force her to confess the truth: "Did he touch you with those hands all covered with rings?" (109). Begging forgiveness, she admits that he has, and Orphée recoils in horror: "I shall always see you with that man's hands on you" (111). Pronko emphasizes that, by altering the Greek myth, Anouilh

> changes the entire meaning of this crucial point in the myth. . . .
> Orphée's inability to see Eurydice is no longer a problem of
> ideality or a dream taking place in the underworld or the
> subconscious, lying in the realm of the eternal. It is reduced to
> a definite temporal reality, . . . on this side of death. And his
> breaking of the condition imposed upon him . . . is not so much

an indication that Orphée could have lived with Eurydice had he not looked at her as it is a demonstration of Orphée's inability to make the compromise demanded by love on earth . . . [and by] the ugliness of life. (197–98)

When Eurydice is thus killed a second time, Orphée is left alone with M. Henri and his father, suddenly back and full of gratitude that his son has not deserted him. In their debate about life and death, they offer Orphée two sharply contrasted choices. In long, pompous, digressive speeches, his father keeps insisting on how wonderful life is, in spite of all that he has suffered, and how through "will power" one can accept life with all its imperfections (Anouilh 117). Cynically capitalizing on the bumbling banality with which this paternal advice is delivered, M. Henri offers Orphée the immaculate perfection of death. "You heard your father talking about life just now. It was grotesque, wasn't it, but that's what it is like" (116). In life Eurydice would be soiled, "covered with finger marks," but in death Orphée can possess the "Eurydice of [his] first meeting, eternally pure and young, eternally herself" (116). Because this untouched ideal is what Orphée wants, he decides to join Eurydice in death. Thus, he leaves his father twice, initially to consummate his love for Eurydice and finally to possess her forever. The child does not stay.

In Munro's "The Children Stay," Brian, commenting on Orphée's decision to die, recognizes his death as a rejection of both his father and his father's philosophy and admits, "Logically I can see killing yourself so you won't turn into your parents. . . . I just don't believe anybody would do it" (198). His comment is significant because, in contrast to the parent-child relationships in Anouilh's play, those in Munro's story are much more complicated: they involve not two generations but three. Pauline and Brian are the parents of two girls, a five year old and a toddler.

But even though Brian is a father, he cannot detach himself from his parents. Unlike Anouilh's Orphée, he wants to maintain intergenerational connection. An "only son" (193), he needs "to have his wife and his parents and his children bound together, . . . to involve Pauline in his life with his parents," and to connect her and their children "to his own childhood" (195). To satisfy this need, the younger Keatings and the senior Keatings always vacation together on Vancouver Island. Brian cannot "imagine a summer without this shared holiday," even though Pauline is unhappy because they cannot "do anything by themselves" (194). She is also unhappy when the principal of the school where Brian teaches refers to her husband as "[y]our boy" (194), a reference that echoes Dulac's patronizingly addressing Orphée as "my boy." Brian's physical appearance, his body "still almost as skinny as a teenager's," is another sign that in spite of fatherhood he is not so much a parent as a son (195).

As the difficulties of Brian's family roles demonstrate, another way in which Munro's casting complicates Anouilh's is that Munro assigns her characters multiple functions that combine the roles of the French characters. Jeffrey is a paradoxical combination of M. Henri and Orphée because his sexual power over Pauline permanently changes her life. Although she mentions M. Henri a few times, she never identifies his role in the play. But Brian, by teasingly referring to Jeffrey as "Monsieur le Directeur," establishes the parallel between the symbolic French director and the Canadian drama teacher (196). Like M. Henri, Jeffrey is powerful, both intellectually and physically. Intensely opinionated, he loves to argue and challenge opposition, and his sexual potency imbues him with an astonishing "live energy" (190). Even when he falls asleep after vigorous intercourse, "[c]onviction and contentiousness seem . . . to radiate" from his "warm" body (208). But like M. Henri's direction of the fated drama of Orphée and Eurydice, Jeffrey's role as the director of *Eurydice* is inseparable from the idea of death. His first name echoes that of Henri, and when Jeffrey and Pauline are introduced he jokes that his last name, Toom, is "Without the B" (184). The word *tomb* is initially associated with the "sordid" hotel where Jeffrey works as a summer night clerk: a prostitute has been murdered there, and guests "check . . . in to O. D. or bump themselves off" (184, 185). But the "dusty" rehearsal room in the old Victoria building in which Jeffrey and Pauline secretly make love also acquires tomblike qualities when he bolts the door before intercourse (188): "The sound of the bolt being pushed into place, the ominous or fatalistic sound of metal hitting metal, gave her a localized shock of capitulation" (190).

That Jeffrey's power is dangerous to Pauline emphasizes his second function: as her lover, Jeffrey also plays the role of Orphée. When they first meet, he looks "directly into Pauline's eyes — impertinently and searchingly" (185–86). Remembering this meeting, she rehearses her lines from the last act of *Eurydice*: "'Don't look at me. Don't look. Let me live'" (186). Her quoting Eurydice's plea at this point clearly labels his act as symbolic of the decision that he later forces on her. But, unlike Orphée, Jeffrey does not operate alone. Brian also compels Pauline to choose, not only between her lover and her husband but also between two kinds of living death.

Jeffrey, however, is hardly aware of the difficulty of her choice because, although he combines the roles of M. Henri as director and Orphée as lover, there is a crucial role that he does not play: he is not a parent. His total obliviousness to what being a parent means is initially indicated by his suggestion that Pauline bring Mara, her toddler, to his mother's house for an afternoon tryst. Seizing the opportunity presented by the absence of his mother for the day, Jeffrey phones Pauline with an invitation into his bed, but she refuses. When she explains that she has to take care of Mara, at first he does not even recognize her name, and then he suggests bringing her along. He sees his mother as a supervisor to get rid of, but Pauline cannot get rid of her maternal responsibility to supervise her child. She fears not only the possibility of physical danger for Mara in a house that has not been toddler-proofed but also the potentiality of psychological trauma: "Mara might be storing up time bombs — memories of a strange house where she was strangely disregarded, of a closed door, noises on the other side of it" (201). Jeffrey's reply to Pauline's refusal, "I just wanted you in my bed," shows that in his "urgency" Jeffrey is thinking only of his own hands on her body (201, 202). Unlike Orphée, obsessed with the other hands sticking to Eurydice, he is almost totally unaware of the other hands clinging to Pauline.

She is covered, not by the symbolically defiling fingerprints of lustful men, but by the literally sticky, sandy handprints and footprints of two children playing on a saltwater beach. This difference is introduced by the name that Mara calls her, not Mommy, but Paw, Paw, for Pauline. Mara's childish mispronunciation suggests not only "Papa," with the implication that Pauline is more of an adult authority figure than the child's father, but also "paw," colloquial for "hand." The children's hands and feet and Pauline's own hands acquire increased significance when Jeffrey, who has pursued Pauline, telephones her again, just as oblivious to her situation as before, and she is summoned to the public phone in the hallway of the lodge at the beach. While she talks, she shifts the squirming, sand-caked toddler, who weighs "a ton," from one hip to another, but then Mara begins "bumping and scrambling against Pauline's side, anxious to get down" (203, 204). Simultaneously, five-year-old Caitlin goes into the lodge store, "leaving wet sandy footprints" (204). As Pauline tries to watch both children and to talk to Jeffrey, she reads the bulletin board signs beside the phone: "NO PERSON UNDER FOURTEEN

YEARS OF AGE NOT ACCOMPANIED BY ADULT ALLOWED IN BOATS OR CANOES," and an advertisement for palm reading, "YOUR LIFE IS IN YOUR HANDS" (205). Because she has just been holding her child, the phone conversation that initiates the permanent change in her life and the lives of her children makes the metaphor painfully literal as well as figurative. The definition of children as persons under fourteen, however, is ironic: by being only literal and not figurative, it is insufficiently inclusive.

Munro structures the long penultimate section of her story to withhold the figurative and fully inclusive definition until the climax. The next morning, in a motel room where Pauline and Jeffrey have repeatedly made love, she recalls her second telephone conversation the day before, her announcement to Brian that she is leaving and the "impossible" condition that he imposes: "The children stay" (206, 212). Although Munro does not specify this condition the first time that Pauline recalls the second conversation, its psychological effect emerges from the subtle intertextualization of a scene in the last act of *Eurydice*.

In this intertextualization, Munro combines the roles of Orphée and Eurydice in Pauline. The disoriented Orphée does not know where M. Henri has taken him until he sees a living Eurydice "standing on the same spot where . . . [he] saw her . . . for the first time" (Anouilh 104). Similarly, in "The Children Stay," as Pauline speaks to Brian at the lodge, she can clearly hear that he is standing "where she stood not so long before, in the public hallway of the lodge," where she read the fateful sign about her life in her hands (205). As Pauline recalls standing there, she, like Orphée, is so shaken and disoriented that she hardly knows which phone she is calling from now: at the end of their strange and stunningly short conversation, she comes "out of the phone booth beside a row of gas pumps in Campbell River" (206), where Jeffrey has taken her to the motel. Her disorientation suggests that like Eurydice she has crossed some kind of boundary between life and death, but unlike Eurydice she has incurred a permanent pain, losing her children. Because she chooses to give up the life that she has literally held in her hands, it is not Jeffrey but Pauline who is Orphée.

But she experiences a terrible dilemma, a choice between her lover and her children. The motel room, in which she is painfully aware of where she is before opening her eyes the next morning, resembles the miserable hotel room in *Eurydice*, with junky, "broken" furniture, a "noisy air-conditioner," and a cheap, torn bedspread (206).

"[H]ard-used between the legs," Pauline tells herself that her adultery is not so much a question of love as of sex (210). Although she reaches for romantic literary parallels in Anna Karenina and Emma Bovary, she tries to be totally honest: "None of this would happen if it wasn't for sex" (209). In sharp contrast to Orphée's disgust with Eurydice and Eurydice's own shame, Pauline argues earlier that Eurydice "probably . . . enjoyed" sex, even with Dulac, "because after a certain point she couldn't help enjoying it" (197). Based only on Dulac's conceited opinion, this argument emphasizes that Pauline fully enjoys her own sexuality. Although she is orgasmic with both her husband and her lover, "she believes" that it is only under Jeffrey's "weight . . . on her" that she is fortunate enough to experience "the inevitable flight, the feelings she doesn't have to strive for but only to give in to like breathing or dying" (210). Like Jeffrey's casting, however, what she sees in him is something that only she can see. Munro's repeated use of the word *believe* signals a characteristic passage of narratorial disparity, longer and more emphatic in the following revised version than in the original *New Yorker* version (102), in which Munro distances herself from her protagonist to qualify Pauline's conviction that Jeffrey is her fated lover.

> That was what Pauline must believe now — that there was this major difference in lives or in marriages or unions between people. That some of them had a necessity, a fatefulness, about them that others did not have. Of course she would have said the same thing a year ago. People did say that, they seemed to believe that, and to believe that their own cases were all of the first, the special kind, even when anybody could see that they were not and that these people did not know what they were talking about. Pauline would not have known what she was talking about. (*Love* 208)

But even though Pauline admits that "There's a lot she doesn't know" about her lover, including his widowed mother's "mysterious but important . . . role" in his life (210), she is convinced that, if she were to give Jeffrey up, she would suffocate: it "would be like tying a sack over her head" (209). Giving up her children, however, is also tantamount to dying.

When Pauline goes out into the motel parking lot, once again she recalls her phone conversation with her husband. In another subtle intertextualization of a scene in *Eurydice*, she alludes to Eurydice's death in the crash of the bus and the truck. As a truck on the highway comes toward Pauline, she thinks of "a large bleak fact coming at her," Brian's insistence that the children stay (211). After furiously asking "what about the kids?" (211), he answered his own question: "'The children,' he said, in [a] . . . shivering and vindictive voice. Changing the word 'kids' to 'children' was like slamming a board down on her — a heavy, formal, righteous threat. 'The children stay,' Brian said" (212).

This simile completes Munro's analepsis in two ways. First, it derives its fatal force from her perhaps unconsciously self-reflexive repetition of a scene at the end of "The Peace of Utrecht" (*Dance* 190–210), in which the narrator is told a terrible fact about her mother's last days. When her dying mother tried to escape from the hospital, she was brought back and coffined alive. To prevent another escape, "They nailed a board across her bed," thus literally nailing her into her deathbed as if into her coffin (208). Second, the sound of the figuratively slamming board echoes "[t]he sound of the bolt being pushed into place" when, near the beginning of "The Children Stay," Jeffrey locks the rehearsal room before he makes love to Pauline (190). By placing these sounds at the beginning and at the climax of her story and by making them so similar to each other, Munro combines the roles of Jeffrey and Brian in the triangle. Like Orphée, neither man will let Pauline live. But when they box her in by forcing her to choose, once again she becomes both of Anouilh's lovers at the same time. Unlike Eurydice, however, who is passive because she is simply killed a second time, Pauline is active because, like Orphée, she chooses to "die."

After an intensely traumatic conflict that transforms the philosophical debate between M. Henri and Orphée's father into counterpoised but contrasting pressures on her remembering body, Jeffrey's "weight . . . on her" hips and Mara's "weight . . . on her hip," Pauline chooses to give up her children (210, 212). But giving them up is an "acute pain" that she knows "will become chronic": "You won't get free of it, but you won't die of it," she tells herself, realizing that she must "carry [it] along and get used to [it] until it's only the past she's grieving for and not any possible present" because her children have grown up (213).

The first meaning of the story's title, therefore, is painfully and paradoxically double. Because the children stay with their father, they also stay with their mother: they are a permanent burden of guilt and grief for the parent who does not stay. The title's second meaning is the most obvious. Although all children grow up physically and most eventually leave their parents, some may nevertheless remain children emotionally and stay with their parents. This figurative definition of children excludes Pauline but includes both Jeffrey and Brian, who keeps "hang[ing] around" his parents (213). In the adulterous triangle, Pauline, unlike the "child" Eurydice, is the only grown-up because she makes her terrible compromise without blaming either her husband or her lover. She realizes that nobody will blame Brian because he tried to "make her see what she was doing" (212). Jeffrey, on the other hand, cannot see what he is doing to Pauline. After her phone conversation with Brian, which Jeffrey naïvely considers easier than Pauline expected, he clumsily articulates what she has been thinking, that perhaps Brian was "subconsciously" expecting her to leave him. When her silence begs Jeffrey "not to say any more," he apologizes (206). But just as he fails to see the impossibility of their making love when a toddler is in the next room, so too he is unable to comprehend the emotional price of her choice. Pauline realizes that "It isn't his fault. He's still an innocent or a savage, who doesn't know there's a pain so durable in the world" (213). The Anouilh *sauvage* is a character who is innocent, incorruptible, and intransigent, even though deeply scarred by pain and suffering (della Fazia 63, 49–52). Jeffrey is clearly not a savage in this sense. By making him a stranger to suffering, Munro argues that such innocence can come only from emotional inexperience. Although he shares this childishness with Orphée, he is not Orphée, because he does not have to die — that is, to give anything up to possess his Eurydice.

In the story's typical Munro epilogue in the present, Pauline's adult daughters, who neither "hate" nor "forgive" their mother, refer to her going "away with Orphée" (*Love* 213), but she repeatedly corrects them: "It wasn't Orphée" (214). Because their father has jokingly told them that their "mother ran away with Orphée," they confuse Jeffrey with the actor who played Orphée (214). Pauline's corrections, however, are also a metafictional comment on Munro's subversive recasting of Anouilh's characters.

Because it is Pauline who actively chooses as both Orphée and Eurydice, her comments on Anouilh's lovers constitute Munro's self-reflexive analysis of her story and her rejection of Anouilh's conception of love. Comparing the lovers, Pauline argues that "Eurydice is more realistic" than Orphée and "loves him better in a way than he loves her" (197). Pauline is also more realistic than Jeffrey because, although she is only a year older than he is, she is an adult and he is still a naïve child, unaware of how much better she loves him. Both explicitly and implicitly, Anouilh's conception of an intransigent, pure, and fated love is also presented as childish for several reasons. Pauline tells Brian, "It's a beautiful play in one way but in another it is so silly," because its adolescent insistence on perfection and its refusal of compromise reject the tough decisions that facing reality daily demands (198).

In dramatizing the desperately disruptive force of Pauline's sexuality, Munro shows that Orphée's rejection of Eurydice's sexuality is also adolescent. In an unpublished interview with Barbara Martineau, Munro defined sex as "the big thing," not only the physical act itself but also "the whole thing of emotions that radiate out from good sex, which seems to me so central in adult life, and so irreplaceable" (qtd. in Ross 79). Caught up in these irreplaceable emotions, "her secret life disturb[ing] her like a radiant explosion," Pauline is a woman whose sexuality "shockingly" outweighs her sense of maternal responsibility (*Love* 200, 209). In two sentences added to the revised version of the story, Pauline, discussing the play with Brian, "dreamily" tells him that "Everybody has choices" (198), but, at the moment when she finally chooses to give up her daughters, a nightmarish reality solidifies around her. "A fluid choice, the choice of fantasy, is poured out on the ground and instantly hardens [into] . . . its undeniable shape" (213). This metaphor, like the bolt being pushed into place and the board slamming down on Pauline, emphasizes the consequences of her choice: now she has boxed *herself* in. Thus, another meaning of the title perhaps implies that women who fantasize about sex without recognizing the potentially dangerous power of their sexuality remain children ignorant of reality.

The final reason behind Munro's rejection of Anouilh's conception of love is thus paradoxical. In spite of all her analytical arguments, Pauline decides to join Jeffrey because she believes that their love, like that of Orphée and Eurydice, is fated. But the epilogue's retrospective recasting of roles shows the most fundamental reason why Jeffrey was not Orphée: he was not the fated lover that Pauline had once mistakenly believed him to be. "It wasn't Orphée," she tells her daughters, but "somebody else connected with the play," with whom she "lived . . . for a while" (213). When her daughters repeat, "Not Orphée," she insists, "No. Never him" (213). After thirty years, the disillusioned dissonance of "for a while" and "never" rejects Jeffrey as Orphée much more emphatically than does the original *New Yorker* ending: "It wasn't him" (103). Subverting her own argument, Pauline has miscast her lover and has finally been just as wrong about love as Anouilh. The shatteringly ironic contrast between "What we think is happening and what we understand later on . . ." is Munro's recurrent theme (Munro, "Interview" 90).

NOTE

[1] For earlier examples of Munro's use of ironic intertextuality, see Carrington; and Munro, "Hired Girl" and "Wilderness Station."

WORKS CITED

Anouilh, Jean. *Eurydice (Legend of Lovers)*. Trans. Kitty Black. *Five Plays*. New York: Hill, 1958. 55–120.

Carrington, Ildikó de Papp. "Double-Talking Devils: Alice Munro's 'A Wilderness Station.'" *Essays on Canadian Writing* 58 (1996): 71–92.

———. "Other Rooms, Other Texts, Other Selves: Alice Munro's 'Sunday Afternoon' and 'Hired Girl.'" *Journal of the Short Story in English* 30 (1998): 33–44.

della Fazia, Alba. *Jean Anouilh*. Twayne's World Author Series 76. New York: Twayne, 1969.

Graves, Robert. *The Greek Myths*. Vol. 1. Harmondsworth, Eng.: Penguin, 1964. 2 vols.

Hutcheon, Linda. *Splitting Images: Contemporary Canadian Ironies*. Toronto: Oxford UP, 1991.

Munro, Alice. "The Children Stay." *New Yorker* 22 and 29 Dec. 1997: 91–96, 98–100, 102–03.

———. "The Children Stay." *The Love of a Good Woman*. Toronto: McClelland, 1998. 181–214.

———. *Dance of the Happy Shades*. Toronto: McGraw-Hill, 1968.

———. "Hired Girl." *New Yorker* 11 Apr. 1994: 82–88.

———. "An Interview with Alice Munro." With Geoff Hancock. *Canadian Fiction Magazine* 43 (1982): 74–114. (Rpt. in *Canadian Writers at Work: Interviews with Geoff Hancock*. Toronto: Oxford UP, 1987. 187–224.)

———. Unpublished interview. With Barbara Martineau. 16 Feb. 1975. The Alice Munro Papers, Special Collections Division, U of Calgary, series 37.20.20.

———. "A Wilderness Station." *Open Secrets*. New York: Knopf, 1994. 190–225.

Pronko, Leonard Cabell. *The World of Jean Anouilh*. Berkeley: U of California P, 1968.

Ross, Catherine Sheldrick. *Alice Munro: A Double Life*. Canadian Biography Series. Toronto: ECW, 1992.

The Luxury of Excellence:
Alice Munro in the *New Yorker*

CAROL L. BERAN

The *New Yorker* would seem to be the magazine that has everything. An illustrious 73-year history. A powerhouse editor. Prominent writers. Buzz.
Everything, that is, except a profit.
— Robin Pogrebin (C1)

While the *New Yorker* competes intellectually with small-circulation publications like *The Atlantic*, it competes financially with mass-market heavyweights like *People*.
— Robin Pogrebin (C6)

FOR A WRITER, publication in the *New Yorker* signifies a high degree of success. Yet the magazine is a commercial enterprise that must please both its audience and its advertisers in order to please its publishers. What does publication in the *New Yorker* mean to the art of a serious yet widely read writer such as Alice Munro?

Between March 1977 and October 1998, the *New Yorker* published thirty-four stories by Munro.[1] "Royal Beatings" appeared in the 14 March 1977 issue. Catherine Sheldrick Ross describes how Virginia Barber, Munro's literary agent, brought about the publication:

> By the mid-seventies, Alice Munro was definitely established as a major writer. In 1974, Virginia Barber of New York wrote and asked to be her agent. Coming from thrifty Huron County, Alice didn't want to pay ten percent of her royalties to an agent unnecessarily. . . . Two years later, she changed her mind, which paid off immediately when Barber sold "Royal Beatings" to the *New Yorker*, thereby beginning a long-standing relationship that now includes a contract for first refusal. (82)

However, a good agent cannot be given all the praise: in his correspondence with Munro, Charles (Chip) McGrath, her first editor at the *New Yorker*, says that the magazine should have published a story by Munro sooner (18 Nov. 1976, Alice Munro Papers [hereafter cited as AMP], MsC 37.2.30.1a). "The Beggar Maid" appeared in the 27 June 1977 issue, and by late 1977 correspondence filed in the Alice Munro Papers at the Special Collections Division of the University of Calgary Library shows Barber congratulating Munro on her right-of-first-refusal contract with the magazine (12 Dec. 1977, MsC 38.2.63.9a). "The Moons of Jupiter" appeared in the 22 May 1978 issue, and by the end of the year Munro's contract had been renewed. Publication by the *New Yorker* brought — and still brings — Munro prestige, money, and a wide audience for her stories.

McGrath, a writer of both essays and short fiction, came to the *New Yorker* in the early 1970s after attending graduate school at Yale, worked first as a proofreader and copy editor, became a fiction editor in 1977, and then became a co-managing editor for fiction. In 1987, he became deputy editor under Robert Gottlieb and continued in that position under Tina Brown until becoming head of the *New York Times Book Review* in March 1995 ("McGrath"). McGrath seems to have been an ideal editor for Munro. His letters to her generally follow the same pattern. He begins with compliments, frequently reactions to the story being edited. Then, with much tentativeness and respect, he identifies a few editorial problems, generally regarding clarity or fact. For example, he suggests in a letter of 18 November 1976 that Munro specify the Canadian setting for an audience likely to assume a setting south of the border unless otherwise informed (AMP, MsC 37.2.30.1a), and in a letter of 2 May 1980 he notes that the phrase "light on his feet" means homosexual, which he does not think Munro means in "Dulse" (AMP, MsC 38.2.4.5a). He asks for information about what "insulbrick" is or where "the Beaches" in "Labor Day Dinner" are located (17 Sept. 1980, AMP, third accession, 396/87.03.1.16). He insists that he edits only for clarity, not to alter her style (18 Nov. 1976, AMP, MsC 37.2.30.1a); when he queries her on matters of style, he generally does so in a way that privileges the writer's art, asking, for example, if a repetition is intentional (11 Nov. 1977, AMP, MsC 37.2.30.3f1) or whether Munro or the character in "The Moons of Jupiter" is misquoting a poem about "trackless seas" where the original has "shoreless seas" (26 Apr. 1978, AMP, MsC 38.2.4.2a). Frequently, proofs from the *New Yorker* add clarifications such as "he thinks" or "she said" or request information about the relationships between the characters. At times, Munro provides an additional sentence or paragraph in response to such queries. At other times, she inks "no cut" in the margin. Often the editors restore cuts that she disagrees with, such as those in "Wood" (6 June 1980, AMP, MsC 38.2.4.7). Munro sometimes seems to anticipate objections, altering the opening of "The Moon in the Orange Street Skating Rink" before McGrath requests changes (24 Sept. 1984, AMP, third accession, 396/87.03. 1.16) and surprising him with a new version of "The Progress of Love" (12 Sept. 1985, AMP, third accession, 396/87.03. 1.16). The Macmillan typescript of *The Moons of Jupiter* suggests how satisfied Munro was with editing by the *New Yorker*: of the five stories that appeared in the magazine, four were given to Macmillan directly from the pages of the magazine without further revision; only "Dulse" appears as a typescript (AMP, third accession, 396/87.03.5.1 and 5.2).[2] Comments such as those that McGrath provides no doubt can annoy an author, but they also flatter, signifying careful attention to helping the writer perfect her work. McGrath's letters frequently reassure Munro that she has the last word.

Ross records Munro in an unpublished interview speaking with deprecating humour about McGrath as an editor:

> Munro says that the *New Yorker* editor Charles McGrath always writes, saying "we are so honoured to have your story; it's wonderful; hardly anything needs to be done to it." But then, in a week, along comes a letter detailing changes — Mr. Shawn upstairs questions the need for the paragraph about toilet noises in "Royal Beatings," et cetera. Mr. Shawn upstairs, who recently retired as editor in chief, also didn't like stories with writers in them or autobiographical stories, which is why he rejected the autobiographical "Chaddeleys and Flemings." Finally, Alice wrote to McGrath and said, "I don't believe in your Mr. Shawn. You're just making him up. Show me a picture." (82–83)

William Shawn did, indeed, exist. After joining the *New Yorker* as a reporter in 1933, he became associate editor, then managing editor, and in 1952 editor, following the death of the magazine's founding editor, Harold Ross. During his long tenure as editor, Shawn enhanced "the reputation of the well-known magazine by emphasizing serious social and literary subjects" ("Shawn, William 1907–1992" 422). "Shawn brought to the *New Yorker* 'the glow that the magazine had lacked,' wrote *Time*'s Stefan Kanfer. 'The world that the reader now entered became far more real and gritty, far less trivial and debonair'" ("Shawn, William 1907–"). Shawn "achieved near-legendary status for the luminous roster of writers he attracted to the magazine" ("Gottlieb" 174). The qualities that Shawn brought to the *New Yorker* made it an ideal place of publication for writers such as Munro. He has also been characterized as "a perfectionist" ("Shawn, William 1907–") who "oversaw every word that was published throughout his thirty-five year tenure and essentially controlled editorial policy" ("Shawn, William 1907–1992" 422). McGrath says of him, "He was almost never satisfied, and was determined that the next issue would be an improvement" ("Remembering" 134). Robert Gottlieb writes that Shawn "was unrelenting in his insistence that everything in the magazine be accurate, clear, and above all, judicious, yet he published work of great feeling and daring, and work that took large risks" ("Remembering" 144). These aspects of Shawn as editor dictated which stories by Munro were selected for publication and affected her use of certain kinds of language and description.

The editorial dislike of autobiographical stories apparently arose because of a lawsuit about a supposedly fictional work by another author; McGrath informs Munro that the magazine's legal department wants to be sure that the names in "The Moons of Jupiter" are fake (26 Apr. 1978, AMP, MsC 38.2.4.2b); later, Munro is asked to sign a legal document stating that "The Turkey Season" is fiction (11 Dec. 1980, AMP, MsC 38.2.4.13), and McGrath suggests that she give the narrator a name to clarify that the story is not autobiographical (1 Dec. 1980, AMP, MsC 38.2.4.12b).

The *New Yorker*'s editorial policies regarding language and descriptions that might offend conservative readers created small conflicts between the magazine and Munro. In his letters, McGrath respectfully requests that Munro delete language that Shawn disapproved of, such as the passage on toilet noises and the rhyme about "pickled arseholes" in "Royal Beatings" (18 Nov. 1976, AMP, MsC 37.2. 30.1b), noting that both the magazine and its audience are fairly conservative. Although McGrath reassures Munro that she has the final say, he doubts that he can persuade Shawn to retain language that exceeds the magazine's standard. Yet ultimately the *New Yorker* did print the rhyme about "pickled arseholes," but not the passage on toilet noises or the vivid passage about a flasher; horses that wouldn't "pull your tail out of a pail of lard" in the magazine wouldn't "pull your cock out" in the book version of "Royal Beatings" (see *New Yorker* 14 Mar. 1977: 39, 44; and *Who* 12, 11, 22). Editorial policy shortened "bullshit" to "bull" and transformed "toothprick tricks" into "toothpick tricks" in "Labor Day Dinner" (17 Sept. 1980, AMP, third accession, 396/87.03.1.16). Although such cuts are a form of censorship, Munro did not restore the second syllable of "bullshit," and "toothpick tricks" still substitutes for "toothprick tricks" in the book version of "Labor Day Dinner" (*Moons* 155, 153); "crap factory" still replaces the objectionable "shit factory" in "The Turkey Season" (17 June 1980, AMP, MsC 38.2.4.8b; *Moons* 63).

Even in the mid-1980s, the *New Yorker* under Shawn's editorship was making sex scenes in Munro's stories less earthy. The repeated reference to "the rat" between Dina's legs in "Lichen" becomes "the pelt" to tone down the image and avoid repetition (15 Oct. 1984, AMP, third accession, 396/87.03.1.16; *Progress* 55). Language was still being censored too. The *New Yorker* version of "Lichen" uses "You're kidding" (15 July 1985: 27) where the book version uses "Holy shit" (*Progress* 36). In the 31 March 1986 issue of the magazine, the scene in "The Moon in the Orange Street Skating Rink" that appears on page 146 of *The Progress of Love* lacks the details about "that tuft of dead looking hair," how "their wet had soaked one stocking," how Callie was "[c]old and sticky where Edgar had wet her," and how "Callie wiped herself with the dust rag — granted, it looked to be a clean one — and said it reminded her of when somebody blew their nose." In the magazine version of "White Dump," the bedroom scene reads, "But she just stroked him. That was effective" (28 July 1986: 35), omitting the phrase that the book version places at the end of the first sentence: "as if impatient for further and faster activity" (*Progress* 297). This phrase is important to the scene because it emphasizes how Isabel puts keeping others happy above fulfilling her own needs, and it is important to the story because it provides one motivation for her to leave her marriage.

Censorship of language and description seemed to continue after Robert Gottlieb succeeded William Shawn in 1987 and Daniel Menaker took over as Munro's editor in 1988. Gottlieb, president and editor in chief at Knopf, was known for looking for a "distinctive voice" in Knopf authors; he believed that "An editor is essentially performing a service job" to "help the writer achieve his voice" (qtd. in "Gottlieb" 174). Menaker, who joined the *New Yorker* in 1969 as a researcher and later became copy editor and then in 1976 fiction and fact editor, and who published a volume of short stories entitled

Friends and Relations in 1976 and *The Old Left and Other Stories* in 1987, writes, "I believe that every word counts. I admire most writers who combine control and imagination" (qtd. in "Menaker"). Menaker edited Munro's stories for the *New Yorker* beginning with "Five Points" in 1988 and ending with "The Albanian Virgin" in 1994. The first letter from Menaker to Munro details small bowdlerizations in "Five Points" (18 Jan. 1988, AMP, receipt no. 900103.1.1). The *New Yorker* page proofs of the story contain a note in Munro's handwriting asking that the passage describing swollen pudenda and leaking semen that the editors have queried be left in; Munro agrees to tone down the description of Maria's pimples, which Maria scratches until they bleed (AMP, receipt no. 900103.1.7.14 and 11). Ultimately, both the magazine and the book printed the same fairly explicit passage:

> Now she feels a pain between her legs. Not unusual after one of these sessions. If she were to stand up at this moment, she'd feel a throb there, she'd feel the blood flowing back down through all the little veins and arteries that have been squashed and bruised, she'd feel herself throbbing like a big swollen blister. (*New Yorker* 14 Mar. 1988: 40; *Friend* 42)

Another indication of changes in editorial policy at the *New Yorker* is evident in "Five Points": Neil says "shit" (34), one of the words apparently forbidden by Shawn.

The magazine's prudishness has varying degrees of significance for Munro's art. For readers who might be upset by profanity and graphic descriptions, the *New Yorker*'s censorship removes potential barriers to appreciating the story. Whether a character says "bull or "bullshit" is not likely to alter significantly the reader's sense of what that character is like, although the softened language does make the character's speech less transgressive, less shocking, than it might have been. Munro's depiction of lower-class people in rural Ontario becomes slightly less authentic when the genteel image of the *New Yorker* excises their characteristic impoliteness and deliberate lack of gentility. However, with descriptions relating to topics such as excretion, genitalia, and sex that have been surrounded by even stronger cultural taboos in North America than have four-letter words, cuts seem more detrimental to Munro's art, because her use of such material generally functions to question or subvert cultural assumptions. The explicitness of unpleasant details in the sexual-initiation scene in "The Moon in the Orange Street Skating Rink," for example, mocks prevalent myths of the romantic nature of such moments. The censored phrase in the bedroom scene in "White Dump" subverts notions of sex as romantic and mutually pleasurable while establishing characterizations that prepare the reader for Isabel's breaking out of her marriage to find sexual pleasure. That some of these descriptions appear in the book versions of the stories suggests Munro's awareness of their importance; clearly, not all editors require as much gentility as those at the *New Yorker* do. Munro knew of the magazine's conservative policies before the publication of her first story there, yet she continued to send her editors stories containing the types of language and description that she knew they would censor. This tells not only of her perseverance but also of how her vision of her art remained strong in the face of editorial opposition. Censorship seems not to have altered her art ultimately, though it altered what some readers saw of it.

The *New Yorker* often joins several of Munro's consecutive short paragraphs into a single paragraph. No doubt the longer paragraph blocks look better in the magazine's narrow columns; however, this change does alter the effect of a story. Munro's alternation of longer paragraphs with a group of short ones establishes a characteristic rhythm that is lost in the magazine versions of some stories. At times, the joined paragraphs also obliterate an emphasis key to the story. In "White Dump," for example, the word *freedom* receives emphasis as it begins a new paragraph (*Progress* 303), emphasis that is lost when that paragraph is joined to its predecessor (*New Yorker* 28 July 1986: 38).

I found no evidence in the Alice Munro Papers that editorial demands by McGrath or Menaker were responsible for marked differences between the magazine version and the book version. For example, changes in narrative point of view in "Dulse" from first person in the magazine to third person in the book and in "The Progress of Love" from third person in the magazine to first person in the book seem to have been authorial choices as Munro continued to rethink her work.

The cuts and revisions detailed in letters from editors at the *New Yorker* never required the sort of drastic changes that an editor of another magazine requested: elimination of one thousand words from "Eskimo," obliterating the character of Rhea (undated letter forwarded to Munro by the Virginia Barber Literary Agency, 16 Jan. 1985, AMP, receipt no. 880812.1.9). In fact, McGrath accepted some stories, such as "Prue," virtually without changes (19 Jan. 1981, AMP, MsC 38.2.14.14). Rather than demand extensive changes, the *New Yorker* editors rejected many stories that Munro submitted under her right-of-first-refusal contract. Two early versions of "Simon's Luck" were rejected because Simon seemed too vague (3 Aug. 1977, AMP, MsC 37.2.30.4a; 5 Dec. 1977, AMP, MsC 38.2.63.9b). "Providence" and "Spelling" were judged inferior to "Royal Beatings" (17 Nov. 1976, AMP, MsC 38.2.63.6). "Eskimo" seemed too forced and "Fits" too unclear (26 Sept. 1984, AMP, third accession, 396/87.93.2.3). The ending of "Circle of Prayer" was too unresolved (16 Sept. 1985, AMP, third accession, 396/87.03.2.3). "Jesse and Meribeth" was judged good but below Munro's usual standard (15 Feb. 1985, AMP, third accession, 396/87.03.2.3), and McGrath preferred "White Dump" to "A Queer Streak" (25 June 1985, AMP, third accession, 396/87.03.2.3). "Hold Me Fast, Don't Let Me Pass" seemed too contrived to Menaker (18 Jan. 1988, AMP, receipt no. 900193.1.1).

Rejection by the *New Yorker*, however, did not prevent these and other stories from appearing in other magazines and in book form. Rather, publication by the *New Yorker* has given readers access both to stories that have not appeared elsewhere and to stories before they appear in book form. Two Munro stories published in the *New Yorker* have not yet appeared in book form: "Wood"[3] and "Hired Girl." Five stories that appeared in the *New Yorker* after the publication of *Open Secrets* appear in the recently published collection *The Love of a Good Woman*: "The Love of a Good Woman," "The Children Stay," "Save the Reaper," "Before the Change," and "Cortes Island" (Munro's author's note indicates that they appear in "a very different form" in the collection [n. pag.]).

Tina Brown's editorship of the *New Yorker* from 1992 until her resignation in July 1998 brought a new flavour to the magazine that has affected how Munro's stories appear and broadened the audience for them. Brown made the *New Yorker* "sharp, rude, timely" (Lacayo), a "timely read among the movers and shakers" ("Talk"). Although she "preserved in every issue a large core of thoughtful material," she enlivened the look of the magazine with photographs, and, most significantly for Alice Munro's fiction, Brown allowed the *New Yorker* to be "unblushing about sex," introducing "the same erotic preoccupations and four-letter words that serious books had discovered decades ago" (Lacayo).

Although the correspondence in the Alice Munro Papers breaks off shortly after Menaker became Munro's editor and Gottlieb became editor in chief, well before Bill Buford and Alice Quinn became Munro's editors and Brown became editor in chief, it is clear that stories recently published by Munro in the *New Yorker* have been current in their subject matter, as her stories have always been; consequently, they suited Brown's desire for timely material. "The Love of a Good Woman" contains a scene of brutal sexual harassment of a patient by a doctor, a dream of child molestation, and hints of possible abortion and euthanasia. In "The Children Stay," the father demands and apparently gets custody of the young children when the mother leaves with her lover. "Save the Reaper" presents the beginnings of a lesbian scene, with a lonely woman aroused by a girl's practiced attempt at seduction. Brown's policies regarding profanity and sex have allowed the word *fuck* to appear twice in "Save the Reaper" (127) and descriptions of the sort formerly censored to be printed in "The Love of a Good Woman" and "The Children Stay." In the former story, Munro discusses ugly physical details of glomerulonephritis:

> Her urine at present was scanty and had a smoky look, and the smell that came out on her breath and through her skin was acrid and ominous. And there was another, fainter smell, like rotted fruit, that seemed to Enid related to the pale lavender-brown stains appearing on her body. (117)

Enid dreams of having sex with "fat squirmy babies," being "slick with lust" as she "set to work with roughness" (127). Mrs. Quinn tells of the optometrist "puffing away getting his fingers slicked in and puffing away"; then he would "thump her like an old billy goat" and "try to bash her into pieces. Dingey on him like a blowtorch" (132). In "The Children Stay," the central character is "hard used between the legs, swollen and stinking. Urinating takes an effort and it seems she's constipated" (102).

Brown's detractors, however, tell the story of her reign at the *New Yorker* slightly differently. Alexander Cockburn complains that "The dumbing down has been relentless":

> In its best days the *New Yorker* was a literary magazine. Now a short story has to come from Sarajevo, or has to tie into the women's issue or the music issue or the black issue. People who like the new *New Yorker* like that it is more topical, quicker to jump on today's news or apologise for Clinton. It's a handy conversation tool for busy liberals.

Cockburn accuses the editors of preferring "Dahmer-generation stuff" about sensational topics such as seducing and eating boys. In James Martin's assessment, the *New Yorker* "demonstrates weekly" an "abject devotion to affluence," evincing attitudes of "feigned ignorance" and "smug detachment" about poverty (23). John Garvey asserts that the magazine "wants to appear tolerant and liberal — where fashion dictates tolerance and liberalism" (10).

For Munro, Brown's editorial policies meant less censorship of previously restricted types of language and description; however, because the magazine has become less conservative and less genteel, Munro's irony and subversiveness seem less shocking as she breaks taboos. Her sensational material loses impact slightly because it is echoed elsewhere in the magazine. The wider readership — Brown raised the magazine's circulation by nearly 30% to 809,000 ("Talk") — combined with the "dumbing down" may have changed the quality of the audience. The "devotion to affluence" and the "smug detachment" about poverty in the magazine as a whole affect how readers are likely to respond to Munro's stories of lower- and middle-class, nonaffluent people, who may seem like museum pieces or objects of anthropological or historical interest rather than of current significance to the reader. In addition, the goal of making the magazine profitable has necessitated more advertising. Adding zip has meant breaking up full pages of text with more insertions and marginalia. Although the *New Yorker* has always contained cartoons, sketches, poems, and ads, the number of interruptions per story has increased in recent years. "Royal Beatings" appears on nine consecutive pages of the magazine interrupted by one poem, two sketches, and seven cartoons. Title and author frame the story: the title is centred over two of the three columns on the first page, written in slightly larger capital letters than those used in the story; Munro's name appears in smaller capital letters below the final sentence of the story. Even relatively few interruptions of the text no doubt affect readers' experiences of the story. However, the number of elements that break up a text has increased greatly since 1977; "The Love of a Good Woman," for example, appeared in the *New Yorker* recently with an astonishingly large number of interruptions: 122.[4]

In "In Memoriam A.H.H.," Tennyson writes, "But clear from marge to marge shall bloom / The eternal landscape of the past" (143). For the reader of "The Love of a Good Woman" in the 23 and 30 December 1996 issue of the *New Yorker*, the landscape of the 1950s blossoms not from margin to margin but from margin to ad, or from margin to brief article or poem, or from margin to sketch or cartoon. Those who believe that art is a self-contained object, self-explicating within its margins, would consider the story to be the same whether they encounter it in a book of short stories or in the *New Yorker*. However, I believe that reading experiences are affected by what is outside a story: both how a story means and what it means change as readers' experiences with the text vary with the context.

Readers of "The Love of a Good Woman" in the *New Yorker* find the story surrounded by thirty-three ads for hotels, resorts, and vacation packages; thirty-four ads for collectibles; eight ads for services related to health and beauty; six ads for compact disks; fifteen ads for books and videos; two ads for a television show on A&E *Biography*; six ads for food, wine, and gifts; and one ad for certificates of deposit at a socially conscious bank (thirteen of these ads use one colour to attract attention among the profusion of black-and-white ads); five full-page, full-colour ads; one page of Reader Service Value Program listings; three cartoons; four sketches (one in four colours); one brief article illustrated with a sketch; one poem; and one black-and-white photograph with a quotation from the story underneath it. All these elements interrupt the thirty-two pages of text. The initial effect of this clutter is to prevent the concentration that stories printed in books with blank margins evoke in readers. Reading one of Munro's stories in a book, readers enter the world of Jubilee or Carstairs or Walley intensely, getting carried away by fictions that seem more and more real as each new story affirms the reality of the place and the people who inhabit it. Magazine readers of the same story, however, are constantly in danger of being carried away from the story by the marginalia.

Such distractions are an integral part of the experience of reading the magazine. Munro's stories themselves are disjunctive reading experiences; abrupt shifts in time and locale keep readers actively creating the story for themselves out of the pastiche of its presentation. Marginalia become additional elements of the collage out of which the reader reconstitutes the story and establishes meaning. "The Love of a Good Woman" thus becomes, in the *New Yorker*, both a story of the 1950s and a story of the 1990s, Munro's story and the story of each reader who encounters it.

I believe that Munro would applaud such a reading experience, because she describes her own experiences of reading stories by other writers as transgressing the linearity of the text, and she suggests that her own stories should be read this way:

For one thing, I can start reading them [stories written by other people] anywhere; from beginning to end, from end to beginning, from any point in between in either direction. So obviously I don't take up a story and follow it as if it were a road, taking me somewhere, with views and neat diversions along the way. I go into it, and move back and forth and settle here and there, and stay in it for a while. It's more like a house. Everybody knows what a house does, how it encloses space and makes connections between one enclosed space and another and presents what is outside in a new way. This is the nearest I can come to explaining what a story does for me, and what I want my stories to do for other people. ("What" 332)

For readers of a Munro story in the *New Yorker*, the house includes a yard with many lovely flowers to sniff, trees to admire, and hedges to meander through as the story "presents what is outside in a new way."

One of the delights in reading fiction is escapism. Readers escape into the world of the story, leaving behind their everyday lives with their joys and sorrows; later they return to the daily world renewed, energized, given fresh vision. For readers of "The Love of a Good Woman" in the *New Yorker*, part of this effect is reversed. The story presents a difficult and unattractive world of poverty, repression, sexual domination, and abuse of power — the sort of world that Cockburn refers to when he accuses the editors of the *New Yorker* of preferring sensational "Dahmer-generation stuff." Munro's view on writing about depressing material is that "People can accept almost any amount of ugliness if it is contained in a familiar formula, as it is on television, but when they come close to their own place, their own lives, they are much offended by a lack of editing" ("What" 334). The *New Yorker* context provides readers with a familiar formula for dealing with Munro's sensational yet depressing material: the marginalia offer readers a delightful fantasy of joining the elite community of subscribers to the *New Yorker* who have sufficient disposable income to live the good life.[5] Why discipline the imagination to stay in Walley among impoverished people (some houses don't have electricity) with serious problems (a drunken father, a chronically ill mother, a crippled father, a blind great aunt, a dying wife) when you can dream of "The Rose Pin" ($45 in sterling silver or $220 in 14k gold) with matching earrings ($75 or $440) in a "Velvet Box" (*New Yorker* 23 Dec. 1996: 116) or envision golfing or strolling on the beach at the Cloister on Sea Island, Georgia:

Vanity? Hardly. More a choice between anonymity and relationship.

On our part, something we learned serving families for as many as five generations. For you, an intangible comfort when you leave home for a distant shore.

The Cloister. Sea Island. Mobil Five-Star accommodations with spontaneous warmth. World class golf. Wonderful dining. Yes, five miles of private beach, tennis, spa, skeet and horseback outings, too. (141)

A drunken character in Munro's "Memorial" thinks, "The only thing we can hope for is that we lapse now and then into reality" (*Something* 178). Because many of her stories are set up in such a way as to make the reader question what is real, which reality is *the* reality, or whether we can speak of reality at all, perhaps the character's statement describes accurately readers' experiences of lapsing into reality occasionally while reading a Munro story.[6] Reading the magazine version of the story heightens the effect: the schizophrenic experience of parallel realities created by the presentation mimics the drunken one of escaping from and reentering reality.[7] On the one hand, the ads, cartoons, sketches, and mini-articles exist without significance to Munro's story; on the other hand, they establish an antithetical reality that disrupts the story's realism. The ad for a hotel on St. Lucia, for example, shows a spacious, nearly empty room with two chairs invitingly set by a cocktail table in front of huge windows that provide a breathtaking mountain view. "Enticing * Remote * Lush," the ad proclaims (*New Yorker* 23 Dec. 1996: 127). Walley of the 1950s is remote but not enticing or lush. Enid, a practical nurse, notices a high school textbook at the house where she is caring for the sick wife:

She could see the dark-green, softened cover of a book called "History of the Renaissance and Reformation." It was second-hand, or tenthhand — nobody ever bought a new textbook. Inside were written all the names of the previous owners, some of whom were middle-aged housewives or merchants around the town. You could not imagine them learning these things, or underlining "Edict of Nantes" with red ink and writing "N.B." in the margin.

Edict of Nantes. The very uselessness, the exotic nature of the things in those books and in those students' heads, in her own head then and Rupert's, make Enid feel a tenderness and wonder. It wasn't that they had meant to be something that they hadn't become. Nothing like that. Rupert couldn't have imagined anything but farming this farm. It was a good farm, and he was an only son. (125–26)

The only use of their education in daily life is to supply a seven-letter word for "Bread of the Amazon" for a crossword puzzle (126). For the characters in the story, cassava exists only on paper; for the readers of the *New Yorker*, "Expedition cruises aboard Russian icebreakers" to Antarctica (131) may be only an 800 number away, unless, of course, they prefer to see the Caribbean and "Discover the world of private luxury yachts with crew. Golf, tennis, diving, all water sports. Superb cuisine/world class chefs" (114). In contrast, Walley exists only on paper.

The word "FICTION" above the title "The Love of a Good Woman" (102) ensures that readers of the story in the *New Yorker* do not mistake Munro's writing for documentary or sue the magazine because they see themselves presented in the characters and situations; this word extends the invitation to escape reality and enter a parallel world. Yet, for the publication of this story in the volume of the O. Henry Award stories for 1997, Munro reveals in her section of "Contributors' Notes" that the story has some basis in fact:

What did I first know about this story? A man and woman disposing of her lover's body. This happened on an island off the B.C. coast — they put him in his own boat and towed him out into open water. . . . The sudden switch from sex to murder to marital cooperation seemed to me one of those marvelous, unlikely, acrobatic pieces of human behavior. Then the lover got transferred into a car, and it all went on in Huron County, and the boys got into it, and their families, and Enid, who took over the story as insistently as she took over a sickroom. And there is the boat, still, waiting by the bank of the Maitland River. (443)

Munro's comment suggests that her fiction begins in fact, becomes altered by her imagination, and then returns to fact at the end when it has taken on a more ambiguous meaning because of the imaginative transformation that being fictionalized has worked on it.

Between the title and Munro's name are printed in italics the phrases

"A murder, a mystery, a romance." This dignified enticement promises the diverse pleasures of three of readers' favourite fictional genres in one story. However, because we are in both Munro's house and the *New Yorker*'s house, we can linger in any one of the rooms for as long or short a period as we please, and at any time we can escape to the pleasures of the garden rather than endure the discomforts of the house. If solving the mystery seems overly interrupted by details about the families of the boys who discover the body, or if deciding whether the death was suicide or a crime gets lost in descriptions of two women's actual and imagined sexual encounters with real and imagined men, or if the romance progresses too slowly as the nurse waits for the wife to die, readers can consider *Dog Love*, a book by Marjorie Garber on "a subject of majesty and a mystery of extraordinary complexity and utter simplicity," "a joy to contemplate," assured that, "of recent dog books, this is easily the pick of the litter" (125). Or they can plan a getaway weekend at the "San Francisco Lover's Hotel" with its "Continental breakfast and wine hour" (114).

The page facing the start of "The Love of a Good Woman" contains a black-and-white photograph by Andrea Modica. The caption below the photograph quotes a section of the story describing Enid (126): *"She had what she thought of as romantic dreams, in which some man would have his arm around her or even be embracing her, but they were nothing, nothing at all compared to the dreams that she was having now"* (103). In the photograph, a woman's forearm with fingers outstretched reaches up to touch the hem of a filmy nightgown hanging on a plastic "boutique" hanger (an anachronism for Munro's story) suspended from a piece of bent wire hanging from the ceiling of a rather bare room with part of an open doorway visible to the right. The romantic and nostalgic tone of the photograph and the quotation is misleading because the quotation is taken out of context. The whole passage describes "ugly dreams" that fill Enid with "disgust and humiliation" (126, 127): "she would be copulating or trying to copulate . . . with utterly forbidden and unthinkable partners. With fat squirmy babies or patients in bandages or her own mother. She would be slick with lust . . . and would set to work with roughness and an attitude of evil pragmatism" (127). Munro's story subverts the gently melancholy evocation of the past signified in the *New Yorker* illustration.

Running heads in capital letters on twelve separate pages seem to imply that "The Love of a Good Woman" is a sensational story involving guns ("SHOULD'VE BROUGHT A TWENTY-TWO" [105]), dangerously contagious sickness ("RUPERT, YOU SHOULD BE QUARANTINED" [119]) and death ("I'M NOT MUCH FOR FUNERALS" [127]), mystery ("THEY ALL KEPT THEIR MOUTHS SHUT" [113]) and solutions to mystery ("A PLACE THAT HAS NO SECRETS" [141]), a conflict of good ("BEING THE MOTHER OF A SAINT" [125]) and evil ("THE UTTERMOST TRESPASS" [117] and "SOMETHING DELIBERATELY VILE" [129]), and, of course, sex ("HER LEG SHOWED BARE" [131] and "SHE DISLIKED THIS PARTICULAR BODY" [121]). Only "DINNER AT A CROWDED TABLE" (111) and "WAS IT SPECIALLY DIFFICULT THIS TIME?" (137) hint of a less sensational, more everyday story. The running heads are all quotations from Munro's story, yet pulled out of context and taken together they promise a conventional sort of sensational story; they fail to direct readers to notice the sophistication, emotional complexity, and sensitivity of Munro's story. Instead, they focus readers' attention on how the story touches on popular media images without hinting at the ways in which these phrases in this story signal subversions of such images. Looked at in context, these phrases actually point to deconstructions of societal myths in the story. The boys discover an unattended dead body; a gun would be useless to them because they themselves encounter no violence. Blushing is not likely to start a dangerous epidemic requiring quarantine, though a man blushing breaks a gender stereotype. As a practical nurse, Enid attends at deathbeds but not funerals. The boys don't keep their mouths shut for long, and the careful reader realizes from perusing the beginning of the story that the mystery, unlike those in popular books and films, remains unsolved. Munro's portrait of Enid subverts the stereotype of the self-sacrificing nurse. The "uttermost trespass" simply concerns telling a man that his fly is open. The "deliberately vile" thing is merely laughter. The bare leg is part of a sex scene, but not a pleasant one, and the disliked body marks the practical nurse's unprofessional reaction to a diseased body. With such phrases, Munro raises conventional expectations in order to deflate them. "Was it specially difficult this time?" is a seemingly conventional question that in context hints at all the complexity of Enid's unconventional actions and reactions to the death of her patient. Thus, the running heads imply for the skimming reader that the story presents the sensational elements familiar to anyone exposed to North American popular culture. For the careful reader, however, the running heads point to moments when Munro evokes and then subverts conventional images and responses, calling into question many of the assumptions accepted and promoted by mass culture.

"The Love of a Good Woman" begins with a description of an anonymously donated item in a museum of local historical/nostalgic objects in Walley: a red box of optometrist's instruments that had belonged to D.M. Willens, who drowned in 1951. The detailed descriptions of the ophthalmoscope and the retinoscope might come from a medical catalogue were readers of this dry prose not startled by the comparison of the former to "a snowman" and the latter to "an elf's head" (102). The precise noting of evidence familiar to readers of the crime and mystery genres explodes into a realm where things seem like things they are not. The images evoke a world of childhood, magic, and transformation, a parallel world in which imagination defines fact. The story is indeed, these images announce, fiction.

The museum objects also announce the theme of preserving the past, of giving it to the present as a reminder of stories and customs now gone; "butter churns and horse harnesses" evoke fantasies of simple, gently paced, self-sufficient country life (102).[8] As the story progresses, this myth of happiness in the idyllic 1950s is subverted by characters and incidents that reveal the decade's less attractive aspects. Readers of the story in the *New Yorker*, however, need not suffer the confusion and consternation of losing a cherished myth.[9] Instead, they can let their attention wander to the ads in the margins; purchasing antiques and collectibles (by phone or mail order) allows one to reconstruct the past to one's own liking, depending neither on what Grandma left behind nor on what Munro has conjured up. "Distinctive Jewelry for the Discerning Collector" is available from the Golden Club: "Between 1880 and 1930, a master jeweler meticulously carved his life's work into steel models. These works of art are now being struck and cast again from the original dies in 18kt. gold" (120). Male readers might prefer a "Handcarved Philippine Mahogany" replica of the "Martin M-130 China Clipper" at 1/72 scale or a "Carbide Cannon" that shoots "with terrific BANG!" with an "Authentic turn-of-century design. Handsome decor when not in use" (120, 140). Cultures frequently locate disturbing events "within routine structures of understanding" (Biel 24); this is what the *New Yorker* context offers for the disturbing aspects of Munro's story.

The action of "The Love of a Good Woman" begins with three boys out for adventure on a Saturday morning. The nostalgic connection for readers quickly dissipates as the boys discover a dead body in a car and go home to the midday meal weighed down with the problems of whether to tell of their discovery, what to tell, and whom to tell; each boy's relationship with his family is troubled. Cece's father's drunken rampages include threats to "flatten his [Cece's] face on the hot burner" (110); Bud's sister asserts that "Bud ought to get his face smashed" (111); and, in Jimmy's house, "Drawbacks and adversity were not to be noticed, not distinguished from their opposites" (111), as the family copes with a blind great-aunt, a disabled father, and too many people for the small house. The boys cannot tell their families about the dead body: "It was just that their houses seemed too full. Too much was going on already" (112). What reader would not, at this point in the story, gladly stray to the *New Yorker* marginalia, exchanging the nostalgic boys' adventure gone astray for the glittering adventures promised in the ads? "Villas, farmhouses, apartments . . . simple to luxurious" can be rented for a family holiday in Italy, or an "Intimate, European family style B & B" in Taos, New Mexico, can provide the adventure of skiing as well as the chance to meet "Fascinating guests" (116). Boyhood adventure, valued as a partially recoverable mythic memory, is first deconstructed by the story that Munro tells and then overshadowed by the hope of future pleasurable adventures that the ads promise.

As "The Love of a Good Woman" shifts its focus from the boys to an unmarried practical nurse, a woman's quest for a safe home evokes for readers the conventions of the romance genre. Surely she is the good woman whose love will save the man who will in turn save her from that fate worse than death, spinsterhood. However, again Munro's treatment deconstructs the myth uncomfortably. The hero may be the villain, the murderer. The heroine may have consciously contributed to the death of her patient. The good woman's nobility may be naïveté. She may find herself drowning rather than being offered matrimony as the two enter the boat and Munro's story stops. Enid, assuming that Mrs. Quinn's deathbed confession is to be believed, imagines herself subtly persuading Rupert Quinn to confess to having murdered the optometrist, his wife's abusive lover:

"I am not going to tell, but you are. You can't live on with that kind of secret."

You cannot live in the world with such a burden. You will not be able to stand your life.

If she had got so far, and he had neither denied what she said nor pushed her into the river, Enid would know that she had won the gamble. It would take some more talking, more absolutely firm but quiet persuasion to bring him to the point where he would start to row back to shore. (137–38)

Yet Enid imagines "a different possibility": "Through her silence, her collaboration in a silence, what benefits could bloom. For others, and for herself" (140). The fearful possibilities inherent in this situation remain open to the end of the story, upsetting readers whose expectations have been nurtured on the romance genre, in which the nurse always marries the wronged husband after the evil wife/patient dies. But troubled romance readers, like frustrated mystery readers, find escape at hand because the *New Yorker* marginalia provide less disturbing fantasies of health and intimacy. At the Carolina Wellness Retreat on Hilton Head Island, "Life's a Beach . . . and Then You'll Diet," while receiving "Training and facts for a real lifestyle change" (137). At Long Bay in the British Virgin Islands, a couple walk on a secluded beach with palm fronds in the foreground (138), unperplexed by mysteries and murders. "The warmth — and the romance" of a wool cape from Casco Bay Fine Woolens (138) might soothe other readers jarred by Munro's subversion of generic conventions.

The marginalia surrounding Munro's story in the *New Yorker* not only disrupt concentration and provide escape from the difficult problems presented by the story but also alter the emotional effect of the story. Reading it becomes an act of penitence for desiring the luxuries advertised so appealingly on each page, for having education and opportunities that the characters in the story so evidently lack. The "imagined community" of the *New Yorker*'s readers overlaps with the "imagined community" of Munro's readers: each is imagined because the members of the community "will never know most of their fellow-members, meet them, or even hear of them, yet in the minds of each lives the image of their communion" (Anderson 6).[10] But only one of these groups experiences the full penitential effect of the story. Readers of the *New Yorker* can sneer together at a cartoon in which "Hamlet's great-great-great-great grandson contemplates show business: . . . whether 'tis nobler to be a flavor of the month, or not to be a flavor at all" (105), feel mutually affirmed in their intellectual status because they can identify the allusion in the title "Hemingway's Hat" whether or not the poem makes sense to them (108), and laugh knowingly with other art aficionados at the cartoon of a woman saying to a friend, "For big, important things, it's the Met and the Modern, of course — but the Whitney is great for stocking-stuffers" (122). The poverty and the lack of education of the characters in "The Love of a Good Woman" offer these readers a look at "the other" (without making any financial demands or insisting on involvement, because the characters are safely out of reach in the 1950s); by observing, readers do penance for having disposable income and pleasures and privileges so much more innocent (if more expensive) than the pleasures and privileges enjoyed by the optometrist (sadistic sex) or the practical nurse (possible euthanasia, possible obstruction of justice) in the story. The combination of story and context produces a catharsis, not of violent emotions purged, but of violent emotions soothed by distance in time and space and transmuted by the promise of immediately accessible pleasures.

Munro's story contains a nostalgic effect, which is subverted by the unappealing nature of the nostalgic time (the 1950s) and place (the country) in her re-creation. The contrast of this iconoclastic effect in the story is both strengthened by immediate juxtaposition with the pleasures of the present in the city (or on an exclusive vacation in landscapes purified of hardship and pain) and overshadowed by the glamorous aura that the ads lend to the lifestyle valued by this imagined community of magazine readers. Even those "stocking-stuffers" from the Whitney conjure up an urban present more elegant and desirable than anything that Walley has to offer.

The aspects of the mystery and romance genres that Munro deconstructs in the story similarly are both emphasized and undercut by the presence of the marginalia that announce loudly their continued existence and value. While sex in the story is ugly, making us turn our imaginations away in shame, sex in the ads is romantic, reminding us of more appealing possibilities. Watching the optometrist Willens take advantage of Mrs. Quinn, we do penance for the ills that the educated have inflicted on the uneducated, men have inflicted on women, the privileged have inflicted on the underprivileged:

> Oh, Missus, would you like me to examine your eyes for you, just sit down here and just you relax and you just shut one eye and keep the other one wide open. Wide open, now. It was like the same game every time, and she wasn't supposed to suspect what was going on, and when he had the thing out looking in her eye he wanted her to keep her panties on, him the dirty old cuss puffing away getting his fingers slicked in and puffing away. Her not supposed to say anything till he stops and gets

the looker thing packed up in his box and all and then she's supposed to say, "Oh, Mr. Willens, now, how much do I owe you for today?"

And that was the signal for him to get her down and thump her like an old billy goat. Right on the bare floor to knock her up and down and try to bash her into pieces. (132)

And then we escape, thankfully, having acknowledged and thereby atoned for our sins of privilege, to the sophisticated world enjoyed by members of the imagined community. We can "Holiday in Vanderbilt Style" at the Fisher Island Club, "one of the world's most exclusive private island communities" (131).

The mystery of how Willens died seems to be solved in the story; the mystery of whether another murder is about to happen at the end of the story is not. Mrs. Quinn's illness may be the result of an attempted abortion:

> "Because you hear one thing and another," Mrs. Green said. "You hear that sometimes a woman might take some pills. They get these pills to take for when their period is late and if they take them just like the doctor says and for a good purpose that's fine, but if they take too many and for a bad purpose their kidneys are wrecked. Am I right?"
>
> "I've never come in contact with a case like that," Enid said. (118)

And Mrs. Quinn's death may be a brutal form of euthanasia. We learn that "Enid did not call the doctor" as Mrs. Quinn's condition worsens (134), that she does not inform family members, and that "She had never absented herself like this before with anybody who was dying" (135); she obliterates all traces of struggle after the patient dies before letting anyone else into the room. For us as readers, the intellectual satisfactions of solving the mystery become overlaid with the concerns from our own time and place regarding abortion and withholding medical care for the dying. However, like Willens, we look through a special instrument — the story — pretending to be engaged in serious work, as we let ourselves roam into other activities, leaving the house for the garden.

The good woman of the title, whose love should redeem those around her, may herself be a murderer, like the man she wants to save. Her love for Rupert may have drawn her to neglect to do good, thereby doing evil to Mrs. Quinn. Her sins of omission and commission leave the romance without a heroine, the unredeemed man without a woman to rescue him. For readers of the story in the *New Yorker*, moral choices exist in the world of the story but not in the world of the marginalia. The imagined community of magazine readers need not grapple with the problems of sin and salvation on a day-to-day basis. The ads clarify that the choice is not between damnation and redemption but between one exciting or restful vacation or another, one valuable collectible or another. The events of the story are safely in the past, represented in the present only by the optometrist's instruments in the museum in Walley.

But if the story is an optical instrument, like the snowman of Munro's simile, then it is a work of human hands that resembles a man but is fanciful and vanishing; like the elf of Munro's simile, the story is something magical that is seen only by select people. The reader is the victim of the author, who seems to be doing one thing with the story while doing something else with it: presenting "a murder, a mystery, a romance" while subverting these genres. Yet, reading the story in the *New Yorker*, the reader may be victimizing the author, seemingly looking at life through the lens of the story while actually looking at it through the double lenses of the story and the ads. The marginalia have the power to strengthen the effect of Munro's story by presenting immediate versions of the aspects of contemporary culture that the story deconstructs. However, as the story alerts us to the fantasies inherent in the ads, presenting "what is outside [the house] in a new way" ("What" 332), the effect of the marginalia can overpower Munro's story, reminding us how attractive we find what it subverts.

At best, the context that the *New Yorker* provides for "The Love of a Good Woman" produces a lively tension between the two versions of reality presented in the story and the marginalia, enhancing the emotional impact of the story. At worst, the marginalia distract readers from the deepest forms of engagement that art offers, allowing them to wander idly among the flowers in the garden instead of confronting the demons inside the house. Munro describes her goal in creating the house that is her story this way:

> So when I write a story I want to make a certain kind of structure, and I know the feeling I want to get from being inside that structure. . . .
>
> There is no blueprint for the structure. It's not a question of,

"I'll make this kind of house because if I do it right it will have this effect." I've got to make, I've got to build up, a house, a story, to fit around the indescribable "feeling" that is like the soul of the story, and which I must insist upon in a dogged, embarrassed way, as being no more definable than that. ("What" 332)

the *New Yorker* readers who prefer the veneer of culture to "the soul of the story" can avoid being made seriously uncomfortable by "The Love of a Good Woman." Each reader must construct Munro's story out of the fragments of the story and the fragments of the marginalia. The power of the story of the 1950s can be defused by the stories of the 1990s or enhanced by them, as each reader chooses. Either way, how and what this story means for readers of the *New Yorker* will be substantially different than they will be for readers who encounter the story in a book with blank margins.

Alice Munro's twenty-one years of publishing in the *New Yorker* and her annually renewed contracts of right of first refusal have probably had less effect on her writing than on how it is read. Does the *New Yorker* support her art at its best? Ross names the qualities for which Munro is famous:

For stories written with such emotional honesty, compassion, and intimacy that in them readers recognize their deepest selves. For stories so rich they seem like compressed novels, juxtaposing past against present, one point of view against another. For creating an indefinable "Munro country" based on her own experience of Huron County, Ontario. For presenting ordinary life so that it appears luminous, invested with a kind of magic. (15)

These qualities — in spite of some censorship — are all available to the large numbers of readers of Munro's thirty-four stories in the *New Yorker*. To those who live in the world of luxurious and conspicuous consumption offered in ads such as those that surround "The Love of a Good Woman," Munro's stories may be an ultimate luxury:[11] something truly excellent, something worth collecting, a place worth visiting and revisiting, a place of relaxation and renewal, of challenge and new awakening. Because art is not static, varying contexts open new ways of appreciating it. The newly appointed editor of the *New Yorker*, Pulitzer Prize-winning nonfiction writer

David Remnick, has said that he will try "to edit a magazine of hilarity, deep reporting, literary quality and moral seriousness" ("New Editor"). I suspect that Munro's stories will thrive under his editorship, for those are salient qualities of her art. Her humour has a subtlety that surpasses the glibness of many cartoons in the magazine. Her extraordinary use of details captures more of daily life than does much journalism. Few writers today equal her artistic excellence. And Munro's nonjudgemental vision opens serious age-old questions of morality while recontextualizing them for our time.

ACKNOWLEDGEMENTS

Research for this essay was supported by the Saint Mary's College Faculty Development Fund and the Canadian Embassy Faculty Research Program. The librarians at the Special Collections Division of the University of Calgary Library were particularly helpful during my research among the Alice Munro Papers. I thank Charles McGrath, Daniel Menaker, Alice Munro, the Virginia Barber Literary Agency, and the *New Yorker* for allowing me to cite unpublished materials in this article.

NOTES

[1] Following are the thirty-four stories, in order of publication in the *New Yorker*.

14 March 1977, "Royal Beatings"
27 June 1977, "The Beggar Maid"
22 May 1978, "The Moons of Jupiter"
21 July 1980, "Dulse"
24 November 1980, "Wood"
29 December 1980, "The Turkey Season"
30 March 1981, "Prue"
28 September 1981, "Labor Day Dinner"
14 January 1985, "Miles City, Montana"
15 July 1985, "Lichen"
7 October 1985, "The Progress of Love"
31 March 1986, "The Moon in the Orange Street Skating Rink"
28 July 1986, "White Dump"
16 November 1987, "Oh, What Avails"
11 January 1988, "Meneseteung"
14 March 1988, "Five Points"
24 October 1988, "Oranges and Apples"
2 January 1989, "Differently"
20 March 1989, "Goodness and Mercy"

4 September 1989, "Wigtime"
22 January 1990, "Friend of My Youth"
21 October 1991, "Carried Away"
10 February 1992, "A Real Life"
27 April 1992, "A Wilderness Station"
8 February 1993, "Open Secrets"
19 July 1993, "The Jack Randa Hotel"
4 October 1993, "Vandals"
11 April 1994, "Hired Girl"
27 June 1994, "The Albanian Virgin"
23 December 1996, "The Love of a Good Woman"
22 December 1997, "The Children Stay"
22 June 1998, "Save the Reaper"
24 August 1998, "Before the Change"
12 October 1998, "Cortes Island"

   2 The variant versions of "Dulse," including the change from first to third person, are discussed by Robert Thacker in "Alice Munro's Willa Cather" (see, especially, 49–52).

   3 For discussions of "Wood," see Carscallen; and W.R. Martin.

   4 The number of interruptions per story has varied greatly in the last dozen years, with more marginalia appearing in longer stories. For example, "Miles City, Montana" takes eleven consecutive pages and is interrupted by ten cartoons and one poem (14 Jan. 1985). "Lichen" takes ten consecutive pages broken by two sketches and nine cartoons (15 July 1985). Other stories have full-page or even two-page interruptions. For example, "The Moon in the Orange Street Skating Rink" is interrupted by eleven cartoons, one sketch, one full-page ad, five partial-page ads, and one two-page ad (31 Mar. 1986). "Oh, What Avails" contains twelve cartoons, one poem, eight full-page ads, and eleven other ads (16 Nov. 1987). "Oranges and Apples" is broken by ten cartoons, two sketches, two poems, two full-page ads, one two-page ad, and two smaller ads (24 Oct. 1988). Some more recent stories have slightly more marginalia than earlier ones, while others have considerably more. For example, the twenty-eight pages of "Carried Away" are interrupted by four sketches, eleven cartoons, two poems, and twenty-seven ads (21 Oct. 1991). "Save the Reaper" contains one illustration, three sketches, thirty-eight ads, one cartoon, and one poem in its sixteen pages (22 and 29 June 1998). Perhaps because of its length, "The Love of a Good Woman" has a startling number of interruptions.

   5 Founding editor Harold Ross consciously tried to position the magazine in the gap left by "feeble and sophomoric" journals such as *Judge* and *Life*, middlebrow magazines such as *Collier's*, *Liberty*, and *Saturday Evening Post*, and slick but predictable highbrow magazines such as *Vanity Fair* and the *American Mercury* (McGrath 184). The ads in the magazine still seem

to target the same highbrow (or would-be highbrow) audience that Ross hoped to attract.

⁶ See Canitz and Seamon for a discussion of how Munro creates an effect that simultaneously makes her stories seem real and questions literary realism.

⁷ J.R.R. Tolkien asserts that the successful writer "makes a Secondary World which your mind can enter. Inside it, what he relates is 'true': it accords with the laws of that world. You therefore believe it, while you are, as it were, inside. The moment disbelief arises, the spell is broken; the magic, or rather the art, has failed. You are then out in the Primary World again, looking at the little abortive Secondary World from outside" (37). The ads in the *New Yorker* form not a Primary World but an additional Secondary World, and each of these Secondary Worlds has the potential to hold or lose readers' attention, or to form a new vantage point from which to view either of the other worlds.

⁸ Like the museum, Munro's writing does serve to preserve the past of southwestern Ontario; however, it also works to subvert our images of that past.

⁹ A recent news article discusses how Americans want to remember the 1950s in a positive way only: "How do Americans want to remember that chrome-plated, crew-cut Eisenhower decade? More than 8 million votes cast in the Postal Service's choose-it-yourself stamp contest prove that for the most part the public tastes are deep-fried and sugar-coated. The top five vote-getters (in order) were drive-in movies, 'I Love Lucy,' 'The Cat in the Hat,' rock 'n' roll and victory over polio. The Korean War was in last place" (Garchik, *The San Francisco Chronicle*. Reprinted with permission).

¹⁰ I borrow the term "imagined communities" from Benedict Anderson, who uses it to describe members of a nation. He theorizes that "Communities are to be distinguished, not by their falsity/genuineness, but by the style in which they are imagined" (6). the *New Yorker* imagines its community implicitly through the selection of articles and ads that it prints, and each reader tacitly joins the community at least for the time of reading.

¹¹ I owe the idea that Munro's stories are "the fictional luxuries sought by readers of the *New Yorker*" to Robert Thacker, editor of this issue of *Essays on Canadian Writing* ("Munro").

WORKS CITED

The Alice Munro Papers. Special Collections Division, U of Calgary Library.
Anderson, Benedict. *Imagined Communities: Reflections on the Origins and Spread of Nationalism*. Rev. ed. New York: Verso, 1991.
Biel, Steven. *Down with the Old Canoe: A Cultural History of the* Titanic *Disaster*. New York: Norton, 1996.

Canitz, A.E. Christa, and Roger Seamon. "The Rhetoric of Fictional Realism in the Stories of Alice Munro." *Canadian Literature* 150 (1996): 67–80.

Carscallen, James. *The Other Country: Patterns in the Writing of Alice Munro*. Toronto: ECW, 1993.

Cockburn, Alexander. "Alexander Cockburn's America." *New Statesman* 6 Sept. 1996: 31.

Garchik, Leah. "Personals: Remembering the '50s." *The San Francisco Chronicle* 8 Apr. 1998: E8.

Garvey, John. "Of Several Minds: What Tina Hath Wrought." *Commonweal* 16 June 1995: 9–10.

"Gottlieb, Robert A(dams) 1931–." *Contemporary Authors*. Vol. 129. Ed. Susan M. Trosky. Detroit: Gale, 1990. 173–75.

Martin, James. "The Rich Are Different." *America* 27 Jan. 1996: 22–23.

Martin, W.R. *Alice Munro: Paradox and Parallel*. Edmonton: U of Alberta P, 1987.

Lacayo, Richard. "What Price Glory?" *Time* 20 July 1998: 54.

McGrath, Charles. "The Ross Years." *New Yorker* 20 Feb. 1995. 180+.

"McGrath of 'New Yorker' to head 'NYTBR.'" *Publisher's Weekly* 21 Nov. 1994: 21.

"Menaker, Daniel 1941–." *Contemporary Authors*. Vols. 65–68. Ed. Jane A. Bowden. Detroit: Gale, 1977. 406.

Munro, Alice. "The Children Stay." *New Yorker* 22 and 29 Dec. 1997. 90+.

___. "Contributors' Notes." *Prize Stories: The Best of 1997*. [The O. Henry Awards.] Ed. Larry Dark. New York: Doubleday, 1997. 442–43.

___. *Friend of My Youth*. New York: Knopf, 1990.

___. "Hired Girl." *New Yorker* 11 Apr. 1994. 82+.

___. "The Love of a Good Woman." *New Yorker* 23 and 30 Dec. 1996: 102+.

___. *The Love of a Good Woman*. Toronto: McClelland, 1998.

___. *The Moons of Jupiter*. 1982. Markham, ON: Penguin, 1983.

___. *The Progress of Love*. Toronto: McClelland, 1986.

___. "Save the Reaper." *New Yorker* 22 and 29 June 1998: 120+.

___. *Something I've Been Meaning to Tell You*. 1974. Scarborough, ON: NAL, 1975.

___. "What Is Real?" *Making It New: Contemporary Canadian Stories*. Ed. John Metcalf. Toronto: Methuen, 1982. Rpt. in *How Stories Mean*. Ed. John Metcalf and J.R. (Tim) Struthers. Erin, ON: Porcupine's Quill, 1993. 331–34.

___. *Who Do You Think You Are?* 1978. Agincourt, ON: Signet, 1979.

"New Editor at *New Yorker*." *The San Francisco Chronicle* 14 July 1998: A2.

"Remembering Mr. Shawn." *New Yorker* 28 Dec. 1992 and 4 Jan. 1993: 134+.

Ross, Catherine Sheldrick. *Alice Munro: A Double Life*. Canadian Biography Series 1. Toronto: ECW, 1992.

"Shawn, William 1907–." *Contemporary Authors*. Vol. 108. Ed. Hal May. Detroit: Gale, 1983. 442.

"Shawn, William 1907–1992." *Contemporary Authors*. Vol. 140. Ed. Donna Olendorf. Detroit: Gale, 1993. 422–23.

"The Talk of the Town." *Time International* 20 July 1998: 51.

Tennyson, Alfred. "In Memoriam A.H.H." *Tennyson's Poetry*. Ed. Robert W. Hill Jr. Norton Critical Edition. New York: Norton, 1971. 118–95.

Thacker, Robert. "Alice Munro's Willa Cather." *Canadian Literature* 134 (1992): 42–57.

———. "Munro and the *New Yorker*." E-mail to the author. 3 May 1998.

Tolkien, J.R.R. "On Fairy-Stories." *The Tolkien Reader*. New York: Ballantine, 1966. 3–73.

Contributors

Carol L. Beran, St. Mary's College of California
Ildikó de Papp Carrington, Northern Illinois University
Dennis Duffy, University of Toronto
Nathalie Foy, Toronto
Deborah Heller, York University
Robert Lecker, McGill University
W.R. Martin and Warren U. Ober, University of Waterloo
JoAnn McCaig, Calgary
Marianne Micros, University of Guelph
Magdalene Redekop, Victoria University
Robert Thacker, St. Lawrence University